INVESTING IN CREDIT
HEDGE FUNDS

PUTRI PASCUALY

New York   Chicago   San Francisco   Athens   London
Madrid   Mexico City   Milan   New Delhi
Singapore   Sydney   Toronto

2 3 4 5 6 7 8 9 0   QVS/QVS   1 9 8 7 6 5 4 3

ISBN   978-0-07-182903-8
MHID   0-07-182903-2

e-ISBN   978-0-07-182832-1
e-MHID   0-07-182832-X

This publication is designed to provide accurate and authoritative information in regard to the subject matter covered. It is sold with the understanding that neither the author nor the publisher is engaged in rendering legal, accounting, securities trading, or other professional services. If legal advice or other expert assistance is required, the services of a competent professional person should be sought.

—*From a Declaration of Principles Jointly Adopted by a Committee of the American Bar Association and a Committee of Publishers and Associations*

Library of Congress Cataloging-in-Publication Data

Pascualy, Putri.
   Investing in credit hedge funds : an in-depth guide to building your portfolio and profiting from the credit market / Putri Pascualy.
      pages cm
   Includes index.
   ISBN 978-0-07-182903-8 (alk. paper) — ISBN 0-07-182903-2 (alk. paper)
   1. Hedge funds.   2. Investments.   3. Portfolio management.   I. Title.
   HG4530.P347 2014
   332.64'524—dc23   2013028458

Contents

Contents

Acknowledgments

I have been fortunate to be able to work alongside some of the most exciting and brilliant minds in the investment arena. My work as a credit strategist and portfolio manager has placed me in the driver's seat through different investment and economic cycles, and I am profoundly grateful for the opportunity to get to know so many thoughtful and dedicated men and women. I would like to express my deep appreciation for the individuals who have in one way or another been teachers, mentors, colleagues, and friends. Their generosity with their advice, time, thoughts and expertise regarding the credit market and the hedge fund industry has influenced this book as well as my journey and growth as an investor. Errors and opinions expressed in the book are my own.

A most emphatic thank you goes to the following individuals:

Steve Blauner at Solus Alternative Asset Management, LP for his advice on distressed investing as well as for some of the most fascinating stories on bankruptcy cases. Christopher R. Hebble at Cerberus Capital Management, LP for sharing his expertise and thoughts on less liquid and distressed investment opportunities. Gunther Stein and Jenny Rhee at Symphony Asset Management for their candid advice on the credit market and hedging techniques. Joseph Naggar, Ted Roosevelt V, and Vanitha Milberg at GoldenTree Asset Management for sharing their thoughts and market savvy regarding the bank loan, high yield, and structured products markets. Richard D. Holahan, Jr. at Caspian Capital Partners, LP for sharing his wealth of legal and operational experience with credit and distressed hedge funds. John Zito at

Apollo Global Management, LLC for sharing his investment acumen as he navigates through the complexities of the credit world. Alicia Sansone and Meredith Coffey at the Loan Syndications and Trading Association (LSTA) for their tireless work on behalf of loan investors. Cathleen M. Rittereiser, Co-Author, *Foundation and Endowment Investing* and *Top Hedge Fund Investors* for her advice on the writing process and keen observations on the hedge fund industry. John Dyment, Mike Carley and Paul Greenberg at Lutetium Capital for their comments and thoughts regarding financing method as well as on trading and investing practices in the credit market. Ioana Barza at Thomson Reuters LPC for her work in the leveraged credit market. Wingee Sin at State Street Global Advisors for her friendship and sage advice regarding the alternative investment world. Bryan Dunn at MidOcean Partners for his insights on relative value strategies and hedging techniques. Tad Flynn at Houlihan Lokey for his thoughts regarding valuation and liquidity management techniques. Andrew Gordon at Octagon Credit Investors, LLC for sharing his years of experience as an investor in the leveraged credit market and his expertise in the CLO market. Aditya Divgi at New York City Retirement Systems for educating me about investor priorities and concerns. Sabrina Callin at PIMCO, LLC for her advice on the writing process as well as her thoughtful comments regarding the investment management industry. Craig Ruch at Matlin Patterson for his insights on liquidity, trading, hedging and credit risk in the credit market. Shawn Wischmeier, CIO, and Rodney Overcash, Director of Credit Strategies, at the Margaret A. Cargill Philantrophies, for sharing their astute observations and candid perspectives on investing throughout the cycles.

I would like to thank the partnership at PAAMCO for their vision, leadership and continuous support. Thank you for letting me join in the adventure! My colleagues for sharing their wealth of knowledge, in particular Philippe Jorion, Ronan Cosgrave, Sam Diedrich, Josh Barlow, Marc Towers, Leslie Macdonald, Charlie Nightingale and Max Rijkenberg.

Most of all, a personal and deeply heartfelt thank you goes to Rodrigo Pascualy for his never ending support, love and friendship.

CHAPTER 1

Hedge Funds and the Credit Market

Hedge funds have often been classified as an asset class. This definition is changing as many investors are becoming more familiar with hedge funds and recognize hedge funds as a specialized breed of active asset managers. Hedge funds provide investors with ways to access various asset classes and are not restricted to a specific asset class. Some hedge funds are focused on one or two specific asset classes such as convertible bonds, while others invest in a wide range of assets. A multi-strategy hedge fund provides a good example, as it may invest in interest rates, sovereign and corporate bonds, equities, and currencies.

Hedge funds also have the flexibility to invest across geographical areas and in various markets around the globe ranging from developed to developing and frontier markets. Hedge fund managers' investments may cover a wide range of investment and trading styles, such as fundamental bottom-up, trading oriented, macro, and relative value. Hedge funds also invest in instruments across different markets—exchange traded and over-the-counter—as well as in cash and derivatives.

The inefficiencies in and across different financial instruments and markets provide opportunities for hedge funds to add value through active management. We will point out particular inefficiencies that are unique to the credit market. These inefficiencies provide both challenges and alpha opportunities to select credit investors that are able to differentiate among different credits.

BERNIE MADOFF—HEDGE FUND MANAGER?

"Mr. Madoff was not running an actual hedge fund, but instead managing accounts for investors inside his own securities firm. The difference, though seemingly minor, is crucial. Hedge funds typically hold their portfolios at banks and brokerage firms like JPMorgan Chase and Goldman Sachs. Outside auditors can check with those banks and brokerage firms to make sure the funds exist.

"But because he had his own securities firm, Mr. Madoff kept custody over his clients' accounts and processed all their stock trades himself. His only check appears to have been Friehling & Horowitz, a tiny auditing firm based in New City, N.Y. Wealthy individuals and other money managers entrusted billions of dollars to funds that in turn invested in his firm, based on his reputation and reported returns."

Source: Alex Berenson and Diana B. Henriques, "Look at Wall St. Wizard Finds Magic Had Skeptics," *New York Times,* December 12, 2008

HEDGE FUNDS—HISTORY AND INDUSTRY GROWTH

Alfred Winslow Jones, a journalist, was credited with founding A.W. Jones & Co., the first hedge fund, in 1949. He formed a limited partnership with four of his friends to invest in common stocks using leverage and short selling. The structure was exempt from registration under the Securities Act of 1933 and the Investment Company Act of 1940; the partnership shares were offered as a private placement.

In the late 1980s and early '90s, the managers of the endowments for universities such as Harvard, Yale, and Duke started looking into hedge fund investments. These managers were banking on the idea that better risk-adjusted return could be achieved by managers who have fewer investment restrictions than managers who are subject to the '40 Act.[1]

In 2002, the California Public Employees' Retirement System (Calpers) and Pennsylvania State Employees' Retirement System (PennSERS) were two of the first state pension plans to invest in hedge funds. Their motivation was to diversify their investment portfolio beyond the traditional asset allocation mix of bonds and equities.

In the two intervening decades since Calpers and PennSERS started their foray into hedge funds, the industry has changed dramatically, and some hedge fund managers have become household names. George Soros became "the man who broke the Bank of England" in 1992 through his short bet on the British pound. John Paulson was known by his short subprime trade in 2007 and 2008. Unfortunately, another household name related to hedge funds is Bernie Madoff and his $50 billion Ponzi scheme. After the fraud was uncovered in 2008, the ripple effect was felt across the hedge fund industry, and investors went back to the drawing board to reassess the risk management process—both internally and of their asset managers. As of the time of this book's writing, much of the hedge fund assets are concentrated in the world's largest hedge funds. Figure 1.1 shows the world's top 20 largest hedge funds, which collectively manage 25 percent of the total estimated $2.25 trillion total assets managed by hedge funds.

PORTABLE ALPHA

Portable alpha investing is a strategy where the investor separates the alpha and beta exposure of the portfolio. Alpha is the portfolio return achieved over and above the return resulting from the correlation between the assets in the portfolio and the broad market (beta). The investor usually obtains beta exposure through a swap and separately obtains alpha through investing in absolute return investments such as hedge funds.

World's Largest Hedge Funds			
FIRM NAME	**ASSETS UNDER MANAGEMENT (IN BILLIONS)**		
1. Bridgewater Associates	$83.3	11. Adage Capital Management	$25.0
2. J.P. Morgan Asset Management	$44.0	12. Renaissance Technologies	$22.0
3. Brevan Howard	$39.8	13. Elliott Management Corporation	$21.5
4. BlueCrest	$35.3	14. D.E. Shaw Group	$21.0
5. Standard Life Investments	$34.3	15. Canyon Capital Advisors	$20.6
6. Och-Ziff Capital Management Group	$31.9	16. AQR Capital Management	$20.3
7. MAN GLG	$29.6	17. M&G Investment	$19.5
8. Baupost Group	$26.7	18. Davidson Kempner Advisers	$18.7
9. BlackRock	$26.6	19. Farallon Capital Management	$18.6
10. Winton	$25.3	20. Adage Capital Management	$25.0

Figure 1.1 Top 20 largest hedge funds
Source: PAAMCO, Hedge Fund Intelligence

During the same time period, there have also been many changes to institutional investors' attitudes about hedge funds. Over time, many other state and corporate pension plans have overcome their initial reservations about hedge funds as the hedge fund industry started to implement better practices on governance and transparency. Institutional investors such as large corporate and state pension plans have also introduced some innovations into the alternative investment landscape such as portable alpha investing.

The rapid growth of the hedge fund industry as measured by the assets under management and number of funds can be seen in Figure 1.2. The chart reflects estimated data, as hedge fund managers have not been required to report the amount of assets they manage. Since 2000, the amount of assets invested in hedge funds is estimated to have grown from $491 billion to $2 trillion in first quarter 2011, and the number of hedge funds has been estimated to grow from 3,800 to more than 9,000 in first quarter 2011.

Today, many investors are still trying to recover from the market downturn of 2008. The need to meet a return target and do so in a risk-controlled manner has turned many institutional investors toward hedge funds. Institutional investors have made allocation to

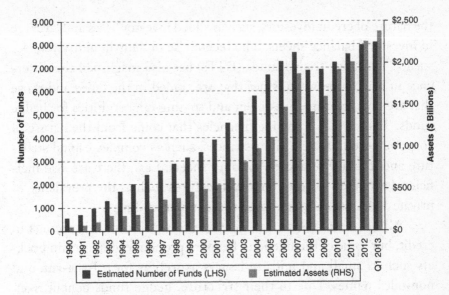

Figure 1.2 Hedge fund industry assets under management and number of funds
Source: Hedge Fund Research

hedge funds to complement their long-only portfolios. For example, long/short equity and credit strategies have been considered as part of their global equity and fixed-income portfolios. Similarly, event-driven hedge funds have been added to complement traditional growth or value equity exposures. In the effort to further diversify the sources of risk and return, investors have also turned to hedge funds and funds of hedge funds to engineer portfolio solutions that can fill a particular need in an institution's investment program, complement existing investments, or provide access to newer or more complex hedge funds and investment strategies.

HEDGE FUNDS IN THE CREDIT MARKET

There are inefficiencies in the credit market, and hedge funds are particularly well suited to benefit from these inefficiencies. In general, the reasons behind the credit market inefficiencies can be broken down into three main groups. The first group is inefficiencies that stem from the nature of credit investors, such as siloed investor bases and leverage in investors' balance sheets. The recent rise of daily liquidity vehicles such as exchange traded funds (ETFs) has also magnified the difference in pricing between issues that are traded in the index and those that are not, creating investment and trading opportunities for hedge funds. The second is the inefficiencies that come from the nature of corporate credit issuers and issuances, such as complex capital structure and leverage on issuers' balance sheets. Last, there are also inefficiencies related to certain market features such as the prevalence of private 144A issuances and over-the-counter trading.

All of these reasons can give rise to significant mispricings in credit, but some of them tend to be more pronounced in certain pockets such as small and midsize issuers as well as for off-the-run and nonindex names. Due to their structure, hedge funds benefit from highly flexible mandates, the ability and willingness to do the necessary legwork to sort out the wheat from the chaff, and the ability to use leverage and short sell to add value for their investors.

SILOED NATURE OF CREDIT INVESTORS

The siloed nature of investor groups in credit where large amounts of capital invest under certain fairly strict constraints such as ratings limitations give rise to opportunities for unconstrained credit investors. There will be opportunities when particular credit instruments fall outside the specific investment parameter and the investment manager will have to sell the instrument, potentially at noneconomic prices. For example, certain investment mandates may have rules that are intended to focus the investment on certain credit quality as measured by rating. The investment manager may only be able to invest in investment grade bonds or may only have a limited amount of bonds rated CCC or below. In an environment of economic downturn where there are widespread ratings downgrades, many bonds may see their credit ratings downgraded by the rating agencies. Many of these bonds may be held by banks, which are subject to capital requirements based on the amount of risk-weighted assets on their balance sheets.

Lower-rated bonds receive higher risk weighting, and more equity needs to be held for every dollar of exposure. From time to time, as banks need to improve their capital standing or meet a new regulatory regime, many have sought to reduce their exposure to lower-rated or otherwise non-capital-efficient bonds, creating opportunities if select bonds become oversold.

The market saw this opportunity playing out during the European peripheral crisis of 2011 and 2012. As banks in both Europe and the United States stared down the barrel and saw Basel III, they faced a very real need to sell risky assets from their balance sheets. The U.S. banks were the first movers to sell assets from their balance sheets. The European and Asian banks were soon to follow. Throughout the crisis, there were opportunities for hedge funds to enter into attractive opportunities ranging from capital relief trade to purchase of whole loans from banks.

Another example of silos among credit investors is in the bifurcation between institutional investors and retail investors. The retail bonds have smaller face value to accommodate individual investors and are pari passu to the bonds issued to institutional investors. However, during periods of market dislocations where retail investors have higher risk aversion and are seeking liquidity, despite having the same rights and seniority as the institutional bonds, the retail bonds can trade at a discount compared to their institutional counterpart.

STRUCTURAL CHANGES IN THE MARKET—LACK OF DEALER CAPITAL

Post Lehman, new regulatory regimes such as Basel III and the Volcker Rule translate into higher capital adequacy ratios and ban on proprietary trading for banks, which has been translated into reduced willingness and availability of banks to take trades onto their own balance sheet. The market implication of this is that there is a marginal buyer base missing in parts of the corporate credit market, particularly for bonds that are smaller, have lower credit quality, or have a complex investment thesis. Banks acted as broker rather than dealer—they would take the trade only if there was the opposite side of the trade. In the past, the bank would step in to provide a bid when a particular name was underpriced. As of late 2012, dealers' inventories are estimated at $45 billion, roughly half a percent of the $8 trillion total U.S. corporate bond market, compared to $250 billion in 2007. The reduction in dealer inventory is expected to be permanent, and this creates opportunities, particularly in names that are not in indices (i.e., not large, not liquid, and likely to have some degree of complexity related to the credit—usually described as "off-the-run"). This opens up room for patient, flexible capital such as credit hedge funds.

STRUCTURAL CHANGES IN THE MARKET— RISE OF DAILY LIQUIDITY VEHICLES

One of the largest new forces expected to change the landscape in credit investing is the rise of daily liquidity vehicles, specifically exchange traded funds (ETFs). Since their inception in 2007, the market has seen new ETFs that invest in the bonds and loans of levered borrowers. ETFs add liquidity and bring additional investment options to the investing public, and at the same time, they change the trading dynamic of certain parts of the corporate bond market. This dynamic is expected to present opportunities to credit hedge fund managers.

ETFs focus only on a certain part of the high yield bond market, typically large, liquid "marquee" bonds—smaller bonds are often overlooked. The lack of coverage from research desks of investment banks, compounded by the lack of dealer capital, often translates into opportunities in names that are excluded from ETFs and bond indices. Figure 1.3 shows the percentage of the ETF holdings by issue size—it shows that the ETFs are largely focused on holding very large to mega issuance sizes, at least $600 million and larger, with the highest percentage ownership seen for issuances larger than $2 billion.

Although high yield ETFs only represent $30 billion of the market or over 3 percent of the size of the total high yield market, it is important that ETFs may cause disproportionate impact in trading volume and volatility for the bonds in the ETF basket. Although there seems to be mixed data on whether ETF bonds are definitively

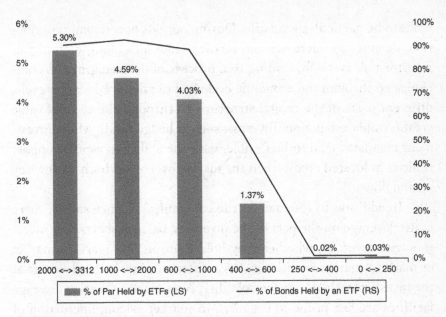

Figure 1.3 High yield ETF holdings by issue size
Source: Morgan Stanley

more volatile than non-ETF bonds, ETF bonds as a group show higher internal correlation—there is little differentiation between bonds in the ETF basket.[2] Lower correlation between non-ETF bonds offers opportunity for credit pickers to add value through credit selection.

LEVERAGE

Most credit hedge funds invest in levered credit, (i.e., capital structure of companies with significant leverage on their balance sheets). Leverage inherently adds volatility, both to the value of debt and equity. Furthermore, market appetite for leverage and the amount of leverage that the market is willing to tolerate on companies' balance sheets is cyclical.

When the economy is strong and the credit market is wide open, there will be more debt in companies' balance sheets. However, leverage magnifies any negative impact of a company's performance, and when high leverage is applied to cyclical businesses, the combination tends to be particularly volatile. During periods of economic contraction, default rate increases and recovery rate falls along with higher investor risk aversion, leading to a process of deleveraging. As companies go through the economic cycle and the financial market cycle, different parts of the capital structure go through the cycle of value creation and destruction. Investors such as hedge funds, whose investment mandates tend to be flexible, have the ability to capture opportunities in levered credit when the market overreacts both on the way up and down.

In addition to leverage on the companies' balance sheets, there is also leverage on the part of the investors' balance sheets. For investors with leverage, whether they hold them in non-mark-to-market or mark-to-market facilities makes a difference in whether leverage at the investor level adds to the volatility. Non-mark-to-market leverage facilities are less prone to the mark-to-market pricing fluctuation of the assets in the market.

Structurally, during the previously unseen volatility of the market in 2008, cash flow collateralized loan obligations (CLOs) were more robust compared to mark-to-market CLO structures. In a cash flow CLO, it is much less likely that price decline in the underlying loans alone would trigger an unwind of the facility (an "event of default") as long as the cash flow from the underlying loans is sufficient to service the CLO liabilities. Mark-to-market leverage facility includes prime brokerage and repo financing, which tend to focus on the more liquid parts of the credit market and where there is a more dynamic and transparent, continuous process for price discovery in the market. For a balanced market, having a mix of mark-to-market and non-mark-to-market leverage facilities is important.

Similar to the credit market for corporate issuers, leverage availability for credit investors also tends to be cyclical. During periods of economic expansion and easy access to credit, investors also have more access to leverage and often at lower cost. A disciplined and judicious use of leverage, both on the part of the issuer and the investor, is the goal. Nonetheless, seasoned market practitioners have observed again and again that this is not necessarily always the case.

During a period where many mark-to-market leveraged vehicles have to be unwound,[3] heavy additional supply of credit instruments presents both risk and opportunities. Investors with existing leverage in the balance sheet will have to watch their leverage facility and defend against certain parameters to stay in compliance with the financing terms. As the forced sellers come into the market, even investors that are not asset sellers will be affected by the downward pricing pressure, hedge funds included.

One way credit hedge funds mitigate this risk is by keeping leverage at a low to moderate level regardless of the maximum amount of leverage that's available to them prior to the crisis. This is an important aspect that many hedge funds focus on when managing risk in a levered credit portfolio because the higher the leverage, the higher the likelihood that the investors won't be able to control their own destiny during a market crisis (the determination to sell an asset is not in the investor's hands and, in many cases, is made at a time that is least attractive to the investor).

Furthermore, credit hedge funds can also add value by having a portfolio manager, risk manager, and back office that are all focused on managing leverage risk. The trader and back office for the credit hedge funds can add value by being actively involved and engaged in tracking market sentiment and appetite for liquidity as well as managing the relationship with their leverage providers. During a crisis, investors that have available spending power ("dry powder") during crisis periods can control their own destiny and benefit from selective asset purchase at very attractive prices. Credit hedge funds are not tightly tied to a benchmark and do not have to stay close to fully invested all the time, which gives them the flexibility to stay disciplined when markets are overpriced and the ability to preserve their buying ability until a market correction takes place.

COMPLEX CAPITAL STRUCTURE

In a capital structure, the value of a company is not distributed evenly. From the senior secured loans in the top of the capital structure to common equity, each layer provides different risk/reward propositions for different investors. In the event of distress, a company's creditors receive higher priority of payment—they are ahead in line relative to the equity investors, who are in position to reap more of the upside in an optimistic scenario. Different parts of the capital structure are not always fairly priced relative to their respective riskiness. Credit hedge funds, with the ability to invest in a concentrated portfolio and flexible mandate, can dedicate the time and skills to determine the part of the capital structure that offers the best reward/risk proposition.

Furthermore, the composition of capital structures tends to vary over time as the appetite for different asset classes changes. As such, the amount of leverage at different parts of a capital structure can vary. Figure 1.4 shows the range of different capital structures for a hypothetical levered borrower. For example, from 2003 to 2007, there was an increase in leverage on the borrowers' balance sheets, and second, the mix of that debt was changing with more of the leverage being located at the senior debt level. The implication for investors is that the thicker loan tranche pushes the high yield bond lower down in the capital structure. Later, when the high yield bond market experienced heavy capital inflows from 2010 to 2012, many levered issuers issued bonds to repay their covenant-heavy bank loans (a "bond for loan" swap). Given this market dynamic, investors such as credit hedge funds need to carefully assess the value of the company and the security package when considering investing in a high yield bond to ensure that the expected return for the high yield bond is adequate compensation for the deeper subordination. The opportunities fluctuate over time, across market cycles, and across companies. In cases where leverage and debt burden on the company is low relative to revenue, cash flow, and growth expectation, certain hedge funds that generally invest in credit may have the flexibility to invest in equity (e.g., multistrategy credit funds and distressed debt funds).

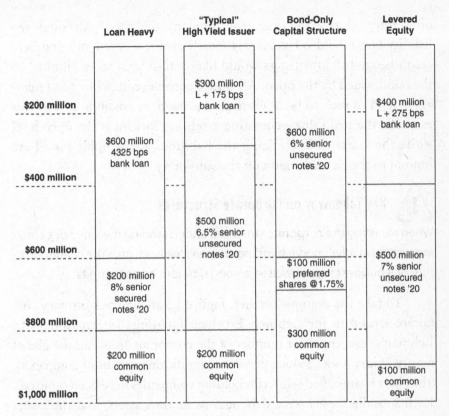

Figure 1.4 **Various capital structures for a levered borrower**
Source: PAAMCO

As investors are faced with more complex capital structure, this presents greater opportunity for astute credit hedge fund managers to add value from a thorough understanding of the capital structure. Figure 1.4 shows variations of a basic capital structure of an issuer with a single entity (i.e., with no parent or holding company relationship). In practice, many issuers are part of a corporate structure with many entities, some of which may reside in different countries and issue debt outside their domiciled address and in foreign currencies. Take, for example, a corporate structure with one parent entity and a single subsidiary. In market parlance, the parent company is often referred to as the holding company, or "holdco," and a subsidiary is often referred to as the operating company, or "opco." Although the liability of the holdco level is technically senior secured and first lien, credit hedge fund managers would likely consider it more "junior" to the bond issued by the opco. All things equal, credit hedge fund managers tend to seek to be as close to the assets as possible, and in this example, the real value-generating assets are located at the opco level while the assets collateralizing the liabilities at the holdco level are limited to the parent's claim on the subsidiary.

 Key Takeaway on Corporate Structures

When investing in a corporate structure, understanding the value of a credit instrument involves understanding where value lies within the capital structure of a business unit as well as among different business units.

To take the example further, Figure 1.5 shows the summary corporate structure for Lehman Brothers Holdings International.[4] In Lehman's case, the sheer number of the corporate units and the global nature of its presence alone present a significant amount of complexity (the chart is simplified—interim holding companies have been omitted). Each subsidiary may issue debt against its own assets, and the assets may or may not be subject to claims of creditors of the parent company in addition to the creditors of that particular subsidiary. In addition, there are complexities regarding guarantees from the parent company (Lehman Brothers Holdings International) to various subsidiaries.

 Key Questions on Corporate Structures

If you are investing in the loan or debt of a subsidiary, what are the assets of that subsidiary? Does that subsidiary have assets beyond the assets on its own balance sheet such as parent guarantee or guarantee from another subsidiary? Does that subsidiary have off-balance-sheet liabilities or provide guarantee to the parent or other units?

PRIVATE ISSUANCE AND FLEXIBLE STRUCTURES

In any investing situation, there is always an issue of information asymmetry between borrower and lender. However, the information

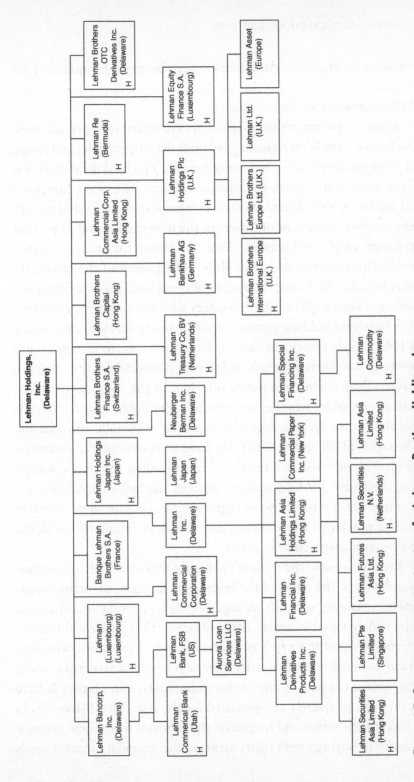

Figure 1.5 Summary corporate structure for Lehman Brothers Holdings Inc.

Source: Lehman Brothers Company Overview. H denotes subsidiaries whose obligations are guaranteed by Lehman Holdings, Inc. (LBHI)

asymmetry in the secondary market may be more pronounced for leveraged corporate credits due to the prevalence of private issuance and the number of smaller issuances.

Many corporate credit instruments are issued on a private basis. Some bonds, namely investment grade and the largest high yield issues, tend to be publicly issued, but many are not. The bank loan market is still predominantly a private market, and a large slice of the high yield bond market is also private. Private companies are estimated to represent roughly 85 percent of issuers in the loan market and 35 percent in the high yield bond market.[5] Rule 144 allows for private issuance to sophisticated investors, while Rule 144A improved the secondary market liquidity for bonds, as trading of the privately issued bonds can happen between sophisticated investors who are no longer restricted by the two-year holding period. In the primary market, an investor in a 144A private placement benefits from the access to management's projections and certain details of internal historical analysis that are not typically available in a public offering. In the secondary market, investors can select whether to remain in the public realm ("outside the wall") or to receive access to material nonpublic information (be brought "inside the wall"). If they have access to material nonpublic information, investors are restricted from trading the public securities of the issuer. In the secondary market, the lack of publicly available information provides some opportunities because some investors would be precluded from buying due to lack of familiarity with the issuer or with a particular issuance.

Because most of the deals are privately negotiated between investors and issuers, the terms of the investment (coupon, maturity, amortization, covenants, security package) are highly negotiable and as such can be widely variable across different deals. This structural flexibility accommodates the needs of both issuers and investors, who may demand customization that suits their regulatory or structural needs or may accept the issuer's request for a unique structure if they believe that they are adequately compensated for the risk. The differences in the investment terms and investors' rights mean that a new investor interested in buying credit instruments in the secondary market needs to have the time, expertise, and access to the information network in order to properly assess the investment opportunity.

Standardization of terms tends to reduce the information asymmetry between borrowers and lenders as well as among lenders and increase secondary market liquidity. Among other factors, the greater extent of variation across deals and the fact that waivers and renegotiations can change the terms of a deal over time create a higher amount of complexity, which makes the information asymmetry a particular feature of the corporate credit market. The information asymmetry tends to be more pronounced in cases where there is no or little publicly available information about the borrowers. An example would be where the borrower is privately owned and has no public equity or bonds in the capital structure.

Opportunities and challenges in dealing with this asymmetry are two sides of the same coin. Credit hedge funds can benefit from the limited buyer base willing to invest in a situation that is difficult to understand and where information is limited. Leveraged companies also face higher probability of needing covenant waivers or to restructure their debt from time to time (see earlier point on leverage). In such a case, lenders and borrowers will need to engage in a negotiation process to restructure the terms of the investment and additional capital infusion may be needed to keep the company as a going concern. In this stage, some investors typically exit the position. Some investment managers may be restricted by their mandate (they are unable to invest in a company in default), others may not be able to participate in adding capital (they have no access to additional funds or "dry powder" or run funds with very little cash); others sell because the liquidity profile of their investors does not match the investment horizon (funds with daily liquidity tend to exit early and be rather price insensitive at the exit). Consequently, credit investors with the ability and willingness to do a deep dive on the investment case, engage in negotiations and workout, and hold investments that need time to work out can benefit from the structural limitations that preclude many other investors from participating in these opportunities.

MARKET STRUCTURE

Unlike the public equity market, the corporate credit market does not have a centralized marketplace where buyers and sellers can meet and conduct trades. Most publicly traded equities trade in stock exchanges (physical or electronic) around the globe, while secondary trading in the corporate credit market largely takes place in the over-the-counter market. The market is fragmented, where trading takes place with various broker-dealers and in the inter-broker-dealer market. Trading in the bond market typically is dominated by large institutional investors and dealers. Large institutional buyers and sellers need to negotiate the trade either directly or through a broker.[6]

At the time of this writing, the need to deleverage and an expected increase in capital requirement for banks have largely led to banks being more likely to act as brokers rather than dealers. For example, an institutional investor wants to sell a bond in the secondary market and calls the bond desk in an investment bank. The investment bank can act as a broker or as a dealer. As a broker, if the bank already has a buyer, the bank will act as the middleman that matches the buyer and the seller. If the bank does not already have a buyer, it will try to find a buyer, and a transaction occurs only if a buyer can be found. As a dealer, if no buyer can be found, the bank may buy the bond from the seller and put it in its inventory because it believes that it will be able to find a buyer at the same or higher price later. In the latter case, the bank uses its balance sheet capital to provide liquidity to the market and takes some risk of the event that the price of the bond declines.

The absence of the capital buffer has a twofold effect: on one hand, it means potentially even more "patchy" liquidity and higher volatility in certain parts of the corporate credit market. On the other hand, it translates into opportunities for credit hedge funds, which now play an even more important part as the marginal buyer of levered corporate credit. Having a flexible investment mandate, trading skills, and ability to capture some liquidity premium can translate into alpha.

RANGE OF INSTRUMENTS EQUALS MORE LEVERS TO PULL

Given the nonuniform nature of value distribution and the wide range of instruments within a corporate capital structure, a credit hedge fund can draw from a variety of tools to express its view depending on investing style and background. A fundamental credit investor may prefer to go long on the most attractive credit instrument in a capital structure while shorting the least attractive part of another issuer. A relative value credit investor has the option to pair long exposure with short exposure to another part of the capital structure of the same issuer, which provides a natural way to hedge the overall company risk of the long exposure. For example, hedge fund managers may pair a long/short trade to reflect their view on the relative value of two bonds from the same issuer but with different maturity or subordination. They may also use equity, equity options, and other equity derivatives as liquid alternatives to hedge the credit exposure. In addition to the cash instruments, there are a variety of credit derivatives to choose from. Credit default swap (CDS), option on CDS (CDS swaption), and CDS indices (CDX) in many cases also provide a liquid, capital-efficient way to obtain long and short exposure to particular corporate credits. When shorting bonds on credit default swaps, the protection buyer may not need to post any margin or need to post only a minimal amount of margin (lower than what would be required if shorting the cash bond). This is another option available to credit hedge funds, which can choose how to express their view depending on their view on liquidity, technicals, cost of shorting, and cash management preferences.

LIMITED UPSIDE ON SHORTS

The unique feature of many credit instruments is the limited amount of price upside (downside for short exposure). Unlike an equity short position where the downside is theoretically unlimited, when one is shorting a bond that is trading at par or near par, the upside/downside is very attractive, as the upside price movement is limited while the price can theoretically move to zero.

CONCLUSION

- Many opportunities arise in corporate credit investing because of the inherent volatility of leverage, both on the borrowers' and investors' balance sheets.
- When looking at a particular bond or loan, just like equities, other parts in the same capital structure or similar instruments from comparable companies can provide some indicator of value.
- When comparing two bonds, in addition to the financial health of the issuers, an investor needs to discern where the bond lies in the capital structure, relative rights, and specific terms attached to each bond.
- The complexity in the corporate credit market (whether from capital structure or the nature of negotiated deals) combined with market structure that relies more heavily on over-the-counter trading and leverage means that comparable instruments often don't move together.
- Due to structural reasons, pricing inefficiencies and value dispersion may exist for longer periods before being arbitraged away. Investment managers who are disciplined on their entry points and who have the ability to hold the investments until the expected catalysts materialize can realize alpha in corporate credit investing.

CHAPTER 2

High Yield Bonds

Corporations form one of the largest groups of bond issuers[1] and thus are a source of many investing opportunities. In this chapter, we will discuss how credit hedge funds can capture the inefficiencies in the market for leveraged ("high yield") companies.

Out of more than 2,000 current outstanding issuances in the U.S. high yield bond market, approximately two-thirds of the issuance by number is smaller than $500 million. Figure 2.1 shows the market by issuance size. Due to the significant percentage of high yield bond issuance done via 144A private placements[2] (i.e., the issuers do not have to file public registration statements with the SEC), there are pockets of greater information asymmetry in the high yield bond market relative to the investment grade bond or public equity markets. A greater amount of complexity and information asymmetry in the space can give rise to investors who are able to do the deep dive to add value through credit selection coupled with hedging the main exposures, thereby capturing alpha. Outside of the United States, the Western European high yield bond market is estimated at $381 billion[3] and the Asian high yield bond market is estimated at $41 billion.[4]

Therefore, many investors see value in having a meaningful exposure to hedge funds whose core expertise and investment skill sets are focused on high yield corporate bonds. Unlike traditional asset

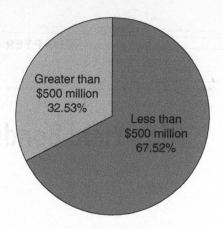

Figure 2.1 The U.S. high yield bond market by issuance size
Source: PAAMCO, Bloomberg

management, the hedge fund structure offers investors additional flexibility via the ability to gain short credit exposure, the ability to go to pockets of the market that are overlooked by traditional benchmark-bound investors, the ability to use a wider variety of synthetic instruments, and the ability to use higher levels of leverage when the opportunities warrant it.

HIGH YIELD BONDS

Many institutional investors largely classify the corporate bond universe into two categories. Using ratings as a standardized template with which to compare various bond issuances, the corporate bond universe is largely split into investment grade and below investment grade issuances. Bonds with ratings below investment grade (anything rated BB– or Ba and lower) are often referred to as "high yield" or "junk" bonds. Many investors have some degree of familiarity with investing in investment grade and high yield bonds, albeit perhaps not through the hedge fund structure.

According to the Securities Industry and Financial Markets Association (SIFMA), on December 31, 2010, the U.S. corporate debt market exceeded $7.5 trillion, making it the third largest fixed-income market within the United States after Treasuries and mortgages. Out of the total corporate U.S. debt market, more than $1 trillion is in the form of corporate debt with ratings below investment grade. Relative to the European, Asian, and emerging markets, the U.S. high yield market is currently the largest and broadest, with more than 1,000 corporate issuers and 2,100 securities in more than 60 industries.[5] However, given the triple-digit percentage growth in the market for European, Asian, and emerging market high yield debt in 2009 and 2010, investors can expect continued new opportunities in this particular asset class.

In the early days of the high yield market, most of the high yield bonds were investment grade at issue but later downgraded (i.e., "fallen angels"). Leveraged companies at the time had little choice when they needed financing—their financing choice was largely limited to borrowing from the banks. Indeed, the heavier reliance on bank lending is a phenomenon that we still observe in other markets where the high yield market is not yet as developed as the U.S. market, such as many emerging markets.

However, in the 1980s the high yield desk at Drexel Burnham Lambert, led by Michael Milken, popularized sub-investment grade bonds to a whole new group of investors. Mutual funds, insurance companies, and specialty finance companies were attracted to the market by the higher yield on these bonds, which more than compensated for the higher losses from default. Investors' demand for new high yield issuance increased, and a new mainstream asset class was born. Corporations and bankers responded to the demand for this new asset, and the 1980s saw the creation of some of the most innovative financing methods for leveraged issuers. Leveraged buyouts and other corporate activities such as mergers and acquisitions or dividend recapitalizations were popularized. One seminal example of a leveraged buyout transaction was Kohlberg Kravis Roberts' (KKR) taking RJR Nabisco private in 1989. The winning bid was for $25 billion, with $4 billion issued in the form of high yield bonds. Figure 2.2 shows the growth of the U.S. high yield market since 1989.

In this chapter, we will discuss hedge fund investment strategies that involve instruments that typically fall below bank loans but ahead of common and preferred equity in terms of seniority.

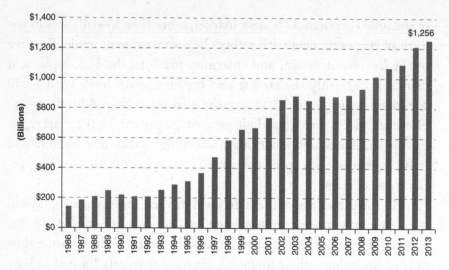

Figure 2.2   Growth of the U.S. high yield bond market
Source: Credit Suisse Leveraged Finance

XYZ Corp.

Senior Secured Bank Loans

Senior Unsecured Bonds

Junior Unsecured Bonds

Senior Subordinated Bonds

Junior Subordinated Bonds

Hybrids (incl. Convertible Bonds)

Preferred Stock

Common Stock

Figure 2.3   Capital structure of a hypothetical corporate issuer
Source: PAAMCO

Figure 2.3 shows the capital structure of a corporation in terms of seniority. When credit hedge funds refer to high yield bonds, they are usually referring to senior unsecured debt as well as junior unsecured or subordinated debt. Given that naming of a bond is not always consistent with its features, this chapter will use the phrase *high yield bond* as a broad term. The key driver for risk and return in high yield investing is the need to do due diligence on the specific features of an issue, as the rights of investors can vary significantly on a case by case basis. For example, although *notes* typically refers to instruments that are less than 10 years in tenor (time until maturity) when issued, there are notes with 20 and 30 year tenor.

High yield corporate bonds are typically issued on an unsecured basis, although in 2009, some less known, more highly levered, or fundamentally weaker issuers issued more secured bonds in place of senior secured loans. Unlike unsecured bonds, which fall under general obligations of the company, secured bonds are backed by specific collateral. Unsecured bonds are not backed by particular assets, however bondholders retain a general claim on the issuer. In liquidation, unsecured bondholders are classified as general creditors of the company. Holders of unsecured bonds may reap some benefit from the value of the company's assets, even assets that have been pledged to secured lenders. This is because the assets that have been pledged as collateral to secured lenders can be used to satisfy general creditors, but only the value in excess of the secured claim. Without the assets of the borrower pledged as collateral and providing an additional layer of protection, holders of bonds typically require a higher coupon payment than bank loan lenders, whose loans are collateralized by the assets of the borrower.

 ## Key Takeaway on the Naming Convention of Bonds

Assuming where a bond lies in the pecking order based only on its brief description can sometimes result in an incorrect analysis. The key point is for fund managers to understand the pecking order of the bond they are holding relative to other "IOUs" of the issuer and the asset coverage relative to that pecking order.

The rights of bondholders are contained in bond indentures, which may have provisions prohibiting the borrowers from certain acts that may have a negative impact on the value of the bondholders' claims. The indenture of a bond can limit the borrower's ability to incur more indebtedness, particularly at the same seniority level as the original bond. Typically less stringent are the provisions that allow the borrower to add borrowing on a subordinated basis, and the borrower may be subject to certain tests such as having to stay below the maximum allowable amount of total leverage as measured by the ratio of total net debt to earnings.

Another provision that may be contained in the indenture of an unsecured bond is the negative pledge provision, which may be found for issuers that have no secured debt on the balance sheet at the time of the unsecured bond issuance. A negative pledge may specify that should the borrower decide to issue secured debt in the future, the existing debt will be secured on a pro rata basis with the debenture. This gives the bondholders (technically an unsecured debt) equal claim on the company's assets with the secured debt that is issued later. This protects the claim value of the unsecured debt holders by preventing future secured lenders from leapfrogging to the front of the line in terms of the seniority of claim on the borrower's assets.

Many leveraged corporations, when they are prohibited from issuing more unsecured bonds, may also issue subordinated bonds. The term *subordinated* implies that these bonds are below unsecured bonds in seniority. One of the sweetener terms to make these bonds more attractive to investors is sometimes the addition of convertibility provisions, which allow the holders to convert the value of their bonds into equity at a certain conversion rate. This gives the holders of these bonds the benefit of the upside when the equity price of the company increases.[6] (Please see Chapter 5 for a separate discussion on convertible bonds.)

Key Takeaway on Different Market Practice Regarding Seniority

As an example of how market practices change over time, many convertible bonds issued after 2008 are pari passu to bonds of the same issuer.

Importance of the Primary Market

The process of issuance of high yield debt is similar to that of issuing investment grade debt albeit with typically a higher variation and negotiability around the coupon. As a reminder, the bonds can be collateralized or unsecured by the company's assets, and the issuance can be either privately or publicly placed.

Key Takeaway on Relative Attractiveness of Different Credit Asset Classes

For managers who focus on high yield debt, it is important to be aware of the relative attractiveness of the loan market, as many issuers will issue wherever it is cheaper. The relative cheapness of either market may be dependent upon macroeconomic factors. There is a strong correlation between the level of issuance and secondary market liquidity.

Another important institutional detail is the difference and hence pricing of public versus private debt. The SEC specified that bond issuers cannot use the private placement market to circumvent the registration requirement: if there is a similar bond by the same issuer that's publicly traded, the issuer cannot issue a bond through private placement. High yield issuers can issue eligible bonds without registering with the SEC if the bonds are only offered to those considered by the SEC to be sophisticated investors—those who have "sufficient knowledge and experience in financial and business matters to make them capable of evaluating the merits and risks of the prospective investment," which is often referred to as the 144A exemption.

Key Takeaway on Bond Terms

The terms of each new bond issuance can vary dramatically, and many things such as covenants, cash vs. payment-in-kind coupons, and conversion rights are negotiable.

When it comes to market issuance and subsequent secondary market liquidity, it is key to keep in mind that the high yield bond market is largely flow driven. The flows into and out of the high yield market greatly affect trading levels in the primary and secondary market. As a result, the high yield market tends to be highly cyclical. The market is either "open" (good liquidity, which usually corresponds with a bullish credit market) or "closed" (poor liquidity, usually corresponds with a bearish credit market). One of the advantages of investing in credit via the hedge fund structure is the ability to be disciplined in purchases and sales. When the market is strongly bullish and many parts of the market are overbid, a credit hedge fund manager does not have to continue to add to his position just to keep up with his benchmark. Similarly, when the market is overly bearish and the fund manager is finding many opportunities, an astute credit hedge fund manager can treat this as a buying opportunity.

 ## Key Takeaway on the Importance of Primary Market

Pay attention to the primary market even if the portfolio only invests in bonds traded on the secondary market. There is a strong correlation between the liquidity of the secondary market and the level of primary issuance.

Secondary Market

In the early days of the asset class, the market for sub-investment-grade corporate bonds was small and was dominated by buy-and-hold investors. There was virtually no secondary market for high yield corporate bonds. Secondary trading for high yield bonds was improved by Rule 144A, which was adopted by the SEC in 1990. Previously, the secondary trading of privately placed bonds was restricted by a two-year lock-up after purchase. Rule 144A modified the lock-up requirement, allowing privately placed bonds to be traded between "qualified institutional buyers" (QIBs). QIBs are typically defined as investors with at least $100 million of assets under management or banks with $25 million of capital.

 ## Key Takeaway on Trading Private Placements

When investing in hedge funds with less than $100 million under management, be sure to understand whether they qualify as a qualified institutional buyer (QIB) and thus can trade private placements.

Over time, technological advances have pushed more transactions to be conducted via electronic trading platforms,[7] which have helped to improve efficiency in price dissemination and discovery, thus changing the pricing characteristics of select pockets in the high yield bond market. That being said, the bond market is still dominated by large institutional investors and broker-dealers that trade on their own behalf, with most of the transactions occurring in the over-the-counter (OTC) market. Large "block" trades are common. Block trades refer to privately negotiated transactions that are executed outside physical or electronic exchanges.[8] The standardization of conventions for bond trades (yield calculation method, settlement practice, and quoting convention among other things) has helped a tremendous amount in improving secondary market liquidity in this market. The fragmented nature of the OTC market can add particular challenges to capturing market information such as pricing and liquidity. Figure 2.4 shows how a dealer market is organized and the role of the interdealer brokers.

Over time, market practices have moved toward improving price transparency in the secondary corporate bond market. In 2002, the National Association of Securities Dealer (NASD) launched the Trade

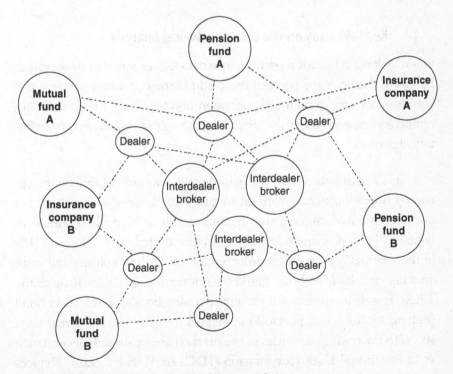

Figure 2.4 **Illustration of a dealer-driven market**
Source: PAAMCO

Reporting and Compliance Engine (TRACE), a vehicle to improve price transparency in the U.S. corporate debt market. Broker-dealers that are members of the Financial Industry Regulatory Authority (FINRA)[9] are required to report OTC bond transactions to TRACE within 15 minutes of completing the trade. TRACE collects secondary market information, namely price and volume, for investment grade and high yield corporate debt as well as convertible bonds. At the end of each trading day, TRACE disseminates the trade information for the most recent trading activities in the OTC corporate debt market on an aggregated basis. The TRACE website reports the volume of trades by number of issues and par volume as well as the number of advances and declines and the number of issues that are seeing 52-week highs versus lows. The daily statistics, which are available on the TRACE website, offer investors access to some information that may be useful in measuring the depth and breadth of the high yield bond market.

 ### Key Takeaway on the Use of Historical Analysis

When looking at historical performance data (either actual or back-tested), be aware that in many parts of the credit markets, trading patterns and liquidity can vary dramatically between periods. Thus, future volatility, opportunities, and sources of mispricing may differ significantly from historical periods.

It is worth noting that the information for transactions on unregistered bonds between qualified institutional buyers is collected, but not disseminated. Since a significant amount of high yield bonds are issued as 144A placement and are therefore traded only between QIBs in the secondary market, the information on trading volume and price on a big chunk of the bond market is not readily available through the TRACE website (unlike for exchange traded bonds). High yield bond traders, analysts, and portfolio managers (people who need real-time access to the trading activities in the market) use fee-based services such as International Data Corporation (IDC) or Markit. These services provide information on prices and volume of the most recent transactions on particular bonds.

RISKS OF INVESTING IN HIGH YIELD BONDS

This section briefly reviews the risks of investing in high yield bonds as it pertains to credit hedge funds.

Interest Rate and Credit Risk

Market participants often divide the yield of a high yield bond into the risk-free rate as measured by comparable Treasuries and a spread above Treasuries. Out of these components, the risk-free rate is the easiest to observe and calculate. After decades of continued downward movement on interest rates, rates are at their historical lows. The likelihood of upside (continued rate compression) is low compared to the potential downside (rate increases). For the years after the 2008 credit crisis, a significant amount of the gains in high yield indices can be attributed to gains from reduction in interest rates.

 Key Takeaway on Interest Rate Risk

High yield bond managers, sometimes for the first time in their entire careers, now have to worry about managing their interest rate risk.

The spread above Treasuries is often divided into credit spread and risk premium, which often includes liquidity premium. When discussing a spread, the spread may or may not be adjusted for embedded options in the bond.[10] Therefore, it is important to verify whether the spread quoted is option adjusted. Estimating the market expectation of default probability is an iterative process. In practice, one method is to assume a reasonable level of loss given default (typically based on historical levels) to back out the market's implied default probability on a particular high yield bond, keeping in mind that historical data has shown there is an excess positive spread between the yield of sub-investment grade bonds and actual default losses,[11] which shows that high yield investors can earn a premium for taking risks.

During market dislocations, the spread above Treasuries can increase far beyond the increase in default probability. This is usually attributed to the increase in risk premium (which is often taken to include liquidity premium). During periods of dislocation, usually there is a flight to quality where investors demand significantly higher compensation to hold risky assets. This means what may look like the reasonable credit risk exposures in a normal environment may result in significant losses during a "risk-off" environment. Combined with a high level of short-term financing, this is one of the key reasons behind many credit hedge fund "blowups." Leverage amount and hedging that may seem appropriate in a normal risk premium environment may be proven excessive and inadequate in a stress situation.

 Key Questions on Hedging

- How is the amount of hedge determined? How do you determine which instruments are best used as hedges?
- Are these calculations based on normal or stressed risk exposures? What are the scenarios?
- Note that there is no correct answer. Hedging may be inadequate. Actual stress test or scenario analysis based on past events may not appropriately reflect current market risks.

Other Risks

Other risks, beyond those of traditional long-only investing, that are highly relevant to high yield–oriented hedge funds include legal and political risks. Due to their flexible mandate, many U.S.-based credit hedge funds may invest in the debt of non-U.S. issuer if the opportunity warrants it. One of the risks of investing in the debt of a non-U.S. borrower is nationalization of the company through which the government of the country where the issuer is domiciled assumes the debt. In that case, investors' rights lie in the hands of a foreign judicial system and investors may find themselves facing a new set of rules in an unfamiliar jurisdiction. Furthermore, treatment and rights of creditors vary significantly across jurisdictions, and the local court system may be influenced by political considerations that are adverse to creditors' interests.

The case of investors in the bonds issued by Allied International Bank illustrates these points. When its assets declined dramatically in the 2008 credit crisis, the bank was nationalized by the Irish High Court. The court then decided to exclude foreign bondholders from the bank's rights offering, essentially forcing foreign bondholders to take a loss on the bonds without the ability to own the bank's equity and therefore losing on the valuable option of the bank's future value as a going concern.[12] Even in the case of "Yankee bonds," which are almost exclusively issued under New York governing law, bondholders may have a difficult time enforcing the decisions of New York courts if the issuer and its assets are located in another country.

INVESTMENT STRATEGIES

Given that the myriad of investment strategies used by credit hedge funds often have some degree of underpinning in fundamental credit analysis, it may be worth dedicating time to some nuances of fundamental credit analysis. The process of evaluating the creditworthiness of a particular high yield investment can be broken down into three major components:

- The first is the company's ability to pay. It is important to focus not only on interest coverage but also on the company's ability to refinance.
- Second is investors' rights and behavior. Many credit hedge funds consider the other investors in the company as a very important part of the credit analysis. In a sense, part of fundamental credit analysis is akin to game theory where the expectations about the actions of others (fellow investors, whether more senior, similar, or junior in the capital structure, management, and equity holders) have an impact on one's decision-making process.
- Third is the value of the collateral behind the debt. This is critical to determining the recovery value if default takes place. In addition, some managers may use activist strategies to improve the value of the collateral.

Covenants are meant to provide protection to creditors by limiting the issuers' ability to do things that may reduce the amount or quality of collateral backing the debt. Generally the creditors seek protective covenants in three areas: cash leakage, asset encumbrance, and debt incurrence. Many credit managers look at covenants as part of their due diligence process. However, the extent to which they evaluate and understand the complexities of certain covenant language can make or break the outcome of the investment. Complexities often arise from exceptions ("carve-outs") to the typical covenant terms, particularly during times when the high yield market is booming and issuers can get away with looser terms.

Covenants can broadly be classified into two types: maintenance covenants and incurrence covenants. Maintenance covenants are more commonly seen in loan agreements, while bond indentures typically contain incurrence covenants. Between the two, maintenance covenants place greater restrictions on the borrower because the borrower needs to meet specific financial ratios every quarter. Incurrence covenants are less restrictive because the borrower needs to comply with them only when the borrower wants to do specific things such as issue more debt or pay dividends.

Certain covenants such as the maximum leverage provision may apply beyond the issuer but also to some of its subsidiaries. Understanding whether a subsidiary is restricted (subject to the bond covenants of its parent company) has an impact on the analysis of the bonds of the parent as well as the analysis of the bonds issued by the subsidiary. When a company needs to issue bonds to buy assets but is prohibited from doing so by the covenants of its existing bonds, the company may create a certain subentity or a special purpose vehicle (SPV). The SPV, if unrestricted, is then able to borrow outside the covenants against the parent.

An example of a covenant intended to preserve cash availability to bondholders is the restricted payment covenant. This covenant limits the ability of issuers to pay dividends to equity holders or to direct payment to various subsidiaries of the company. Traditionally, the restricted payment bucket may be limited to a certain portion of the company's net income and subject to meeting the fixed charge coverage limit.[13]

However, issuers with private equity owners have an incentive to loosen the restricted payment covenant. From time to time, there have been aggressive structures where the restricted payment bucket is not limited in size, allowing large cash dividend payments to the sponsor.

Other types of covenants that provide protection to bondholders include limitation-on-lien covenants, where the typical language states that the issuer has limited ability to issue more senior secured debt and thus protects the unsecured bondholder from subordination. During the 2012 great hunt for yield, some of the newly issued bonds did not have the limitation-on-lien covenant. Bonds were issued at such attractive coupons that issuers were not willing to promise that they would keep assets unencumbered because they did not expect to gain any pricing advantage by doing so. Bondholders also saw less protection, as bond issuances were done without the debt incurrence test. This test limits the ability of the bond issuer to issue new debt, which would create additional claim on the company's assets. Similarly, some issuers did away with the change-of-control clause in their bond issuance. This clause protects the bondholders by giving them the right to put the bond at par or par plus a premium if the issuer is sold.

Relative to their benchmarked peers, there is a greater focus in the hedge fund community on finding disparities between the traditional credit metrics used by rating agencies and what managers believe is the true case. The managers tend to do this because, unlike in a traditional account, they have more flexibility in guidelines and are not required to stick within certain limits of rating buckets. Credit hedge funds also tend to pay greater attention to complex capital structures (and the corresponding impact on priority of payments), covenants, and subtle behavioral issues with management.

When evaluating credit hedge fund managers, it is important to keep in mind that these strategy classifications are subjective in nature. Hedge funds can and do use different ways to describe their strategy, sometimes emphasizing one approach over others depending on market appetite for a particular approach. It is particularly important for investors to find out in detail about the investment styles and strategy used by a hedge fund given the inherent flexibility in the mandates for many credit hedge funds. Two managers may have similar background and describe their respective portfolios using similar catchphrases or description but have portfolios with very different exposures and performance depending on how these strategies are executed. A multistrategy credit fund may combine any and all of these strategies at a particular given time, although one style may be the dominant approach in how they view the world depending on the background and particular strength of the lead portfolio manager (PM). For example, if the lead PM's background is from proprietary desks of investment banks, he or she is most likely to view the world from a trading perspective, although this strong trading orientation may be combined with deep research capabilities from other parts of the firm. The investor's challenge is to disentangle the contribution from the basket of approaches that a manager uses. Determining whether a particular approach actually adds value over time is part science, part art.

Fundamental Long/Short Strategy

The fundamental long/short high yield bond strategy essentially seeks to obtain long exposure to bonds that are underpriced and short exposure to bonds that are overpriced. In this sense, this strategy has many similarities with the classic Graham and Dodd long/short equity investing strategy familiar to many investors. Key differences include looking for specific catalysts that will bring value realization (see section titled "Event-Driven and Special Situations"); evaluating the ability to trade the positions; and finally, the ability to maintain not only the short borrow but also the typically very high interest payable on the short positions.

When looking at fundamental high yield hedge fund portfolios over the economic cycle, the portfolio can be long biased or close to net neutral. Some managers add value through their management of gross and net exposure of the portfolio in addition to their fundamental credit selection. The portfolio in this case may be relatively diversified or concentrated depending on the manager's risk tolerance and degree of conviction on the portfolio positions. In this strategy, typically the portfolio gets relatively more diversified as the fund gets larger ($1 billion or larger). The likelihood to see a diversified portfolio in this strategy is tied to the PM's appetite for liquidity and inversely related to the liquidity of underlying positions. It is a function of the typical investment size that makes sense for the fund "bite size." Let's take an example of two fundamental high yield hedge funds, A and B. A has $1 billion in assets under management and B has $250 million. A 3 percent position is $30 million for A and $7.5 million for B (assume both buy bonds at par; as such, market value of the bond is equal to the face value of the bond). If both funds A and B were to invest in bond X and the bond typically trades anywhere from $30 to $60 million in a given trading day, B's exposure is relatively more liquid than A's, all things being equal. If the manager of fund A wishes to improve the liquidity profile of his investments, then he will need to either invest in more liquid bonds (larger issuance size, higher daily trading volume, better coverage by the sell-side, etc.) or reduce the size of his exposure.

Comparing a hedge fund to a typical long-only portfolio, a diversified hedge fund portfolio will still be relatively more concentrated. Measuring concentration by the range of position sizes as percent of net asset value (NAV), a typical diversified fundamental credit hedge fund portfolio may define a 1 to 2 percent position as small, a 2 to 4 percent position as medium, and large positions can be anywhere from 5 to 10 percent of NAV. Some credit funds with customized mandates that are specifically tilted toward concentration may see core positions well in excess of 10 percent of NAV. In contrast, a typical long-only credit portfolio may see a fair number of positions smaller than 1 percent of NAV and very few positions larger than 5 percent.

 Key Questions on Position Sizing and Shorting

- Do you have a maximum position size? At cost or at market? Is it a hard limit?
- What is the current largest position in your portfolio? How has the size changed over time?
- How do you maintain your borrow? Will you use credit index hedges? Equity puts or calls?

Edge Being Captured

Compared to public equities, the high yield bond market has a higher amount of informational inefficiency, particularly if there is no listed equity for the issuer, as is often the case with LBOs or other private equity deals. The information issue is compounded by the fact that creditors' rights for different high yield bonds (e.g., seniority, collateral package, call and put features) can vary significantly across issuers of different credit ratings and across different issuances of the same issuer over time. Unlike in the equity market where there typically is one class of shares, the existence of parent and operating company relationship with respect to cross-company guarantees or pledges combined with cross-default provisions are some of the examples that add complications to a company's capital structure. In a world where business is globalized, having the bond issuance and the company's value generating assets in different legal jurisdictions can also add significant complexity to the credit analysis. When combined with the greater informational asymmetry in the high yield market, there is room for investors who are willing and able to do the deep fundamental work to add alpha.

The inherent flexibility in the investment mandate and structure of hedge funds can serve to better capture the inefficiencies in the high yield market. For example, many high yield investors cannot invest in unrated and privately rated bonds, or have certain restrictions about the amount of exposure to CCC and defaulted bonds.

In addition, as was the case many years ago with equities, there are relatively few players in high yield that focus on shorting the relatively overvalued bonds. Compared to shorting equities, shorting a bond near its call price provides much better risk/reward opportunity to the investor. When shorting cash equity, the maximum gain to the investor is the price of the equity, while the maximum loss is theoretically infinite. When shorting a bond near its call price, the maximum gain is the price of the bond, while the maximum loss is the difference between the call price and current price of the bond.

As with any long/short mandate, managers can add value through management of the gross and net exposure of their portfolio. In expectation of a bearish credit market, a fundamental credit hedge fund can bring the net exposure of the portfolio to neutral or negative by adding a significant amount of short exposure to issuers that are expected to show fundamental deterioration in their creditworthiness or run into liquidity problems. Similarly, when the credit and economic environments are expected to be benign (widely available credit, low default, positive and steady growth environment), the hedge fund manager has the flexibility to increase the gross and net exposure of the portfolio.

 Key Takeaways on Stop Losses

Due to its liquidity profile and the way technicals affect the high yield bond market, stop losses can be difficult to implement and may result in selling the position at or near market bottom. Unlike equity hedge funds, credit hedge funds with a fundamental investment approach tend not to employ stop losses.

Risks

In the case of fundamental long/short credit managers, the biggest risk is that the managers are mistaken on their fundamental credit analysis. In this scenario, the concentration of the portfolio can compound the losses from taking the wrong bet on the fundamentals. Another risk is that the managers are correct on their fundamental analysis, however, the market is not recognizing it and the bond remains under- or overpriced due to market technical or other nonfundamental reasons. Particularly on the short side, the relatively high coupon interest payable can be substantial, which makes holding nonperforming short positions very painful. It is highly possible the portfolio will exhibit negative carry, as the yield on the short side (the lower quality securities) may be greater than that of the long side.

While this strategy focuses on fundamental valuation, one must not forget that these are fixed-income securities. For example, the portfolio may take unintended yield curve risk if the average maturity on each side is significantly different. In addition, when performing a liquidation or stop loss analysis, one must remember to take into account the bid-ask spread, which is wider than those seen in equities. Finally, while the high yield market is large, many players are buy and hold, so the market impact of any trading must also be factored into the analysis.

In certain cases, if managers are unable to express their fundamental view through cash instruments, they may use synthetic credit instruments to express their view. A trade that is often seen is buying protection via credit default swap to express a negative view on a company's credit fundamentals. Expressing a short view via CDS as opposed to shorting the cash bond may provide certain benefits—for example, for many bonds the CDS may be more liquid. However, there is a risk that the CDS does not track the performance of the cash bond. The manager may be right and the spread on the cash bond may widen, but the spread on the corresponding CDS may stay relatively flat or widen less than the cash bond. The different performance between cash and CDS bond is often referred to as the cash-synthetic basis.

 ## Key Questions for the Short Side of the Portfolio

- How do you prefer to express your short view—cash or synthetics?
- Is your portfolio negative carry?
- How do you think about the cash-synthetic basis in your portfolio?
- What is the liquidity of the CDS of (a particular bond)?

Event-Driven and Special Situations

In the credit space, some of the more popular events (listed from the most concrete or definitive "hardness" to the less explicit "softness") include Chapter 11 restructuring or bankruptcy, liquidation, asset sales, spin-offs, demergers, asset injections, maturity or refinancing, change of control, activism, and value investing with catalyst. An event is harder if it meets two criteria: the impact on the security is quantifiable with a higher degree of certainty and the timetable of event realization is well defined. In this strategy, the thesis may include a series of events within the investment horizon, and each event may be viewed as an option on a stream of cash flows with its own attached value.

Oftentimes, there may be some sort of overall macroeconomic hedging as well, particularly if managers see a macroeconomic event (e.g., results of an election) as having outsized impact on their event-driven longs. This approach tends to rely on fundamental research as, in many cases, a particular event was unearthed as a result of having done the fundamental work on a particular bond or bond issuer. The key difference is that there is no real attempt to have a diversified short side of the portfolio; rather the short positions are used to reduce exposure to the overall macroeconomic environment.

On the long side, one may search for a company that is expected to be the target for purchase by a larger company and the bond (which may be expensive, particularly if the new owner is more highly rated) is expected to be called at par plus call premium in the next six months. This would be classified as a hard event because it is very specific. Another example would be a company that is currently negotiating its labor contracts and is expected to be able to cut costs, improving the company's credit metrics and cash flow. The negotiation is expected to last three months, with cost-cutting impact showing on the financials for the next four quarters. This would be classified as an operational improvement and would be considered a soft event. Another example of a hard event is a company engaged in a litigation battle against its competitor, who claimed it infringed on its valuable patents. The case is currently in the last appeal stage, and a final decision can be expected within the next three months. This style is often referred to as a litigation play and would typically be considered a hard event even though the time frame may be uncertain.

On the short side, an example of a negative event would include a company whose revenues are highly contract driven (resulting in long-term predictable cash flows) and is operating under a set of contracts and contracted pricing that are scheduled to expire within the next 6 to 12 months. A lot of these contracts are not expected to be renewed at current pricing, if at all, which may lead to reduced revenue and cash flow.

Edge Being Captured

The aim of the event-driven strategy is to profit from the tendency for company- or asset-specific events to move in a way that's uncorrelated with one another. As such, the ability and willingness to embrace situations that are complex and/or misunderstood by many market participants is a source of alpha. The nonhomogeneous nature of access to and quality of information in the high yield market gives advantage to investors with insight toward future events on a specific bond and bond issuer. In order to keep the noncorrelated nature of the portfolio, it is important to have overall macroeconomic hedges in place for variables such as general levels of interest and/or credit risk.

One reason that this strategy is attractive is that bond indentures contain language that provides specific triggers for catalysts. For example, a bond may have a provision in the indenture where if the company is late in filing its quarterly reports with the SEC, then the bonds become due in full shortly after the filing due date. The company may be in good financial health and have good access to the capital markets; however, a recent change in accounting methodology (which does not affect creditworthiness) may have delayed the filing. This is a provision that is likely to be discovered by close reading of the bond indenture, and doing so enables the hedge fund manager to anticipate an event where a bondholder can put the bond back to the issuer in short order, realizing highly attractive internal rate of return for a short-term investment with low credit risk.

Risk

There are two main risks of this strategy. The first is event risk. Similar to the fundamental long/short strategy, there is risk that the manager is proven to be incorrect in regard to the anticipated catalysts or where the manager is correct when it comes to the catalyst but is mistaken on the timing (execution risk).

The second main risk is that if the overall macroeconomic conditions deteriorate, these portfolios often decline by more than expected. In a bear market, many of these events have positive correlation to the overall macroeconomic environment. This can translate into not only a significant delay in the events, but also their cancellation as the corporation reevaluates its actions, thus resulting in an even greater loss in these positions.

Finally, if the position is a short position and the manager is expecting a negative catalyst, an extended horizon for the catalyst increases the risk of being short squeezed (if shorting a cash bond) or the fundamentals being overshadowed by technical strength in the CDS market (if shorting through credit default swap). Given where yields can be, shorting high yield bonds can also be an expensive proposition for the portfolio. The longer the short is on while waiting for the negative catalyst to materialize, the higher the hurdle the investor has to overcome before the trade reaches breakeven.

 Key Questions for Event Credit Managers

- How do you define an "event"?
- Give me an example of a soft event you would not invest on.
- What are the time horizons of the events in the portfolio?
- How frequently is the thesis reevaluated? What if events do not materialize as expected?

Capital Structure Arbitrage or Relative Value

Capital structure arbitrage or relative value trading typically involves taking a long exposure combined with a paired short exposure. This type of trade can be done within the same capital structure of the same company, or of different companies. With equities, a classic example of this trade is taking a long exposure in the equity of Coca-Cola and shorting the equity of Pepsi. Convertible bond hedging is not usually considered capital structure arbitrage even though it fits the definition; rather it is considered its own well-defined substrategy.

In credit, there are a number of variations on the trade. One is to buy Coca-Cola bonds and short Coca-Cola stock. This trade is a reflection of a view on how value will move between different parts of the same capital structure. For example, if the company announces a reduction in demand for soda, the market could punish the bonds and the equity similarly. Or, alternatively, the market may feel that— despite the negative announcement—Coca-Cola remains well positioned to pay its debts, and the equity may be punished more than the bonds. This capital structure arbitrage can also take a distressed angle. For example, should Coca-Cola file for bankruptcy and the assets of the company not be enough to satisfy the full claims of the bondholders, the bonds are likely to become the fulcrum security. In other words, in the bankruptcy process, bondholders may receive part of their claim in cash and the rest in ownership of the company, while the equity holders may lose their entire investments or receive only a minimal amount.

Edge Being Captured

This strategy captures value that arises from the fact that the complexity of corporate capital structure and different supply and demand dynamics of various asset classes often mean that value is not evenly distributed in various parts within the capital structure. In a capital structure, seniority and the prioritization of claims in a waterfall structure translate into a pecking order for various classes of bondholders. Understanding where value lies in parts of the capital structure and being able to gauge relative price attractiveness between those parts mean that an investor may be able to profit from that relative mispricing while hedging out some of the broader risks.

Risk

The primary risk in a relative value trade is nonconvergence—that the long position suffers a loss while the short position does not respond correspondingly or maybe also suffers a loss. The secondary risk is that, particularly if it is a junior bond on the short side, the short position, due to a squeeze, may be difficult to maintain. It is also very important to differentiate between long on the senior bond and short on the junior and the reverse of the trade, long the junior bond and short the senior. This second position is dramatically riskier than the first because in a bankruptcy, there is much higher probability of losing on both sides of this trade.

Capital structure arbitrage trades also tend to be more highly levered, on both the long and the short side. The portfolio aims to capture small over- or underpricing of instruments, and the portfolio needs enough trade to multiply a small profit per trade into a large enough profit for the entire portfolio. The higher leverage brings with it the amplification of losses (as well as gains) and liquidity risk as well as counterparty risk. The hedge fund manager needs to be cognizant about the potential dry-up in liquidity. Many relative value fund managers are typically careful about staying liquid on both sides of the trade. However, they need to show that they are cognizant of the possibility that the trade may be liquid when put on, but when the trade moves against them, the timing may coincide with a liquidity crisis. If certain positions need to be liquidated in the event that the managers are unable to meet a margin call, the liquidation may take place well below fair value of the assets (a reflection of heightened risk premium). Furthermore, the trade is "printed" at a lower price, and this may negatively affect other positions in the portfolio, leading to more liquidation.

In a capital structure arbitrage, the complexity of a situation can give rise to the risk that the manager is mistaken about the value at various parts of the capital structure. For example, a trade may consist of a long exposure to a high yield bond issued by a subsidiary and short exposure to the equity of the parent company. In this trade, the capital structure arbitrage is between the bond and the equity as well as between the parent and subsidiary—the debt of the subsidiary is typically regarded as higher in seniority relative to the debt of the parent because in many cases the asset of the company is located at the subsidiary level. In certain cases, the debt of the subsidiary may be considered senior to the bank loan of the parent. The original thesis may be that the subsidiary's bonds are underpriced given the asset coverage at the subsidiary level and that if the company hits a negative patch, the equity of the parent company may be affected more than the bond of the subsidiary.

However, if the manager is wrong about the amount of asset coverage at the subsidiary level and the parent company has access to other assets (e.g., other subsidiaries), the value of the equity may remain stable even as the bond drops in value.

Another risk in the relative value trade comes from the different seniority of the long and the short leg. It is common to see a long position of cash bond paired with short via CDS to express the view that the cash bond is underpriced relative to the CDS. The reason why the cash bond traded at a wider spread than the credit default swap may be because the bond is subordinated while the CDS reference entity is senior unsecured (i.e., the CDS reference entity is more senior than the bond). In the case of issuer default, the bond may not be deliverable against the CDS; it is more junior and this is the reason behind the wider spread.

Basis risk needs to be carefully analyzed, as many short positions are implemented using credit derivatives. In a trade example of a long and short position on two different bonds of the same issuer (e.g., a long cash exposure of senior Coca-Cola versus buy protection on the CDS of Coca-Cola where the underlying reference obligation is a junior bond), there is a risk that the CDS spread does not reflect a movement of the spread for the cash bond. In some cases, there may not be a CDS (or a sufficiently liquid CDS market) on a particular bond, and the cash bond may be difficult to obtain or borrow. Anytime the trade involves a cash position versus a synthetic credit instrument, the cash and synthetic basis can diverge. Basis is defined as the difference between the spread of the synthetic credit instrument and the spread of the cash instrument.

The liquidity differential between the instruments used in the long and the short legs of the trade can also present a risk to the investor. A popular trade construction is to have less liquid instruments on the long end and more liquid instruments on the short leg. Some trade examples may include going long on a less liquid high yield bond and shorting the public equity, a bond with better liquidity, or credit default swap with better liquidity. The thesis of this trade is to profit from capturing the liquidity premium, and this trade is more often seen with fund managers who combine the relative value approach with a fundamental credit edge. During certain volatile times, the less liquid bonds may see higher volatility (a $2 million offer may have a large negative impact on price with a bond where the typical market trade is $2 to 4 million compared to a bond where the typical trade is $10 to 15 million), making them potentially better buys for discerning fund managers with sufficient "dry powder." Having a more liquid short may also allow managers to add value through tactical trading or to exit more quickly if the short moves against them. In the event of market dislocation, however, investors in the market may choose to abandon their less liquid positions and rotate into more liquid positions in the form of a "flight to quality." Because this trade is essentially a long liquidity trade, this may cause the trade to incur losses.

Key Questions for Capital Structure Arbitrage

- Which side of the portfolio—long or short—has been the main return generator for the past quarter/12 months/X years?
- Do you think of the short side as a hedge or as an alpha generator?
- If the company files for bankruptcy, which positions will be hurt?
- How do you manage the cash-synthetic basis risk (if at all)?

Trading Oriented or Technical

In the trading-oriented or technical strategy, the investment approach may still be influenced by some fundamental analysis on the company; however, the clear dominant factor is the shorter-term supply and demand dynamics for each bond. This strategy is often used by former dealers who in essence are replicating the dealing function. Thus, the trading-oriented approach typically has a shorter investment horizon compared to the fundamental long/short approach.

Given the variety of approaches, a few examples will help clarify the types of trades in the trading-oriented strategies. For example, a trading strategy is to capture the roll-down impact. As time goes by and the bond rolls closer to maturity or the next call date—a bond that had five years to maturity now has four years to maturity—if the five-year point on the spread curve is 500 bps and the four-year point is 400 bps, the bond is expected to benefit from a 100 bps spread tightening. If the bond has duration of 3.5 years, the 100 bps spread tightening is expected to result in a 3.5 percent increase in the bond's price.

Another variation of this strategy is a combination of a trading orientation and relative value approach. The long leg of the portfolio is as described before, and paired with a short exposure via a 10-year CDS contract where the swap curve is relatively flat between the 5-year CDS and the 10-year CDS. In other words, it is not that much more expensive to buy a 10-year protection on the bond relative to the 5-year protection. Due to the "flatness" of the CDS curve, as the 10-year CDS becomes a 9-year CDS (and the 5-year bond becomes a 4-year bond), the spread narrowing on the short side is less than the spread narrowing on the long side. The trade can also be structured as a neutral or positive carry trade. Because the CDS has a higher sensitivity to credit spread due to its higher spread duration, the fund manager may decide to do the trade on a duration-neutral basis where there are more dollars at exposure on the long end than on the short end. Depending on the relative difference in spread between the long and the short leg, the trade could earn more carry on the long end than what it has to pay out on the short end.

Another example is the upgrade/downgrade trade. This trade is often applied with bonds that are in the "threshold" between investment grade and non-investment grade. The trade is to go long a bond that is expected to be upgraded from BB to BBB—this will significantly broaden the universe of investors who can hold the bond (due to regulatory or capital requirement reasons, for example). The increase in demand in addition to expected improvement in credit quality as proxied by rating is expected to create a positive technical wind for the bond. Similarly, the trade involves a short exposure of a bond that is expected to be downgraded from a BBB to BB.

Edge Being Captured

A trading-oriented strategy aims to profit from the fact that many players in the high yield bond market are subject to constraints that may lead them to make noneconomic decisions combined with the likely mandatory reduction in proprietary books in the major dealers. Because there are no centralized exchanges for high yield bonds like there are for equities, the trading activity in the high yield bond market is dispersed among various subconstituents in the market. For example, there are approximately 40 broker-dealers that are trading in corporate high yield bonds. A liquid high yield bond can be covered by five or six dealer desks, while an illiquid corporate high yield bond may only be traded and covered by the lead bank in the original deal syndicate. When the relevant few players are unable to provide liquidity to the market, it tends to have a more marked impact; thus liquidity in this market is often described as "it's there until it's not" or "patchy."

Risks

The key risk to this strategy is that one is not able to execute the trades at the desired prices. Because there is relatively high turnover in the portfolio and relatively short holding periods, transaction costs are significantly more important in this strategy. This can be illustrated in the case of nonconvergence. The trade is profitable if the dislocation in the market is temporary and the relative prices between the long and the short legs of the trade converge to their normal relationship. However, both the long and the short legs of the trade can remain dislocated for an extended period or even diverge further from historical norms. The risk is that the fund manager is unable to stay in the trade and is taken out before convergence takes place. Leverage presents this risk because if one or both legs of the trade are hit with losses, the fund manager is likely to need to meet margin calls or be taken out of the trade when the leverage provider or swap counterparty liquidates his positions. Usage of leverage is common for the relative value approach, both on the long and the short side of the portfolio. Even when leverage is not used on the long portfolio, the short portfolio will be levered, whether through reverse repo, cash shorts via prime brokerage, or credit derivatives such as CDS and CDX. It is important that fund managers are able to demonstrate to investors that they have a robust process to anticipate margin calls and manage cash as well as a reasonable risk and leverage management process.

Another risk in the relative value trade comes from the fact that the long exposure may not be perfectly matched to the short exposure. This is a good example of how reward and risk are two sides of the same coin.

For example, a trade may include a long cash exposure on a high yield bond that has 10 years to maturity and a paired short exposure via a 5-year credit default swap on the same issuer. The thesis of the trade is that the long cash bond is trading at too wide a spread relative to the spread level of the credit default swap. Here, the mismatch in tenor of the long versus the short leg may be intentional or due to market imposed reasons such as liquidity. If the issuer defaulted on the bond, the trade may end up flat because the loss from the long cash bond position is offset by the gains from the credit default swap. However, if the issuer does not default on the bond, the spread of the cash bond will narrow and converge to the level of the credit default swap. In this scenario, the long position will see positive gains as the short position is flat (no change in mark-to-market), earning the investor a profit on the trade. The investor also benefits from positive carry because the running coupon on the long position is expected to exceed that of the short. However, timing of default is important. If default happens right after the manager puts the position on, the trade may end up in a loss because the up-front points on the CDS are lost immediately.[14]

Another reason that fund managers use a trading approach is to benefit from technical dislocations. Consider a situation in which the fund manager expects that the sell-off in the cash bond market is temporary, for example, if the bond is not very frequently traded, the issue is closely held, and one of the large holders of the issue is forced to sell its bond in the market due to unrelated reasons but buyers are scarce because not many investors are familiar with the issuer or with the issuance. In this scenario, the relative lower liquidity and informational inefficiency of the bond market can provide opportunities for certain investors. The manager may not be able to match the tenor of the long cash bonds because the only tenor available for the credit default swap is the five year.

For a credit portfolio where the cash longs are hedged with credit indices, such as the CDX North American High Yield Index (CDX. NA.HY), basically the manager intends to isolate the credit risk on the long side by hedging the general credit market risk as proxied by the credit index. There are several forms of basis risks in the portfolio such as the credit basis risk—that the long bond positions are different from the bonds that make up the CDX.NA.HY. The CDX.NA.HY is an equally weighted index of 100 most actively traded credit default swaps of high yield companies. If the long portfolio the index is supposed to hedge largely comprises smaller, less frequently traded bonds, there may be times when the index short is not behaving as expected. The long bond positions may see losses due to spread widening as the spread of CDX.NA.HY remains flat or even narrows if smaller, less liquid companies are seeing losses due to decreased appetite for smaller bonds while the investor appetite for bonds of larger, more liquid companies remains robust.

Synthetic instruments such as credit default swaps, credit default swap indices, tranches (segments) of the indices, and options on credit default swaps are widely used by credit hedge funds. For this reason, another common risk in a credit hedge fund portfolio is the cash-synthetic basis risk. Although in theory the spreads of a cash bond and the credit default swap on the same issuer are supposed to trade fairly closely to each other, there are times when the two can diverge. Different funding and margining cost, liquidity, and optionality between a synthetic and a cash bond are some of the reasons that may drive the two instruments to trade differently. The basis (the spread differential between a credit default swap and the relevant cash bond) is said to widen (become more negative) when the spread on the CDS remains at similar level or narrows when the spread on the corresponding cash bond increases. In this case, the synthetic hedges are not going to provide the gains intended to hedge against the spread widening on the long cash bond positions.

Some of the risks in trading high yield bond investing strategies are related to the higher cost of trading and the potential for higher negative impact of a short squeeze. The wider bid-ask spread for a high yield bond compared to a public equity means that investors bear a higher cost of entering into and exiting out of a trade. For example, a liquid high yield bond may trade with a 0.25 to 0.5 point bid-ask spread. On a bond traded at par, this equates to a 25 to 50 basis point cost compared to 4 to 6 basis points for a liquid, large cap public equity. A less liquid high yield bond can trade with a 1 to 2 point bid-ask spread compared to 30 to 60 basis points for a small cap public equity. Furthermore, although shorting high yield bonds and equities both face the risk of being short squeezed, the impact is likely to be more painful for a high yield bond. This is particularly true for high yield bonds that are less liquid. For smaller issues or issuances that are very closely held, should the bond be called and investors required to cover a short position, the ability to do so may be limited. An investor may look at the most recent quote from a broker-dealer that shows that a particular bond is trading at 80 cents on the dollar. However, during certain periods, this quote may not be executable. When calling the dealer, the investor may be surprised that covering his bond short would cost him 85, not 80 cents. Large investors are also more likely to lend out their equities than their bonds, reducing the availability of bond for borrowing relative to equities.

 ### Key Questions for Trading-Oriented Strategies

- What are the reasons behind the technical dislocation?
- Who are the market makers for the bond X?
- What are potential reasons that may cause the technical dislocation to persist?
- What is the bid-ask spread for situation X?
- How long would it take for the portfolio to exit a trade in normal scenario? In a distress scenario?

Correlation Trade

Correlation trade was a particularly popular trade with a subset of credit hedge funds in the few years leading to 2008. This trade typically refers to relative value trades of portfolios and tranches of portfolios of risky credits.[15] The portfolios can be cash or synthetic, and synthetic credit portfolios include credit default swap indices such as CDX North America indices and iTraxx indices as well as tranches of said indices. See Chapter Appendix A for a technical discussion on correlation.

A popular example of the trade in early 2007 was to sell protection on the lowest tranche (e.g., the 0–3 percent or equity tranche) of the iTraxx index and to hedge by buying protection on the next more senior tranche (e.g., the 3–6 percent tranche) of the same index. Depending on the relative notional amount of the long and the short leg, the trade can be structured to meet particular objectives such as being carry neutral or carry positive.

Another example of this trade is to sell protection on the mezzanine or equity tranche of a credit default index (e.g., the 3–7 percent tranche of the CDX IG) and buy protection via CDS on names within the index that are expected to be most likely to default. Similar to the trade above, this trade can also be structured to meet a particular carry objective or to have an overall long or short exposure to credit spread as well as specific credit events.

Edge Being Captured

Credit hedge funds can profit from going long and short different tranches of a portfolio of risky credits due to different reasons. First, different tranches have different sensitivity to changes in risk factors such as implied default correlation, credit spread, and defaults. The sensitivity of a particular tranche to a risk factor is nonlinear, and the relative risk of tranches within a vehicle changes as a risk factor changes. For example, as default correlation rises, the senior tranches becomes more risky relative to the equity tranche. Intuitively, mezzanine and equity tranches care more about idiosyncratic risk (individual default), while the senior tranches care more about widespread systematic default. This means sophisticated investors can earn a premium from taking a view on credit as well as from understanding the complexity of structured credit vehicles.

Second, different tranches have a different natural buyer base with different risk tolerance and return expectation. For example, insurance companies and European banks prior to 2008 were active participants in the senior tranches of the structured credit market as a way to earn additional yield to corporate credit of comparable rating, while hedge funds were natural buyers for the riskier parts of the structured credit market such as mezzanine and equity tranches. The combination of the complex nature of the instruments as well as the siloed buyer base for different tranches can translate into periods where particular tranches can be mispriced relative to each other or to the whole structure.

For example, a credit hedge fund with long credit exposure (sell protection) on the 0–3 percent ITraxx index and short credit exposure (buy protection) on the 3–6 percent credit index generally does so based on the expectation of a continued benign default environment. Given its junior-most status, the equity tranche has the highest expected return compared to the more senior tranches. A credit hedge fund can sell protection on the equity tranche on an unhedged basis and essentially takes on a levered exposure to credit spread and default. The hedge fund that wished to hedge small changes in credit spread can also hedge part of the risk by buying protection on the 3–6 percent tranche.

In the second trade example, a credit hedge fund that generally expects a benign default environment but is concerned about the idiosyncratic credit risk of select names in the portfolio can obtain sell protection on the mezzanine or equity tranche of the structured vehicle (this can be a credit default index or a CDO) and hedges the risk to individual credits by buying protection on the high-risk names via single-name CDS or a custom basket. For this trade to generate more profit than loss (positive P&L), if the risky credits do default as expected, the short leg of the trade would profit, and this profit is expected to more than compensate the losses in the mezzanine or equity tranche.

Risk

Many iterations of the correlation trade are essentially a levered long or short bet to a particular risk factor, such as credit spread. In the years leading to 2008, credit hedge funds that made leveraged bets on continued credit spread compression and low default posted impressive performance. However, when the market took a turn for the worse, the leverage that made such attractive returns possible also amplified losses. Facing rising defaults and spread widening, some hedge funds faced increasing margin pressure from their counterparties and were forced to unwind their trade and, in some cases, the entire fund.

In the first trade example, the risk of the trade became apparent when the default rate rose, the equity tranche suffered great losses, and the gains from the protection on the mezzanine tranche were not enough to overcome the losses. Intuitively, if loss given default in the portfolio does not exceed 3 percent going forward, the market expects loss to be capped at 3 percent; the worst-case scenario of this trade is that the long 0–3 percent equity tranche is wiped out while the protection in the mezzanine tranche does not provide the expected protection.

In the second trade example, the credit hedge fund is exposed to both fundamental or idiosyncratic credit risk and widespread market default. If the overall default rate proves to be much higher than expected and the fund hedged only 3 out of 100 credits in the index, it could be underhedged. Similarly, if the manager is wrong on his fundamental credit thesis and the three names that he hedged are not the three names that defaulted, he would also see losses on the long end of the portfolio while the CDS premium he has paid is wasted.

Additional risks of the correlation trade include counterparty risk, liquidity risk, and basis risk. Since correlation trades often include derivative credit instruments such as credit default swaps, credit default indices (and tranches of the indices), and synthetic CDOs, the trade is typically done bilaterally over-the-counter between the credit hedge fund and a swap dealer. As the Lehman bankruptcy illustrated, the default of a swap counterparty can wreak havoc on your investment, even if the trade itself is working in your favor. Many with positive mark-to-market on their swaps have found their claim (the accumulated unrealized gain or posted margin) reduced significantly when they became the unsecured general creditor of a bankrupt entity.

Another risk to this trade is liquidity risk. The story of Peloton Partners highlighted this risk. Peloton had posted an 87 percent return in 2007, largely by buying a senior-most (AAA) tranche of mortgage-backed structured products and shorting the mezzanine tranches. The trade profited when defaults caused the lower tranches to lose value while the value of the senior tranches stayed stable. Peloton, who at that moment saw the selling as overdone and expected default to moderate, repositioned its portfolio such that it had a long exposure to default. When default continued to rise, the portfolio suffered losses and the fund's counterparties demanded margin calls. In order to meet these margin calls, Peloton had to sell assets, and it sold what it could sell, the most liquid securities. The liquidity crisis faced by the fund was compounded by investor redemptions, which the fund could not meet given the low liquidity of the investments.

Another risk in the correlation trade is basis risk. At different points in the market, technical rather than fundamental reasons may drive pricing in different tranches of the same structured vehicle. For example, in the trade example where a credit hedge fund is long the 0–3 percent tranche and short the 3–6 percent tranche, a rise in implied default correlation should theoretically render the 3–6 percent tranche riskier (and thus there should be positive P&L from the short leg of the trade). However, if many market participants with the same trade decided to unwind the trade, both the long and short leg of the portfolio may result in losses. The long leg sees losses due to default and selling pressure, and the short leg sees losses as the price of the 3–6 percent tranche rises (its yield falls) because of short covering.

Levered Carry

The levered carry strategy has some overlap with the fundamental credit strategy. This strategy might include the trading of a bond that is found to be "money good" through fundamental analysis (the analyst decides that the bondholder is highly likely to receive the payment of principal). This strategy involves buying a liquid, stable bond, typically at or very near par value, and levering up, typically via prime brokerage financing. This strategy tends to be less popular with high yield bonds than with leveraged loans because of the potential for higher mark-to-market volatility for bonds. Furthermore, prime brokerages very rarely provide sufficiently attractive financing to make this trade appealing for hedge funds.

Edge Being Captured

This strategy relies on the carry from bonds on a levered basis to generate the bulk of the return rather than price appreciation. It involves capturing the difference between the carry from the bonds and the lower cost of financing (i.e., borrow at a lower rate and invest in higher yielding instruments). This is a business model behind commercial banks and is also part of the model for investment banks, perhaps until lately. Some of the reasons that mitigate the risks of hedge funds are (1) the borrowing of hedge funds with their prime brokerage is collateralized with the assets of the fund, (2) the collateral is a diversified portfolio of securities, and (3) the leverage of certain hedge funds (measured by borrowing to equity) may be lower than the leverage of some highly levered companies.

Risks

Borrowing short to leverage one's long investments produces what is commonly referred to as leverage risk, which amplifies returns as well as losses. For example, as the trade moves against the investor, the amount of leverage also increases. Calculating leverage market value of assets divided by equity, equity is the first-loss position when value of assets declines until equity is wiped out. Mark-to-market of the asset declines, but the amount of financing stays the same, thus equity falls when asset value falls. This increased value of leverage works for the investor when the market bounces back, as the higher leverage means more impact on the equity when the asset value rises. Thus, this is not to be taken to mean that investors should keep leverage constant as asset price falls. As a matter of fact, in a constant leverage strategy, investors crystallize losses and lose the ability to capture the bounce—it is not a good strategy in a volatile market. Nonetheless, if asset price falls and leverage increases, a further decline in asset value will have a greater impact due to higher leverage.

Furthermore, for investors, the risk is that if the trade experienced enough losses, the leverage provider may liquidate the trade even though the company may not default and may meet its obligations. In essence, losses are crystallized before trade has time to work. Also, because the financing is backed by a portfolio of assets, the leverage provider may liquidate trades indiscriminately, including assets in the portfolio that were performing just fine.

Key Questions for the Levered Long Strategy

- What are the terms of the leverage?
- Why this method of financing rather than others?
- Under what circumstances can the leverage lines be pulled? Is there a cure provision in the event of a breach of covenant?

- How do you monitor your leverage lines? Who is responsible, and how often is it done?
- If credit spreads rise, how do you protect the portfolio?

CONCLUSION

- The global high yield bond market has grown in the past three decades from the "stepsister" of the investment grade market to one of the largest mainstream asset classes in the world.
- It is a highly dynamic market, where industry practices such as naming convention, leverage level, and number and type of covenants can vary meaningfully across issuers and across different periods.
- Most credit hedge funds focus their efforts in the secondary market. Nonetheless, it is important to understand how the primary market can provide an indicator of things such as liquidity and risk appetite in the secondary market.
- Much of the secondary trading is done in the OTC market, which is subject to greater inefficiencies than the market for listed securities. Many bond issuers also do not have listed equities, which means there is limited public information and research coverage available. This gives rise to opportunities for selective and disciplined credit investors.
- Due to the private nature and liquidity profile of many high yield bonds as well as the wide usage of credit derivatives to hedge the portfolio, many risk management techniques and measurements that are commonly used on listed securities are not effective on this market
- Credit hedge funds have the flexibility to use more leverage than a traditional long-only account. Judiciously used, this can translate into better returns while keeping moderate risk. However, investors need to be cognizant that excessive and poorly managed leverage can exacerbate losses and turn a mark-to-market loss into a permanent one.

CHAPTER APPENDIX A: QUICK REFRESHER ON CORRELATION

As a quick refresher, the diversification benefit of holding a portfolio of risky assets depends on correlation between assets. Figure 2.5 shows the formula for calculating portfolio variance for a two-asset portfolio. The benefit of diversification hinges on correlation between assets: portfolio variance is minimized when assets are perfectly negatively correlated. In a portfolio of credits, it is important to understand not just the likelihood of default for individual credits, but also the likelihood of two or more credits defaulting at any given moment. Experienced credit investors understand the cyclical nature of defaults and have noted that default correlation tends to rise as overall default rate rises. This intuitively makes sense because in a normal market environment, defaults tend to be driven by borrower-specific factors such as failed launch of a new product, while in a recession, the default rate rises and poor macroeconomic conditions are the common underlying driver behind defaults.

Pricing on tranches ("slices") on structured credit vehicles such as structured finance collateralized default obligation (SF CDO) or credit default indices (e.g., CDX, iTraxx indices) are quoted using implied (default) correlation. Think of implied correlation in tranche pricing as similar to implied volatility in option pricing. In other words, implied

$$\sigma_P^2 = (w_1)^2 \sigma_1^2 + (1 - w_1)^2 \sigma_2^2 + 2w_1(1 - w_1)\rho_{12}\sigma_1\sigma_2$$
$$= (w_1)^2 \sigma_1^2 + (1 - w_1)^2 \sigma_2^2 + 2w_1(1 - w_1)\sigma_{12}$$

Figure 2.5 Portfolio variance for a two-asset portfolio
Source: PAAMCO
σp = portfolio volatility
$p2$ = portfolio variance
$w1$ = weight of asset 1
$\sigma 1$ = standard deviation of asset 1
$w2$ = weight of asset 2
$\sigma 2$ = standard deviation of asset 2
$p12$ = correlation between asset 1 and asset 2

correlation is an output that can be calculated from observable inputs such as price, attachment and detachment point on the tranche, recovery rate, asset value, asset volatility, and risk-free rate. It is impossible to observe implied correlation; only historical or actual correlation can be observed.

CHAPTER 3

Stressed and Distressed Investing

The stressed and distressed markets have many unique features that can catch inexperienced investors by surprise. Understanding the causes of distress (financial versus operational), the bankruptcy and reorganization process, and the motivation of the parties involved are crucial in successfully evaluating stressed and distressed opportunities in credit. We will also discuss the types of strategies and the risks in distressed hedge funds. The chapter will conclude with a discussion and key questions for the most popular strategies in distressed investing.

To begin the discussion, which of the options in Table 3.1 is the more attractive investment?

There is no simple answer to this question. It depends on many things, one of which is the investor's appetite for risk and target return, but most importantly, *it depends on the price*. Option Two is an example of a distressed bond, and the price at which an investor can buy the bond heavily determines whether it makes for an attractive investment. For many sophisticated investors, there will be a price where the expected return is high enough that purchasing the security is well worth the risk. Importantly, many of the metrics typically used by investors in evaluating performing bonds such as rating, maturity, yield to maturity,

Table 3.1 **Comparison of Two Investment Opportunities**

Option One	Option Two
Issuer: A Corp, a multinational pharmaceutical company	Issuer: B Corp, a global producer of chemicals used in oil drilling
Rating: AA	Rating: BB at issuance, currently in default
Maturity: June 30, 2038	Maturity: September 30, 2027
Coupon: 6.5%	Coupon: 6.6%
Yield to maturity: 6.5% at issuance, currently 5.5%	Yield to maturity: 6.7% at issuance, currently in default
Amount outstanding: $3.0 billion	Amount outstanding: $250 million
Collateral type: Senior unsecured	Collateral type: Senior secured

and coupon do not apply or are irrelevant when evaluating the debt of issuers that are in or near default.

THE DISTRESSED MARKET

Unlike many other security markets, the size of the distressed and stressed credit markets can vary dramatically. Given that the price of the distressed debt is set by the quantity of the buyers versus the supply, understanding and monitoring both the supply and the likely available investor appetite are vital to timing a successful distressed security investing program. It is important to note that because defaults tend to come in waves (i.e., defaults are cyclical), distressed investing tends to be cyclical in nature. Over time, investors' interest in defaulted or near-default debt has grown tremendously due to better understanding of the benefits of adding distressed assets into the portfolio. This growth in the market, among other things, can be attributed to the "Altman effect." The creation of the Altman-NYU Index of Defaulted Debt Securities was a milestone in the distressed debt market. It provided portfolio managers and investors with a common methodology to track the size and performance of distressed assets. Figures 3.1 and 3.2 show the size of the distressed

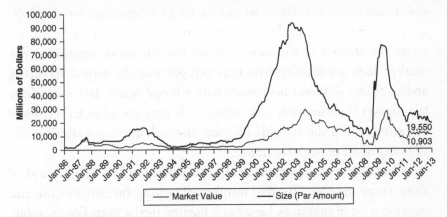

Figure 3.1 Size of distressed sector in the CS high yield index (par amount and market value)
Source: Credit Suisse

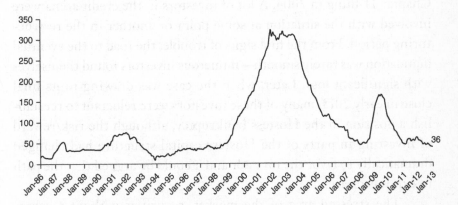

Figure 3.2 Size of distressed sector in the CS high yield index by number of issuances
Source: Credit Suisse

high yield market over time by dollar amount (par and market value) and by number of issuances.

The pricing for distressed assets also tends to be heavily influenced by the idiosyncratic factors commonly found in stressed and distressed situations. The complexity of the situation surrounding a distressed asset tends to be poorly understood. For a typical

distressed borrower, there would be times when negative developments are revealed and there are not many investors who truly understand the impact of the new information. In many situations, the
market does not discriminate between parts of the capital structure
and/or paints different borrowers with a broad brush. In times where
the market is sufficiently risk-averse, it is very common to see many
investors taking the attitude of, "sell first, ask questions later" at the
slightest whiff of negative news.

In cases where restructuring takes place over a long period of
time, there may be a limited number of willing investors at the end
because a lot of investors have been burned in the past. For example,
in the Interstate Bakery Corp./Hostess bankruptcy saga, the borrower had to go through a second Chapter 11 filing[1] in January 2012
after a long and arduous restructuring process related to the first
Chapter 11 filing in 2004. A lot of investors in the credit arena were
involved with the situation at some point or another in the restructuring period. From the first signs of trouble, the road to the eventual
liquidation was rarely smooth—numerous investors found themselves
with significant loss. Later, when the case was drawing to its final
close in early 2013, many of these investors were reluctant to reestab-
lish a position in the Hostess bankruptcy, although the risk/reward
of investing in parts of the Hostess capital structure had changed
dramatically to favor the investor and it could be argued that the path
to exit was clearer.

The stressed area of the market, securities without a corresponding company restructuring or default, can either complement
or replace the distressed security universe. When extremely difficult
economic conditions are accompanied by tight credit, such as during
the 2000–2002 recession, distressed debt opportunities can domi-
nate the investing landscape in credit as companies are forced into
bankruptcy. Conversely, as seen more recently in 2010 to date, when
economic downturns are accompanied by aggressive monetary policy,
the actual numbers of defaults can be quite low as credit instruments
are "amended and extended" instead of creditors forcing debtors into
bankruptcy.

Key Takeaway on Timing in Distressed Investing

The opportunities in distressed investing typically follow a spike in default, and like defaults, distressed investing tends to be cyclical. Post the 2008 credit crisis, we see an increase in large distressed situations related to large leveraged buyouts.

Definition and Cause of Financial Distress

A distressed company typically refers to a company that has failed or is expected to fail to meet its obligations to its creditors. The most common events of distress include failure to pay the interest and/or principal on debt as well as the breach of loan and bond covenants. Currently there is no legal or official definition as to what constitutes a distressed bond or bank loan. Widely accepted industry convention defines a distressed corporate bond as one that trades at a spread of 1,000 basis points or more compared to Treasury bonds of comparable maturity. Another commonly accepted definition classifies as distressed a bond that is trading at a price lower than 40 and a bank loan that is trading at a price lower than 80. Typically, the publicly traded equity of a company with distressed debt and/or bank loans will also trade at marginal value—a few dollars or lower.

Another popular method used to measure the size of the distressed universe is by ratings. One measure is to include the par amount of defaulted bank loans and bonds (rated D or equivalent). Another measure includes all bank loans and bonds that are rated CCC equivalent or lower. Often, bonds and bank loans on which the holders have undergone distressed exchanges or exchange offers, earning the rating of SD (selective default) or its equivalent,[2] are also commonly included in measurements of the distress universe. In a distressed exchange, a creditor's claim is repurchased for cash, while in an exchange offer, a creditor swaps the original claim for another instrument. However, both situations are usually coercive and creditors end up receiving less than the par amount of their original claims, although they may receive more than their purchase price depending upon the price at purchase. Given the ratings, spread, and price-based definitions above, the market usually regards a bond or bank loan to be distressed long before the issuer seeks protection under the bankruptcy laws.

 Key Takeaway on the Definition of Distressed

Given the ratings, spread, and price-based definitions established earlier, the market can regard a security to be distressed long before it files for protection under bankruptcy laws. Be clear as to whether the manager is talking about actually defaulted securities or merely securities trading at a wide spread.

Financial distress takes place when the market perceives a reduction in the value of a company's assets or an inability of the company to meet its obligations as they come due. The market's diminished confidence in the company's ability to meet its financial obligations, whether real or perceived, is reflected in the reduced value of the company's liabilities. Figure 3.3 shows the company's assets and liabilities before, during, and after restructuring for a hypothetical company. In this simplified example, the junior unsecured bond is the fulcrum security: the holders will see partial or full write-down of their claim, and in exchange they will receive equity in the restructured entity. The senior subordinated bonds and below were written down to zero (i.e., their claims are completely extinguished). In the wave of defaults surrounding the 2008 credit crisis, senior secured bank debt made up the majority of the liabilities and was often the fulcrum security.

Assets	Liabilities & Equity Pre-Restructuring	Liabilities During Restructuring	Liabilities Post Restructuring
Cash		Administrative Claims, DIP Loans	
PPE	Senior Secured Bank Loans	Senior Secured Bank Loans	Senior Secured Bank Loans
Inventory	Senior Unsecured Bonds	Senior Unsecured Bonds	Senior Unsecured Bonds
Account Receivables	Junior Unsecured Bonds	Junior Unsecured Bonds (F)	Junior Unsecured Bonds
Intangibles (e.g., Goodwill)	Senior Subordinated Bonds	Senior Subordinated Bonds	Senior Subordinated Bonds
	Junior Unsubordinated Bonds	Junior Unsubordinated Bonds	Junior Unsubordinated Bonds
	Hybrids (incl. Convertible Bonds)	Hybrids (incl. Convertible Bonds)	Hybrids (incl. Convertible Bonds)
	Preferred Stock	Preferred Stock	Preferred Stock
	Common Stock	Common Stock	Common Stock

Figure 3.3 Company's assets and liabilities during stages of restructuring
Source: PAAMCO

There are a myriad of reasons why companies become distressed. The reasons are often roughly categorized either as operational or financial. Operational issues can be summarized as fundamental deficiencies in the underlying operating business. They often include poor management, a poor product mix, an inability to meet changing consumer demand, an unsustainable cost structure, or fraud. Operational results can also stem from being in an industry that's experiencing secular decline, for example, film (Kodak) or traditional advertising (Yellow Pages). Financial issues are largely a function of an unrealistic capital structure, specifically too much leverage. Shipping and energy are examples of sectors with high capital expenditure and high leverage, which would often result in financial distress.

The skill set required for investing in operational situations is dramatically broader than the skills required to invest in purely financial restructurings. In evaluating a financial restructuring, managers can take the cash flow being generated by the underlying business as a given and focus their attention on how the business can be restructured. This requires a strong knowledge of valuation across the capital structure as well as an understanding of the current demand for different security types. Investing in an operationally distressed situation adds a significant level of complexity. Not only does the business need to be financially restructured but one has to evaluate how likely it is that the operational turnaround will succeed. It is for this reason that purely financially distressed situations tend to trade a tighter spread than operational situations when all else is equal.

 ## Key Takeaway on Price as an Indicator of Opportunity

Beware the manager who has a low average price as a selling point for a fund (implying a potentially high expected return). Consider the risk—these are often pure operational turnarounds. While on the surface the portfolio may seem cheaper than a well-diversified portfolio containing both operational and financial restructurings, it should be cheaper given the greater risk level.

It should be noted that in a bullish credit market, a company that is facing deteriorating earnings before interest, taxes, depreciation, and amortization (EBITDA) due to escalating costs may be able to avoid covenant violations and skirt distress by refinancing its debt obligations. In this case, the refinancing may only mean delaying the onset of distress instead of staving it off altogether. However, it does buy the company valuable time during which it may be able to turn around its operational problems.

The case of Bear Stearns provides an interesting example of how the market reaction to troubled companies can lead to a domino or compounding effect. As a reminder, the Bear Stearns collapse did not result in bankruptcy but rather its eventual sale to J.P. Morgan. The main reasons for Bear Stearns's distress can be attributed to excessive leverage, asset/liability mismatch, and the loss of financing. A study by the Government Accountability Office showed that the total leverage as measured by assets-to-equity of Bear Stearns, Goldman Sachs, Merrill Lynch, and Morgan Stanley reached 30x in 2007.[3] Bear Stearns's heavy exposure to illiquid mortgage-backed securities (MBS) took a toll as the market became increasingly concerned about the deterioration in value of residential mortgages, and hence its willingness to finance short-term debt. Given the bank's oversized exposure to residential mortgages combined with its very high level of leverage,[4] the market feared the worst about Bear's financial stability. Once Bear Stearns found itself unable to access the capital market for financing, it was considering a few unpalatable options including Chapter 11 bankruptcy filing before it was sold to J.P. Morgan. The Bear Stearns case highlights an important fact about financial distress: it is arguable that the main underlying causes of the distress take place over a long period; however, the event of distress itself is usually brought to fruition by the company's loss of access to capital.

Options at the Time of Distress

Since most distressed portfolios contain, at a minimum, some debt instruments where the underlying companies have yet to enter bankruptcy, it is important to understand the different options that are available to the company. Having a full command of the underlying business's likely course of action and the ability to "create your own event" is a common attribute of successful distressed investors.

When a company faces financial distress, its options include reorganization and debt restructuring, recapitalization, and liquidation. Reorganization and debt restructuring allow the debtor to reduce the amount of its liabilities. Recapitalization provides the debtor with the working capital it needs to operate its business as it goes through the reorganization process. Partial liquidation of assets may be part of the effort to provide capital. All these options are part of the restructuring process, where the overarching assumption is that the company has more value to creditors as a going concern than in liquidation, although sometimes whole or partial liquidation of the company's assets is inevitable. The end goal is to come up with a restructuring plan that enables the company to operate as a going concern and preserves the maximum amount of value for different classes of creditors. The question is how the pain of any losses is distributed and what the ownership of the company will be after it emerges from bankruptcy. For most of the discussions in this chapter, we will focus on the options for a company whose debt is under the jurisdiction of the U.S. bankruptcy laws. Figure 3.4 shows the decision tree of options for a company faced with distress.

Out-of-Court Restructuring

A typical out-of-court restructuring usually involves an exchange offer in response to an impending distress scenario. If a bondholder chooses to participate in an exchange offer, he would exchange the current

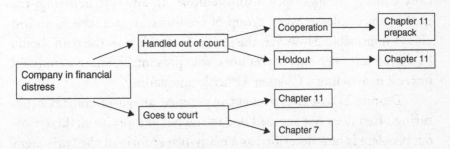

Figure 3.4 Decision tree of options for a company facing distress
Source: PAAMCO

bond for a new bond, usually for a smaller par amount and with a longer maturity date. However, the new amount is typically larger than what the holder could get if he chose to sell the existing bond in the market. The new debt may also have less restrictive cash service requirements and thus offer the debtor better flexibility in managing cash needs, which can be of particular importance in times of distress. The new debt may do so by taking the form of a zero coupon bond or a bond with a payment-in-kind (PIK) toggle. With a PIK toggle, when a coupon payment is due, the company can add the interest to the principal amount of the debt instead of paying the interest in cash, essentially paying off its debt by issuing more debt.[5] In a successful out-of-court restructuring, the debtor reduces the amount of debt on its balance sheet and reduces the ongoing cash burden of servicing its debt obligations.

One of the key benefits of an out-of-court restructuring is that the process is typically faster than a potentially lengthy and cumbersome bankruptcy process. Following the 2008 credit crisis there was a substantial backlog in the U.S. bankruptcy courts, which was exacerbated by the increased complexity of debtors' capital structures. It may take years for the court to adjudicate some of the more difficult bankruptcy cases. In an out-of-court restructuring, debtors can usually reach resolution fairly quickly, sometimes within a few months. The sooner the debtor's fate becomes clear to its suppliers and consumers, the less the uncertainty with regard to the value of the company. Furthermore, by avoiding the legal and administrative fees[6] incurred in an in-court restructuring, an out-of-court restructuring is also typically a much cheaper option for creditors. In any restructuring, the goal is not to please every group of creditors; in fact, this is almost always impossible. However, the goal is to decide how the pain should be shared across groups of creditors, who presumably share a common interest in avoiding a Chapter 11 bankruptcy filing.

Despite its cost effectiveness, in practice, an out-of-court restructuring often does not succeed due to the holdout problem. The holdout problem is best described as a many-player form of the "prisoner's dilemma." The punch line of the prisoner's dilemma is that the optimal solution is for both players to cooperate with each other. However, both sides harbor fear that if they are the first to offer an olive branch, the other side would take advantage of them. As a result, the players end up hurting each other rather than opting for the optimal solution.

Translating this to the holdout problem in an out-of-court restructuring is simple to see. If some bondholders participate in the exchange offer while others do not, the nonparticipating bondholders retain their right to the full amount of the original claims at the expense of the exchanging bondholders. Furthermore, after the exchange offer takes place, the nonexchanging bondholders now have a claim on a healthier company due to the reduction of balance sheet leverage and lower interest payment. This improvement in the company's financial situation is expected to manifest itself in higher market prices for the original bond.

One popular method to overcome the holdout problem in an out-of-court restructuring is by creating downside penalty for nonexchanging bondholders. Often, as a part of the exchange offer, bondholders who do not participate can end up being subordinated to the new bonds. In many bond indentures, subordination of the current bond to the new bond can be effected if more than 50 percent of the outstanding bond amount votes for it. Bond covenants may also allow additional senior and/or secured indebtedness. However, as a practical issue, getting enough bondholders to come to the negotiation table and vote for the exchange offer may be challenging if there are many passive bondholders, each with only a small amount of the total outstanding bond issuance.

Another challenge to the out-of-court restructuring is that, in certain cases, a reduction in cash required to service the debt alone may not be sufficient. For example, if the financial distress were to be caused by a dramatic increase in operating costs, the company might still need an additional cash infusion to finance its higher working capital needs. In the 2008 credit crisis, the market saw some "preemptive restructurings" where the debtor could see financial distress looming in the future and did not wait until distress was imminent before reaching out to creditors with a proposed restructuring plan. Loss of access to liquidity can often be the cause that precipitates the onset of distress. A company that is still in reasonable financial health and still has access to one or more liquidity sources will have a much improved chance for a successful preemptive restructuring. In the event a debtor requires a cash infusion in addition to a successful exchange offer, if it were unable to access additional cash from either its creditors or equity holders, it may need to access debtor-in-possession (DIP) financing, which is available through the Chapter 11 restructuring process.

 ## Key Takeaways on Evaluating Distressed Hedge Funds

One technique for evaluating and comparing the depth and quality of hedge fund manager research is to look at the current portfolio, choose several "stressed," prebankruptcy companies and ask about the likelihood of an out-of-court restructuring. Strong answers include analyses of current market conditions for various types of securities the company could issue; current creditors and their motivations; as well as traditional financial statement analysis.

In-Court Restructuring

It used to be that the investor community was very concerned about the bankruptcy stigma. For example, in the 1980s, it was common for pension plans to restrict their bond holdings to only investment grade rated bonds and Treasuries. However, over time practice has changed. In fact, today, many investors understand that entering bankruptcy to restructure a company may be a necessary step in bringing an ailing company back to health. Corporate bankruptcy filings in the United States generally fall under one of two sections of the United States Bankruptcy Code: Chapter 11 for restructurings and Chapter 7 for liquidations. Contrary to what many may think at first glance, there is often liquidation associated with the Chapter 11 process as well. Because for our purposes the majority of investible restructuring cases occur under Chapter 11, we will briefly review its mechanics.

A Chapter 11 filing rarely comes as a surprise. In fact, many distressed investors are usually aware due to observing free cash flow and covenant ratios that the company has been in financial trouble long before the actual filing takes place. In addition, the larger sell-side research firms often produce lists of companies that may be under financial distress as determined from regulatory filings and financials. Under certain conditions, the company may have first attempted an out-of-court restructuring that turned out to be unsuccessful. In some cases, the filing itself is a nonevent, with the market prices of the bonds or loans of the debtors showing no significant price deterioration or even increasing upon the news of the Chapter 11 filing.

There are multiple forms of Chapter 11 bankruptcy. In a fully prepackaged bankruptcy filing under Chapter 11 (also known as a "pre-pack"), the debtor files for Chapter 11 with a Plan of Reorganization (POR) that already has been circulated, solicited, agreed to, and voted on by *all* the necessary classes of creditors. In this case, the restructuring process is very short, usually months instead of years, and in essence, the filing marks the end of the process. When the company has not either attempted or been able to complete a prepack filing, it is often referred to as a "free-fall" filing.

Unlike an out-of-court restructuring, the Chapter 11 process provides stakeholders with some structural benefits. The first is the ability to provide new financing—debtor-in-posession (DIP) financing on a supersenior priority status, with a claim senior to all prepetition indebtedness. Second, cash is prohibited from being dispersed by the corporation to satisfy prepetition obligations because of the "automatic stay" provision of the Bankruptcy Code. Under the automatic stay, all prepetition obligations of the debtor are "frozen" and no creditor can have access to cash (whether in the form of balance sheet cash or via asset sales) at the expense of other creditors or seek to enforce its prepetition claims.[7]

The Chapter 11 petition can be filed voluntarily (by the debtor) or involuntarily (by its creditors). In practice, involuntary petitions are not common, as only unsecured creditors who are able to allege that the debtor is generally not paying its debts as they come due are eligible to file an involuntary petition. Furthermore, in many cases, when the threat of involuntary Chapter 11 filing is looming, the debtor usually submits a voluntary filing. By doing so, the debtor becomes a DIP and retains control over the restructuring process.

Timing of Events in Chapter 11

The DIP (the management) has the exclusive right for the first 120 days after filing to propose a plan of reorganization. Management also has up to 180 days after filing to solicit creditors' votes for the plan. Both of these periods can be extended by the Bankruptcy Court.

Period of Exclusivity and Solicitation

Prior to the 2005 Bankruptcy Abuse Prevention and Consumer Protection Act (BAPCPA), the extensions could prolong the exclusivity period to multiple years. Post BAPCPA,[8] the exclusivity and solicitation periods are limited to 18 and 20 months respectively. The length of the exclusivity period is of major importance to creditors, particularly unsecured creditors. This is because a protracted stay in the costly restructuring process tends to reduce the value of the company's assets, leaving less value to creditors. Furthermore, customers and suppliers also tend to be wary about doing business with a company whose future is unclear. For example, after GM filed for Chapter 11 in June 2009, many consumers were reluctant to purchase cars from a company that might not exist in the near future. Consumers cited concerns about who would make parts and engines and who would maintain the warranty and conduct future repairs. The infusion of liquidity and quick resolution to GM's restructuring assured potential customers that the automobile company was going to continue to exist, albeit with fewer brands.

Voting

After the exclusivity period ends, if management fails to propose a plan of reorganization, or if the plan that was proposed failed to garner enough votes to be confirmed within the given time period, then different creditor groups can propose their own plans of reorganization. These competing plans would have to be accepted by the different classes of claims that are eligible to vote. Grouping of claims into classes is important: in addition to determining voting eligibility, the U.S. Bankruptcy Code ranks the payment, and right of ownership, of the company's assets by the level of seniority of each class. Secured creditors are the first in line to receive the proceeds from their collateral up to the amount of their claim. If the collateral proceeds are less than their claim, the deficiency is considered to be an unsecured claim. In general, claims under a Chapter 11 plan can be broken into the following in order of most to least senior: secured claims, priority unsecured claims, general unsecured claims, and equity claims. Administrative and priority claims are not classified in a plan of reorganization (POR). Administrative claims include the expenses incurred during the bankruptcy case such as court costs, legal and accounting fees, and trustee expenses. DIP loans typically are the most senior secured claims. Priority unsecured claims include payments due to employees[9] and taxes due. General unsecured claims typically include prepetition trade claims and unsecured bondholders. Equity claims are typically extinguished in the process unless creditors allow some residual value to be allocated to equity holders.

The basic concept in grouping is based on claims that are "substantially similar." However, the bankruptcy courts have been vague on what the phrase really means, and it does not mean that all similar claims will be classified together. The plan of reorganization will specify the recovery of various creditor groups in each class depending on, among other things, intercreditor agreements, liens, and intercorporate guarantees.

 ### Key Takeaway on Claim Name as Indicator of Rights

The name of the claim (e.g., "senior unsecured notes") by itself is not a sufficient indicator of its contractual rights and potential subordination.

Voting eligibility is determined by whether claims within a class are considered "impaired." Investors are considered to be impaired if, in the plan of reorganization, they will receive anything other than the full amount due on their claim, usually defined as par plus accrued interest, whether in cash or in the form of a reinstated claim. One important point is that even an improvement in the claim may be deemed an impairment. A credit instrument is deemed to be impaired if there is any change in the contractual and legal rights. For example, a note due in 2018 that carried a 5 percent interest rate is impaired if the holder will receive a new note with a higher coupon in a less levered capital structure even if the maturity is unchanged. Classes of investors who are considered impaired have the right to vote for or against the plan of reorganization. For every class of impaired investors, the plan needs at least a two-thirds vote and half of the number of investors voting to be approved.

For distressed investors, determining which class is appropriate for a particular claim is complicated by the increased complexity of corporate structures. Some companies have multiple entities. The simplest structure consists of one parent or holding company (holdco) and one operating subsidiary (opco). Valuable assets usually are located at the operating subsidiary level, with senior secured loans often issued or guaranteed at this level. The opco claims are also typically deemed senior to the holdco claims, although guarantees between subsidiaries, from subsidiary to parent, or otherwise can also add complexity to the analysis. Furthermore, investors also need to consider cross-default provisions across subsidiaries and parents. In our example of the simple corporate structure of one parent and one subsidiary, a cross-default provision may mean that if the parent were to default on its bonds, then the loan holders of the subsidiary would have the right to accelerate the payment of the loan (the loan immediately becomes due and payable) even if the opco borrower is not otherwise in default of the loan.

 Key Takeaway on Comparing Distressed Hedge Funds

Be careful when comparing how different hedge funds position in the same bankruptcy. Pay particular attention to exactly which bond or bonds they own both in terms of seniority and in terms of issuer. Holding a secured opco bond may result in a very different view of the situation from a hedge fund that has been providing DIP financing.

Parties in a Restructuring

In a Chapter 11 restructuring, it is important to recognize the various interest groups that are involved, the role they play, and the levers they can pull to influence the outcome of the process. Understanding these actors and how ensuing events are likely to unfold is the central feature of distressed investing.

Debtor-in-Possession

When a debtor files Chapter 11, the debtor becomes a DIP and has all the powers of a bankruptcy trustee.[10] The DIP status gives the management of the debtor the power over the assets of the company and the ability to operate the company as a going concern until a plan of reorganization is voted on by the affected creditors and approved by the bankruptcy court, enabling the company to exit from Chapter 11. The DIP is a fiduciary to the creditors and has the rights and powers of a Chapter 11 trustee. The DIP also accounts for assets of the firm, examines and objects to claims, and provides monthly reporting of the debtor's operations including its monthly income and operating expenses. The DIP also has the right to employ professionals including attorneys, valuation experts, turnaround consultants, and accountants to assist the debtor during its bankruptcy case. In certain extreme cases, the bankruptcy court may substitute an outside trustee. Outside trustees have similar rights as the DIP, plus they have the ability to remove or replace existing management.

U.S. Trustee

Different from the bankruptcy trustee, the U.S. trustee is a U.S. government employee and is appointed by the Department of Justice.[11] During the bankruptcy process, the U.S. trustee monitors the extraordinary activities of the debtor and ensures that the debtor complies with its reporting requirements. The U.S. trustee also administers the public meetings of the creditors.[12] If the debtor fails to fulfill its reporting requirements or is deemed to "fail to take the appropriate steps to bring the case to confirmation,"[13] the U.S. trustee has the right to file a motion with the court to have the debtor's Chapter 11 case converted to another chapter of the Bankruptcy Code or to have the case dismissed.

Bankruptcy Courts

The large majority of the proceedings in Chapter 11 bankruptcy cases in the United States are administered by the federal bankruptcy courts. There is a bankruptcy court for each judicial district in the United States, for a total of 90 bankruptcy districts, and each state can have more than one district. Unlike most of the other courts in the United States, which are considered "courts of law," in other words, they are required to follow judicial precedent, bankruptcy courts are "courts of equity." This means that the decision-making power in a bankruptcy case lies with a United States bankruptcy judge, who is bound to produce an "equitable" result rather than a strict following of legal precedent. This is why you often hear and talk about both the power and importance of the specific judge hearing the case. Most jurisdictions have provided the public with electronic access to court documents for a small fee via Public Access to Court Electronic Records (PACER).[14] Another benefit of the debtor filing voluntarily for Chapter 11 is that it has considerable latitude to choose the jurisdiction in which the case is filed.

 Key Takeaway on Where Filing is Done

Watch out for "forum shopping" by debtors (i.e., filing the bankruptcy in the court that is expected to be most favorable to the debtor or management). A good distressed manager should be able to demonstrate familiarity with previous rulings of the relevant bankruptcy court and/or a particular judge.

Suppliers and Trade Creditors

As the Chapter 11 process goes on, in order to remain a going concern, the company needs to maintain the confidence of its suppliers and its customers while the management negotiates with creditors. Prepetition trade claims typically fall into the general unsecured class along with other unsecured creditors. However, the court has allowed exemptions to this general rule for vendors who are deemed to be "critical vendors." Under this rule, if a vendor whose goods and services are deemed critical to the success of the restructuring will not continue to provide goods and services until the prepetition claim is paid, the debtor may seek to pay such vendors in full prior to plan confirmation.

Official Creditors' Committee

According to the Bankruptcy Code, the U.S. trustee is required to appoint an official creditors' committee. This committee typically consists of the seven largest unsecured creditors. The official creditors' committee acts as a representative of the interest of all unsecured creditors; its goal is to maximize the value of the unsecured claims. In order to do so, the committee will analyze the company's financial situation, which includes projections of the company's prospects, the review of contracts (obligations to customers and to suppliers), an evaluation of cost structure (contracts to suppliers, pension obligations, leases), an asset valuation (inventory, property, plant and equipment, receivables, goodwill and other intangibles), an evaluation of cash flow needs versus cost and ability to access the capital market during and post restructuring. The committee creates a plan of reorganization with the debtor and other constituencies.

There are two important considerations for investors who are considering joining the official creditors' committee. First, creditors' committee members will spend a substantial amount of time and effort due to the extensive legal and procedural responsibilities involved. Second, it is very likely that the committee's tasks will require that committee members have access to material nonpublic information (MNPI) of the debtor. Bondholders with access to inside information can better assess the company's financial and operational health by having access to its financial projections, budget, and management plans. This information is doubly valuable to distressed investors, who often operate in an informational semivacuum because companies often stop their SEC filing after they file for Chapter 11. However, having this access means that the committee members are often restricted from trading their position until the information becomes public. Large bondholders who may qualify to be members of the official creditors' committee may not join the group due to concerns about the extensive time commitment involved and the need to preserve trading flexibility.

 Key Takeaways on Creditors Committee

Typically, an official creditors' committee is made up of investors with significant holdings. If you invest in a manager who is on a creditors' committee, your liquidity and redemption rights may effectively be restricted beyond what the manager may have agreed with you, the investor.

For investors to gain access to MNPI (deemed insiders), they need to sign a confidentiality (confi) agreement and agree to comply with trading restrictions related to being an insider. A party in possession of MNPI may not buy or sell securities.[15] Some investors with MNPI are comfortable trading bank debt and trade claims (but not regulated securities) using a "big boy" letter.[16] Credit hedge funds that invest in stressed and distressed assets usually do not sit in official creditors' committees due to the time commitment and trading restriction.

Ad Hoc Committees

There is no legal definition of, or formal rules as to who can form an unofficial committee in a bankruptcy case. Usually it includes debt holders of similar claims acting together with the goal of maximizing asset value for their class and getting their proposed reorganization plan accepted. Having sizable holdings is important, as it's easier to get management to cooperate if the committee members own sizable blocks of the issuance. However, some smaller bondholders can have more credibility than their size alone would indicate. These bondholders can join forces and devote a substantial amount of time and effort to proposing a plan and building consensus among creditors. By doing so, these bondholders can have a disproportionately large influence in driving the process, particularly if some of the larger holders are not active participants in the restructuring. Many mutual funds, for example, do not have the resources necessary to dedicate to being fully active in the restructuring process and are often passive participants in the process. Skill, network, and relationships with restructuring advisors, bankruptcy attorneys, investment bankers, and crisis managers (in the event you need to replace management), as well as the ability to build consensus, are important in building credibility when trying to garner support among creditors and persuading the debtor to pursue a particular reorganization strategy.

Similar to the official committee, members of an unofficial committee may elect to access MNPI. If they elect to do so, they are subject to the same trading restrictions as members of the official creditors' committee, at least until the MNPI becomes public or stale.

 Key Takeaway on Unofficial Committees

Investors who do not wish to be part of the official creditors' committee can still benefit from partnering with other investors who share similar goals in unofficial or ad hoc committees.

Stressed vs. Distressed Investing

The definitions of popular industry terms such as *stressed* and *distressed* are fluid in nature, and credit hedge fund managers may have narrower or broader definitions in mind when describing their portfolios. There are many similarities in stressed and distressed investing. In both stressed and distressed investing, many credit hedge funds are long-biased investors that rely on deep fundamental credit work to identify and capture value. The difference between the two often lies in the extent of the problems faced by the borrowers compared to their distressed cousins. Stressed companies may face less severe problems (i.e., "distress-lite").[17]

One of the main reasons for getting involved before a bankruptcy has occurred or is imminent is that one may have more valuable options as well as time to cure the cause of distress. For example, say the slowdown in the economy has a similarly negative impact on two consumer-driven companies, Company A and Company B. Company A is expected to be able to reduce production, cut down on inventory, and trim costs by renegotiating its supplier contracts, while Company B is unable to do so due to long-term supply contracts that are costly to unwind. In addition, while it operates on reduced capacity, Company A has access to liquidity via an untapped revolver.[18] As a result of its access to capital while it works toward streamlining its costs, Company A's bonds trade at a stressed level, while Company B's bonds trade at a distressed level.

 Key Takeaways on Stressed vs. Distressed Investing

Stressed investing can be a subset of event-driven credit investing and is sometimes referred to as special situation investing. Think of stressed and special situation investing as "distress-lite."

As time goes by, a stressed company can either recover after fixing its problems or descend into the distressed category as its problems continue to worsen. A stressed investor's profit comes from either credit recovery or early distressed investing. In the credit recovery scenario, an investor with long exposure to the stressed bond can profit when the spread narrows after the company improves earnings from cost reduction and uses the capital drawn from the revolver to create a lower-cost line of products. The investor may choose to adopt a passive stance similar to a typical large-cap, value equity investor or actively engage management in a cooperative dialogue about how to renegotiate its supplier contracts and maximize its liquidity given the available revolving line of credit. In the event that the company fails to renegotiate its contracts, continues to see its earnings fall, and eventually is tapped out of liquidity, stressed investors may find themselves becoming distressed investors. Some distressed investors with long-term capital may recognize certain stressed situations as potential distressed opportunities and enter into distressed situations early.

In this case, the investor typically has a long-term investment horizon and intends to maintain the exposure through the distressed period and the recovery stage with the goal of earning a handsome return when the company undergoes the eventual exit.

RISKS

The risks in distressed investing are many and vary greatly depending on where the investor's claim sits in the organizational and capital structure.

Valuation Risk

Distressed debt investors, just like deep value equity investors, face the main risk of making the wrong fundamental calls regarding the value of the underlying business. This is one of the key risks faced by distressed investors. The fact that distressed investors can enter into their positions at low price points mitigates this risk. However, if loan investors overestimate the value of the collateral securing the loan and bond investors overestimate the value of the debtor's assets, the recovery rate may be lower still than the low entry prices due to additional risks faced by distressed companies. Furthermore, a company in distress is not operating at an optimal level. Distressed investors face the risk that some of the impairment in the value of the business incurred by the distress period may be permanent. Among other things, distress brings additional strain on operations because financing options are fewer and more expensive, management is distracted by the legal and procedural duties related to the restructuring process, sales are lower due to consumer concerns about company viability, and the firm lacks access to vendor financing and vendor discounts. In addition, if poor management is a contributing factor to the distress and investors are unable to replace the team, distressed investors may have the additional burden of having to work with the same management team. The combination of reduced operating flexibility and potentially a contentious working environment rife with conflicts of interest significantly increases the inherent risks associated with this strategy.

Key Takeaways on Liquidity of Distressed Assets

Be aware that although there are some large bankruptcies where there is an active trading market for the distressed bonds (the Lehman bankruptcy comes to mind), in most cases, even though they may be supported by a "broker quote," most distressed bond prices are nothing more than educated guesses, and it is rare that size may be traded without significantly moving the market.

Entry Risk

It is very difficult to time the "bottom" in distressed investing, trying to buy the bank loan or bond at or near the lowest price point. In many cases, the descent into distress begins with a sharp sell-off on heavy volume, followed by periods of sparse trading volume and high price volatility. Often, after the initial sell-off, the price falls further and it can stay low for years before it starts to show meaningful appreciation. Many distressed investors accept the fact that they will not be able to time their entry points perfectly, particularly when combined with the fact that during periods with sparse trading volume, they may not be able to buy as much as they want at the price they want. Accumulating position may take a significant amount of time, patience, and skill; in thinly traded markets, interested buyers have to be careful not to let their interest drive up the price of the asset.

 Key Takeaway about "Timing the Market"

Many distressed hedge funds accept the fact that being a little early or a little late to buy or sell is a risk. However, if they are right on their investment thesis and execution as well as generally judicious in their purchase, the upside is expected to far outweigh the cost of not being able to perfectly time the market.

Exit Risk

Investors face the risk that in certain scenarios, the exit from bankruptcy (and thus value realization and increase in liquidity) may be delayed. In contentious restructuring battles, the process can drag on for years. Interstate Bakeries, also known as Hostess Brands, filed for Chapter 11 in 2004, had a five-year restructuring process, and emerged from Chapter 11 in late 2009, only to refile for Chapter 11 in January 2012. Meanwhile, the restructuring expenses mount and the value of the company is being eaten away by the bankruptcy costs, decreasing the likely recovery to creditors. In the case of Hostess, the company was forced to liquidate after failing to reach a new collective bargaining agreement with one of its larger unions.[19] Unsecured creditors are most at risk, as they occupy a junior status in the investor pecking order. The uncertainty that accompanies a protracted restructuring further erodes the value of the debtor's assets. When widespread restructuring took place in the auto industry in 2009 and 2010, one of the key motivations to have a timely exit for the companies was to preserve the value of these companies. If consumers were comfortable that a company was doing business as usual (the brands would be around, and so would the dealerships and the services), they were more likely to buy from that company.

Key Takeaways about Fund Liquidity Terms vs. Actual Portfolio Liquidity

Understand what the liquidity of the portfolio is through time—this is what drives your end liquidity. Not understanding the likely exit horizon for bankruptcies for which your manager is involved may lead to unanticipated lock-ups.

Chapter 7 Risk

If the Chapter 11 restructuring process fails and the debtor is liquidated in a Chapter 7 proceeding, investors usually receive less than they would have if the company had been restructured as a going concern. This is due to two things: first, because Chapter 7 is usually the second step after a long attempt at a restructuring, the restructuring cost has eaten away some value from investors. Second, the liquidation process may take place during a challenging macroeconomic backdrop or may not be handled well for many reasons (lack of expertise, members of management are going to lose their jobs and thus are indifferent to this process, or creditors can't come to a consensus on the sale plan). This risk is greater for unsecured creditors than for secured creditors, who (at least in theory) are ahead in seniority.

Jurisdictional Risk

Another form of legal risk is the varying degree of creditor rights in different legal jurisdictions across the globe. As investors scour the globe to find the next great distress opportunity, they need to be aware of the treatment of creditors in different regimes. Some distressed investors simply avoid investing in areas where they do not feel that they can sufficiently understand the legal system or feel that the bankruptcy law is not creditor friendly. Many distressed managers are focused on opportunities in the United States and in the United Kingdom. That being said, there are opportunities outside these two areas for the right investors. The key is that unlike in the United States where there is an established legal process and a bankruptcy court system that has dealt with many complex bankruptcy cases, value realization in other areas of the world is much less dependent on the legal system. For example, the equity in businesses in countries such as India and Indonesia tends to be largely family owned. These families are highly influential in local business and politics, and their relationship with the local judges can influence the outcome of the restructuring, which tends to heavily favor equity owners. In these countries, the approach to distress investing is different from investing in U.S. distress. Having a trustworthy local partner with on-the-ground presence and expertise, longer-term investment horizon, and a "softer" constructive approach (not having to rely on winning a legal battle in the bankruptcy court) are some of the key requirements to distress investing where the legal system is less defined.

Case Study: Vitro

Vitro SAB, a Mexican glass manufacturer, provides an interesting example of some of the complexities involved in investing in distressed strategies as well as to illustrate the additional challenges that can arise when investing in non-U.S. distressed situations.

Vitro defaulted on $1.2 billion of bonds in 2009, and the Mexican holding company filed a proceeding in Mexico to reorganize. Some of Vitro's U.S. bondholders filed involuntary bankruptcy petitions in Texas against Vitro's U.S. subsidiaries that guaranteed the bonds. Much to their surprise, the Texas bankruptcy court ruled in Vitro's favor,[20] agreeing that the subsidiaries were "generally paying their debts as they come due," and therefore were not eligible for Chapter 7 relief. This decision came as a surprise to many seasoned practitioners of the U.S. distressed market. The decision appears to say that, for example, if homeowners stopped paying their mortgage, the mortgage lenders should not be able to foreclose because as long as they are current on their electric and cable bills, they are "generally paying their debts," even if they have not made mortgage payments. This decision was later reversed by the District Court. However, at the time the Texas bankruptcy court issued its ruling, it illustrated the legal and process risk associated with investing in a distressed bond.

 ### Key Takeaway on Jurisdictional Risk

The ruling was done by a U.S. court and involved U.S. guarantors—the jurisdiction risk is not because Vitro was a Mexican company. Process and legal risk are not uniquely limited to non-U.S. jurisdictions—there may be plenty of it in U.S. courts too!

The second risk is related to differences in Mexican and American bankruptcy law. The Mexican bankruptcy court approved the reorganization plan proposed by the company, over the objections of the U.S. bondholders. The heart of the U.S. bondholders' objection lay with the action by Vitro's management that, under the control of the family that owned the company, had created intercompany obligations so that the company owed $1.9 billion to its subsidiaries. This enabled Vitro to count its subsidiaries as creditors, and the Vitro-controlled subsidiaries then could outvote outside bondholders in the restructuring process. The company had essentially taken advantage of the fact that the Mexican bankruptcy laws (the "ley de Concursos" or "the Concursos") were silent on intercompany loans and "insider" claims. Under the U.S. Bankruptcy Code, the claims of insiders are not counting when determining whether there is an impaired accepting class of creditors (a requirement to confirm a plan of reorganization). Thus, in a U.S. proceeding, Vitro would not have been able to pull a similar trick to outvote its creditors. Vitro then asked a U.S. court to enforce the restructuring plan approved by the Mexican bankruptcy court,[21] which purported to satisfy and release the claims against U.S. subsidiaries. In 2012, a judge in the U.S. Dallas court denied Vitro's request on the basis that the reorganization plan did not provide sufficient protection to the claims of U.S. creditors. The decision to deny comity to the Mexican reorganization plan was affirmed by the District Court and the United States Court of Appeals for the Fifth Circuit. In plain English, the case is settled. Bondholders received approximately 85 cents to every dollar of claim and their legal fees, estimated at more than $25 million.

Equity Mark-to-Market Risk

When a company exits from bankruptcy, the shareholders of the new entity have the option of allowing the equity to be traded or to keep it privately held. By allowing the equity to trade, the holders may improve liquidity, but they face the risk that the equity may trade at a valuation multiple below traded comparable companies for a time. The lower multiple represents the premium demanded by investors for taking on risks related to bankruptcy overhang, informational limitations, and the potentially lower liquidity of a newly emerged entity. In addition, sell-side analyst coverage tends to be light.

The bankruptcy process typically frees up the debtor from the cause of financial distress and gives it a lighter debt burden. Furthermore, management's tendency to aim for conservative projections in the plan of reorganization makes it easier to show improved financial performance post exit. Nonetheless, it may take a few quarters of improving results to build positive momentum with the broader investing public. It also takes time and resources, both of which may be scarce for a company emerging from bankruptcy, for the company to establish an investor relations team to promote the company to potential investors including sell-side analysts. At this point, potential new investors are limited to those who are able and willing to base their investment decisions on a limited set of information and those with a time horizon that allows them to wait until the broader market recognizes the value of the company.

The period during which a newly emerged company establishes credibility with the market may be longer for stocks traded OTC relative to those traded on an exchange. Pink OTC ("Pink Sheets")[22] is the main collector and distributor of OTC quotes for equities. The main difference between being quoted on a stock exchange and the Pink Sheets lies with the difference in SEC filing requirements. With the exception of foreign issuers, mostly represented by American Depositary Receipts (ADRs), the companies quoted in the Pink Sheets tend to be closely held, extremely small, thinly traded, or have filed for bankruptcy. These companies typically do not meet the minimum listing requirements to be traded on a stock exchange such as the New York Stock Exchange. As such, the lower filing requirements of the Pink Sheets appeal to these companies. Unlike companies traded on a stock exchange, Pink Sheet companies are not required to file periodic reports or audited financial statements with the SEC. This makes it difficult for new investors to find reliable, unbiased information about these companies.

If the equity remains unlisted, the question for hedge funds is how to mark the equity in the fund's net asset value calculation. A common method is to use an earnings multiple methodology. If there is a recent strategic acquisition of a comparable company, the multiple of earnings implied in the sale price is a reasonable number to use. However, in many cases, the multiple is based on publicly traded comparable companies with a discount to reflect the limited liquidity for a private equity position. The question is how much of a liquidity discount is appropriate—if a comparable company is trading at 7× earnings, whether a multiple of 5×, 5.5×, 6×, or 6.5× earnings is the number to use. This is a gray area, and it is more of a problem for a hedge fund structure where investors are able to come in and out of the fund and an incentive fee is charged on an annual basis. If the multiple is too low, then the exiting investors are disadvantaged. If the multiple is too high, entering investors are disadvantaged. The key is to find a reasonable process and to confirm that the manager can demonstrate that reasonable care has been taken in determining the multiple.

For private equity, valuation is an issue because the best that an investor can do is to use public comparables in determining a multiple. In addition, the fact that a stock is traded does not mean that it is liquid. There are a few reasons liquidity may be limited including a limited target market because of the informational issue, limited float, small capitalization size, and the need to market itself to institutional investors.

 Key Takeaway on Equity Risk in Credit Hedge Fund Portfolios

Many distressed managers have significant long-only equity positions as they retain the post-reorganization equity. Don't be surprised to find significant equity risk in these "event-oriented" credit portfolios.

Liquidity Risk

Periods of market distress in OTC markets are often characterized by scarce bids, and when they exist, a wide bid-ask spread. The wide bid-ask spread often reflects the informational asymmetry between potential buyers and sellers. Under normal market conditions, a range of 1–2 points for bid-ask spread for a distressed bank loan and 2–4 points or more for a deeply distressed bond is not unusual. During market turmoil, the spread can widen to up to 10 points for a distressed bank loan and 20 points for a distressed bond. Often, after sellers whose actions are not profit-maximizing ("noneconomic sellers" in industry parlance) have exited the market, new buyers attracted to the new low asset price may be unable to purchase the asset at that price because the majority of the remaining investors are professional distressed investors. These investors are usually committed to holding the asset through the company's restructuring process, are confident that they will be able to realize significant gains after restructuring is completed, and are unwilling to sell unless given a significantly higher bid than the price they paid. However, because the restructuring process can be uncertain in terms of timing and outcome, the low bid of the potential buyer partially reflects the high uncertainty premium associated with distressed investing. The bid-ask spread can be particularly wide for transactions where the buyer does not have access to MNPI[23] and the seller does.

Even in scenarios where the equity of the newly emerged company is traded, the equity is not necessarily liquid. As discussed above, the limited investor awareness and ability to invest in the equity of a newly reorganized company presents liquidity risk. In a company where the majority of the stock is owned by a few large buy-and-hold investors, trading may be infrequent and trading volume observed during a given day low. This may mean that it is difficult for new investors to enter into a position without moving the price significantly. Correspondingly, it may also be difficult for a hedge fund facing a sudden liquidity requirement to sell the equity without negatively affecting the price.

In addition, when the company exits Chapter 11, it may have only a small amount of public float. Many institutional equity investors are liquidity driven and use the amount of the float as a measure of liquidity for a stock. When a company exits from bankruptcy and lists its equity in the public market, a large share of the float may be owned by distressed investors and management. These are typically deemed as insiders, and thus are restricted from trading up to 180 days after the issuance of the stock on emergence. For a hypothetical company with the equity market capitalization of $500 million and 60 percent insider ownership, only $200 million will be considered as the public float. Furthermore, in select cases, only a small amount of public equity may be released at a time. Until the float increases, institutional investors will shrink away from investing in the equity. The limited number of eligible investors translates into limited liquidity for the equity position. Investors who need to exit the equity position during the early stage post exit from the restructuring face the possibility of losses due to liquidity discount.

INVESTMENT STRATEGIES

Investors in stressed and distressed situations can benefit from a source of uncorrelated alpha. Investing in distressed credit instruments is very similar to investing in deep value equity in the way that investors in both strategies aim to profit from their ability to source, identify, and invest in select assets that are overlooked by other investors. However, there are inefficiencies in the distressed corporate credit market that differentiate them from the public equity market and provide challenges and opportunities. Although there are credit hedge funds that can generate alpha on the short side by actively trading their hedges or short alpha positions on stressed and distressed names, many distressed credit hedge funds (particularly those who adopt the "classic" distressed strategy as outlined below) generate their alpha predominantly on the long side.

Edge Being Captured

Investors who are able to profit from investing in distressed assets are capitalizing on their ability to evaluate investment opportunities in a market with high informational inefficiency. In addition, investors who are able to invest in stressed and distressed bank loans and bonds can unearth interesting opportunities because many investors are excluded from investing in the asset class.

Greater Information Asymmetry

Financial distress increases the degree of information asymmetry between a company and its investors. After a publicly traded company files for bankruptcy,[24] the reality of dealing with the burden of bankruptcy usually means that SEC filings may be delayed and/or less informative.[25] The reports filed prior to the bankruptcy will still be available publicly. However, some of the figures may no longer be useful given that the company has now entered into a very different operating situation. Past statements, financial ratios, and operating performance may have little reliability in terms of analyzing the current conditions of the debtor.

 Key Takeaway on Information Efficiency in the Distressed Market

In distressed investing, the difficulty in finding timely and reliable information presents a significant barrier to entry to select investors.

Technology has certainly made it easier and cheaper for investors to access documentation produced in the bankruptcy court system.[26] However, a significant amount of time and expertise is required to read and analyze all the legal documents related to a case. In order to understand the issues related to the restructuring, investors need expertise in corporate finance, accounting, restructuring, bankruptcy law, contract law, and banking and capital markets. The complexity associated with the process increases exponentially if the debtor has a complex capital structure with multiple subsidiaries and intercompany guarantees. Professional distress investors often rely on the expertise of bankruptcy lawyers, restructuring advisors and consultants, bankers, forensic accountants, and financial analysts. This complexity means that even when information is publicly available and readily accessible, there are significant time commitments, expertise requirements, and additional out-of-pocket costs associated with collecting and interpreting the information.

 Key Takeaway on the Nature of Available Information in the Distressed Market

Complexity in distressed situations means that even when information is publicly available and readily accessible, there are significant time commitments, expertise requirements, and additional out-of-pocket costs associated with collecting and interpreting the information.

Wide Range of Skills Required

In addition to expertise in fundamentally analyzing the value of a distressed company, investors need to navigate the complex and potentially lengthy restructuring process in or out of court. In order to be effective in what can be an extensive negotiation process among investor groups, one needs to understand the contractual rights of various investor groups and the levers each group has to influence the process. Here, the ability to analyze and understand loan covenants and bond indentures is of key importance. Furthermore, an in-court restructuring also requires knowledge regarding the workings of the U.S. bankruptcy courts and bankruptcy laws. Even investors who do not intend to actively participate in the negotiation need to understand the extent of the rights of other investors under the law in order to assess their own positions.

Need for Credibility

Reputational value is also very important in the negotiation. An investor who is a "known entity" with the know-how to navigate the process, work with management, and secure financing can wield substantial influence in bringing different parties to the table and increasing the chance for a successful restructuring.

The importance of reputation partially explains the phenomenon that has been observed from time to time in the marketplace: although creditors' committees typically consist of the largest creditors, smaller creditors also have ways to influence the restructuring process through unofficial and working committees. Many investors seem to think that having a large amount of capital and the corresponding ability to hold a larger amount of an issue is a necessary condition to gain profit in distressed investing. This is correct in select cases, particularly if the investor intends to adopt a hostile approach. However, smaller hedge fund managers can benefit from their ability to participate in deals that may be too small for large and mega funds. Smaller funds also tend to attract less media attention and thus lower headline risks, which may be relevant when one is negotiating against a politically sensitive constituency. The Chrysler bankruptcy was a particularly interesting situation where much of the popular discourse at the time was painted as bondholders (hedge funds and Wall Street investors) against auto-workers. Although the decision to put the UAW's claim ahead of the bondholders is inconsistent with the rules of seniority, there was significant media and political pressure against bondholders' efforts to enforce their contractual rights.[27]

The smaller bite size of smaller funds may also allow for greater trading flexibility, which is particularly important given the lower liquidity of many distressed assets. Furthermore, there are instances in which smaller funds have wielded larger influence than the fund size alone would indicate. Even with a small toehold position, portfolio managers with the reputation of ability to maximize value for creditors can "punch above their weight class" by leading and assembling a group of creditors who are actively involved in influencing the course of the negotiation.

 Key Takeaway on Activism in the Distressed Space

Be careful not to assume direct positive correlation between size of a firm or a hedge fund and size of influence in the restructuring process.

OTC Market Structure as Barrier to Entry

Due to certain features of the OTC market and the nature of private issuances, many investors are excluded from participating in the market for distressed corporate assets. This means that when the instrument becomes distressed, potential buyers are limited to those with access to the select group of broker-dealers who traffic in the credit. Locating the broker-dealers with available inventory of the distressed asset may be difficult for professional money managers without the appropriate network in the distressed credit arena.

In addition, all bank loans and many notes are issued as private placements under Rule 144A. Therefore, should a bank loan or a privately issued bond become distressed, the only investors eligible to purchase the asset in the secondary market are accredited investors and institutional investors and/or money managers who are qualified institutional buyers (QIBs).[28]

Some mutual funds are prohibited from owning defaulted securities, and because of this, when a company defaults on a principal or coupon payment and/or files for Chapter 11 reorganization, the mutual fund holders of the debt may be required to sell the asset regardless of market price. During periods of distress in the credit market, market participants usually see a dramatic reduction of liquidity due to the strong imbalance of demand and supply, resulting in depressed sale prices (assuming buyers could be found).

THE FUNDAMENTAL CREDIT OR "CLASSIC" DISTRESSED STRATEGY

For many in the industry, the classic form of distressed investing is largely a long-only or long-biased strategy. By definition, classic distressed investing is a very specific subsection of "event-driven" investing because restructuring (within Chapter 11 bankruptcy or otherwise) and/or liquidation are well-defined events. Distressed investing in its classic form involves buying a bond or bank loan at distressed prices, holding it through an in-court or out-of-court restructuring process, having full or partial conversion of the debt instrument into equities at the exit from restructuring, and finally creating a liquidity event through the sale of the newly created equities. Distressed investors often describe their target investment as a "good company with bad balance sheet." Note this phrase refers to financial not operational turnarounds. A typical distressed debt investor is as much a believer in fundamental value investing as a typical value equity investor in the sense that both of them are investing in securities that they consider to be undervalued by the market.

 Key Takeaway on Evaluating Distressed Funds Using Past Investments

Distressed investing is very specific to each situation. Do not assume that the current portfolio characteristics will be reflected in the future.

A typical distressed credit portfolio can have anywhere from 5 to 20 situations in the portfolio that span the breadth of the distressed timeline. The number of situations should be correlated with the resources, namely number of analysts and distressed expertise, of the manager. There is no "average" portfolio, and the mix of prebankruptcy names, issuers in the restructuring process, and post-reorganization equities can differ significantly depending on where we are in the distressed cycle. At the beginning of the cycle, the portfolio may consist predominantly of prebankruptcy or stressed names, while in an economic recovery, most of the portfolio may consist of post-reorganization equities. In addition, it is important to double check whether there are nonstandard investments such as DIP paper, total return swaps, and foreign exchange hedges where appropriate. That being said, the overall composition and management of the portfolio may on the surface bear a marked similarity to that of a deep value equity investor.

However, there are meaningful differences between distressed debt investing and deep equity value investing. Distressed debt investors' ownership of the company's equity largely happens through the restructuring process. In contrast, equity investors enter their position by buying in the equity market. Due to market inefficiencies we discussed above, a distressed investor is typically exposed to greater liquidity and information asymmetry risks relative to the value investor. On the other hand, a distressed investor whose debt position is converted into equity was transferred from a creditor to an owner of the company without having to pay equity multiples.

Another difference between distressed investors and deep value equity investors is in the appetite for liquidity. Deep value equity investors may wait a long time for event realization; however, in the event that they need to exit the position prior to event realization, they are most likely able to do so relatively quickly (within days if not intraday) and without taking too much of an illiquidity haircut in the process for a reasonable size investment. The range of investment horizons can vary widely in distressed investing. Very liquid distressed bonds (bonds with very large amounts outstanding and dispersed holder base) can be liquidated in days or weeks without much price impact. In contrast, many distress situations involve substantial liquidity risk in addition to complexity and credit risk. The time horizon of classic distressed investors can range from a few quarters to multiple years. In the middle of the process, investors who wish to exit the position may not be able to do so without incurring a significant loss to the position.

Another key difference between distressed investing and deep value equity investing lies in the natural phase of a company's life cycle. Unlike value equity investors, most distressed investors start to be involved with a company around the time of the first signs of distress and throughout the restructuring process. Upon exit from restructuring and conversion of the fulcrum security, distressed investors often find themselves owners of an undervalued equity position. At this point, the distressed investor is a value investor in a private or publicly traded equity position.

 ## Key Questions for a Distressed Fund

- Describe a distressed situation you have been involved in.
- At what stage did you decide to enter into a position?
- What is your exit plan? What if the restructuring does not go as planned?
- What is the typical size of a position at cost? At market? What is your maximum position size? Is it a guideline or a hard limit?
- Do you tend to take on an activist role in restructuring? Describe an involvement.
- How are trades allocated? (for managers who have multiple funds or managed accounts)
- How are positions valued?
- For fair value positions, what is the methodology used? What are the comparables used, and how were they selected?

THE TRADING-ORIENTED STRATEGY

Another type of strategy used in the distressed space is the trading-oriented strategy. It may be used as a stand-alone strategy, or it may be combined with the traditional distressed approach. These strategies have shorter investment horizons (three to six months, for example, instead of two years). Many of these situations tend to involve relatively more liquid situations (large amount of loans and debt outstanding with a well-diversified base of holders), which permits a fair amount of trading taking place even though they are distressed instruments. Examples of these situations include Lehman Brothers, with $691 billion in assets before bankruptcy filing, Enron with $65.5 billion assets before filing, and Worldcom with $104 billion in assets before filing. Figure 3.5 shows the top 10 bankruptcies in U.S. history by assets.

An example of this strategy would be hedge fund managers who invest in the claims of large, liquidating estates such as Lehman Brothers, MF Global, and Madoff. This strategy is essentially a combination of value-oriented and event-driven strategies. A hedge fund manager who is familiar with the value of assets in the estate can take an opinion on how much value will be distributed to the claimants, and he will enter into the position if the claims are trading at a significant discount to what he considers to be fair value. Additionally, the manager may use his expertise on the process to purchase a claim with the expectation of a large upcoming cash distribution.

Rank	Company	Bankruptcy Date	Value at Bankruptcy ($ millions)
1	Lehman Brothers Holdings, Inc.	9/15/2008	$691,063
2	Washington Mutual, Inc.	9/26/2008	$327,913
3	WorldCom, Inc.	7/21/2002	$103,914
4	General Motors Corporation	6/1/2009	$ 91,047
5	CIT Group Inc.	11/1/2009	$ 80,448
6	Enron Corp.	12/2/2001	$ 65,503
7	Conesco, Inc.	12/17/2002	$ 61,392
8	MF Global Holdings Ltd.	10/31/2011	$ 40,541
9	Chrysler LLC	4/30/2009	$ 39,300
10	Thornburg Mortgage, Inc.	5/1/2009	$ 36,521

Figure 3.5 **Top 10 bankruptcies in U.S. history by asset size**
Source: www.bankruptcydata.com

Key Takeaways of the Trade-Offs between Liquidity and Volatility

For tradable distressed assets, there is a trade-off between liquidity and mark-to-market volatility. Many distressed assets including post-reorganization equities have a "kink" in their beta profile—it is idiosyncratic to the market when the market is up, but has a high beta when the market is down.

 Key Questions for Trading-Oriented Positions

- What is the typical time horizon for a trade?
- Describe some of the catalysts that are currently in the portfolio.
- What if a catalyst does not materialize in a timely manner? Give an example.

THE CAPITAL STRUCTURE ARBITRAGE STRATEGY

In stressed situations, a popular strategy involves taking long exposure on the bank loan or senior bond of a stressed company and shorting the more junior part of the same capital structure, usually the equity or the subordinated bond. The best scenario for the investor is a Goldilocks scenario: the company's financial health improves by just the right amount (i.e., not too much). The long position benefits because the prices of the bank loans and bonds appreciate; the short position also benefits as the equity price falls. If the company sees an across-the-board improvement in the prices of its financial liabilities, the investor's profit depends on the relative performance of different parts of the capital structure. Sizing also matters; this is where investors with portfolio management skill can add value through relative weighting of the long and short position.

Consider a hypothetical example of an equal percentage rise and fall in the price of the bank loan and equity of a widget maker. Let us assume that both the loan and the equity saw a 10 percent increase in price. Whether the investor realizes a profit or a loss from this capital structure arbitrage depends on relative sizing of the long and the short positions.[29] If the long and the short positions are equal-weighted as a percentage of a fund's net asset value (NAV), the investor earns neither a profit nor a loss on the trade. If the long position is larger than the short position, the investor realizes a profit. A loss is incurred if the long position is smaller than the short position.

With distressed names, capital structure arbitrage (particularly in the same capital structure) is not common with hedge funds because in most cases there is no equity to short. As the company goes into restructuring, the equity either has been extinguished or is trading so close to zero that shorting it would be pointless from an investment perspective. In addition, the equity may be very difficult to borrow. An alternative to the trade above is taking long and short positions on different stressed and liquid distressed situations. For example, an investor can take long exposure in a stressed bond of a car maker while shorting the equity position of one of its suppliers. If the automotive sector suffers from general economic headwinds, the investor may suffer losses in the long bond position but profit from the short equity position. The thesis is similar to the first type of capital structure arbitrage; however, there is additional potential risk and reward for the investor in the form of basis risk between the two different issuers.

The key additional risk in this strategy is the basis risk between the long and the short position. On the same capital structure, the risk is that there may be an external unseen force such as government intervention where seniority is obviously violated by giving the equity holder (or another junior claim holder) a greater claim than they would have received under strict seniority at the expense of the senior claim holders. On different issuers, the investor faces the risk that the performance of the two companies could differ. If the company with the equity short actually benefits from the distress of its competitor (the long exposure), the equity price may go up as the bond or loan price falls.

THE DEBTOR-IN-POSSESSION FINANCING STRATEGY

By definition, the companies that are in financial distress are usually unable to meet their cash obligations, including interest payments. However, investors in a distressed company can gain attractive interest income and fees from providing much-needed liquidity and working capital via DIP loans. Similar to a bank loan, lenders can sometimes negotiate sweeteners in the form of fees and/or original issue discount (OID).[30] DIP loans typically earn more than senior secured bank loans while enjoying superseniority.

Claims that were created prior to the Chapter 11 filing are referred to as prepetition claims, and claims that were created after are referred to as postpetition claims. This differentiation is important because postpetition claims receive priority to prepetition claims. The source of DIP financing can come from prepetition or postpetition lenders. In restructuring cases of 2009 to 2010, the market saw many prepetition lenders who provided DIP financing enjoy "roll-up" rights. This means for every dollar of DIP financing they provided, a dollar of their prepetition loan received the same superpriority claim as the postpetition claims (it was "rolled up"). DIP loans' attractive terms, superpriority claim, and roll-up rights for prepetition loans mean that prepetition lenders are incentivized to provide as much DIP financing as possible. The superpriority claims (including the rolled-up prepetition loans) also give rise to the DIP's "priming lien"—this means that in the event of asset sale or liquidation, the DIP loans (and rolled-up prepetition loans along with them) are ahead of the other senior secured lenders. With the exception of other priority claims such as court and legal expenses, this means the DIP lender has to be paid in cash and in full before the proceeds of an asset sale or liquidation can be distributed to the prepetition lenders and before a debtor can confirm a plan of reorganization[31] (to exit Chapter 11). Figure 3.6 compares the capital structure of a company before and after roll-up.

Risks

The supersenior position of the DIP loan, the high coupon, and the typically short tenor reduces the credit risk of this strategy. Lenders need to ensure that there is adequate collateral behind the DIP loan, which is usually collateralized by inventory and accounts receivable in addition to property, plant, and equipment (PP&E). There is still the

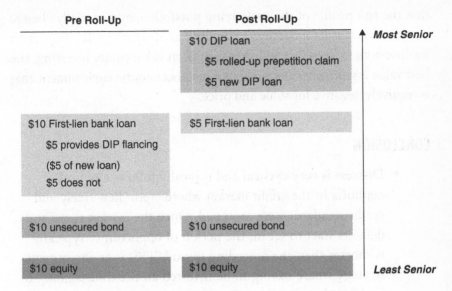

Figure 3.6 **Comparison of capital structure pre and post roll-up**
Source: PAAMCO

risk that the company may continue to deteriorate and the value of the inventory and accounts receivable will be less than expected. In this scenario, the DIP lenders are in a relatively better position compared to other investors.

Potential investors may ask, "Where's the catch?" The reason investors don't see DIP funds being offered widely is that there is typically limited capacity and sourcing. Existing secured investors (lenders and bondholders) are the most likely providers of DIP financing. New providers will usually need to take out the prepetition senior secured debt. Additional risk is liquidity risk, although the DIP lenders typically hold their loan until maturity due to the short tenor, or if they need to exit, they may sell the position to other DIP lenders. Finally, there have been cases where the original DIP financing was not enough and a more senior DIP line was put in later; as a condition of the new DIP, all or part of the original DIP loan is subordinated to the new financing.

In conclusion, few distressed funds maintain the same strategy throughout the overall macroeconomic distressed cycle. Understanding that the risk profile of the underlying portfolio may materially change over time is critical for the investor in distressed securities. It is important for investors to keep in mind that as in deep value equity investing, the best value investments are made in a macroeconomic environment that is relatively negative for value and price.

CONCLUSION

- Distress is very cyclical and typically follows a period of euphoria in the credit market where credit flew freely and credit standards were loosened. Once the market turns and defaults start to set in, the period of opportunity typically is shorter than the preceding period. This is an investment strategy where having to be invested all the time is going to lead to sub-optimal results.
- There is no official or legal definition of what constitutes a distressed asset. Market conventions use ratings, spread, and price-based definition to determine what constitutes a distressed asset.
- The reason for distress can be financial, operational, or both. Bankruptcy or default is often not a surprise to investors. A company can be in operational trouble for a long time before it finally files for bankruptcy or runs out of liquidity.
- Restructuring a distressed company can occur in and out of court. When the stars align for an out-of-court restructuring, investors benefit from a faster and more cost-efficient process.
- In a restructuring or bankruptcy process, fundamental credit analysis alone is often insufficient. Value-oriented credit managers who find themselves owning distressed positions have gotten into "value traps" as the value of the position continues to deteriorate and exit from bankruptcy often continues to move further ahead in the horizon. Negotiation, structuring, legal, and consensus building

skills are crucial to bring the debtor out of bankruptcy and back into health.

- Hedging a distressed position can be extremely difficult. Often, classic distressed strategies are long-only or heavily long-biased strategies because adding a hedge only introduces basis risk.

CHAPTER 4

Bank Loans

In an environment where investors' thirst for yield is high and increasing, many institutional investors are looking beyond the traditional yield instruments such as high yield bonds and dividend bearing equities. In addition to the yield feature, various investment strategies applicable to high yield are also applicable to loans. A bank loan is a confidential, private offering made by a company to qualified investors. Bank loans are typically floating-rate instruments with seniority in a company's capital structure, secured by a lien on the borrower's assets, and have more restrictive covenants than bonds. As a result of these factors, bank loans have historically exhibited lower default rates and higher recovery rates relative to bonds. Even so, there are a number of key risks to investing in bank loans, including credit risk, liquidity risk, and settlement risk.

Bank loans have become an increasingly important instrument in the tool kit of a credit hedge fund manager. The bank loan market enjoyed tremendous growth over the past two decades thanks to increased supply from issuers and increased demand for bank loans from institutional investors. Over time, increased standardization of market practices and documentation also led to a viable secondary market for bank loans and contributed to the substantial growth of the loan market. This chapter will highlight some of the structural features of the loan market that lead to opportunities for hedge fund investors.

BANK LOANS BACKGROUND

Characteristics of Bank Loans

Given general familiarity with bond markets, it is perhaps most straightforward to explain bank loans by highlighting key differences relative to bonds. The first is that *bank loans are not securities.* A bank loan is a confidential, private offering made by a company (the "issuer") only to qualified banks and accredited investors (usually a syndicate of lenders). Unlike a public bond issuance, terms are often negotiated between the issuer and the syndicate,[1] and therefore tend to be highly variable across issuers.

Bank loans are often senior to bonds and most other securities. Bank loans typically sit at the top of a company's capital structure (Figure 4.1). In the event of bankruptcy, loan obligations are secured by a lien on the borrower's assets and therefore senior to unsecured and subordinated bonds, to hybrid instruments, as well as to preferred and common stock.[2] However, one must be careful to check for any operating and holding company relationships. It is possible for a bank loan to have

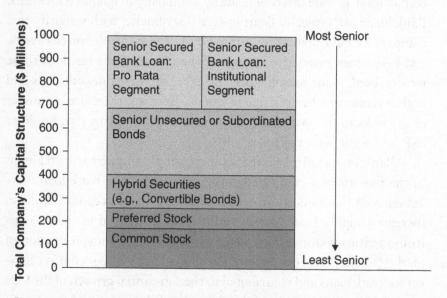

Figure 4.1 Capital structure of a hypothetical company
Source: PAAMCO

the appearance of seniority but, given the overall capital structure of the company, in fact, on an economic basis, be junior to certain bonds.

Bank loans are floating rate instruments. Coupons are typically quoted as a spread above a floating-rate (e.g., three-month LIBOR). In contrast, bonds have fixed coupons. As a result, bank loans typically have lower interest rate duration than bonds. The interest rate component on bank loans is typically adjusted on a quarterly basis as LIBOR changes. Some loans include a LIBOR floor, which makes them attractive when LIBOR remains low for a prolonged period.

Bank loans typically have stronger covenants than bonds. Fitch compared loan covenants against bond indentures for sub-investment grade credits and found that a loan typically had 20 covenants versus 6 for bonds.[3] Covenants provide loan investors with the ability to monitor performance of the borrower and/or limit the ability of the borrower to undertake certain actions that may impair the value of the loan investors' claim. More numerous covenants provide better protection for creditors. Loan covenants often include restrictions or requirements on mergers, while bond indentures rarely contain similar language. In addition, loan covenants typically have a higher degree of enforceability, as they are typically collateralized by a lien on the borrowers' assets.

Bank loans are typically callable at par by the issuer at any time. Recently, more loans have featured a "soft call" provision at 101 or 102, which compensates the investors in a way that's similar to high yield bonds in the event of a call. The callability of the loan means that investors face the risk of being refinanced should rates or spread decrease. In early 2012, Global Blue, a European provider of tax-free shopping service owned by private equity sponsors, repriced €460 million of its loans at 1 percent lower less than a year after issuance.

Bank loans' market practices for trading, clearance, and settlement differ from bonds. Loans and some bonds trade on the over-the-counter (OTC) market.[4] It is also common industry practice for secondary trading of a loan to be done through the agent bank, arguably the bank most familiar with the unique details of that particular loan. Price and volume information on recent trades are not as readily available for bank loans compared to the high yield bond market. Because up-to-date pricing and volume information is important for trading activities of credit hedge funds, they typically access the information via pricing quotes from banks and paid subscription with third-party loan pricing services such as Markit and Thomson Reuters' Loan Pricing Corporation.

 Key Takeaway on the Loan Market

Unlike bonds, there are no public bank loans. All bank loans are privately negotiated contracts.

Over time, the Loan Syndications and Trading Association (LSTA) has worked toward improving standardization of documentation and trading and settlement practices for bank loans. One of the important hallmarks of the organization was the establishment of a standard settlement process for loans trading near face value ("par"[5] or "near par" loans). Industry convention is for par or near par loans to settle in T+7 (the settlement date is the trade date plus 7 business days). Common industry practice in normal market conditions is for distressed[6] loans to settle in T+20. Distressed loans trade on a more complex set of documents than par loans. However, settlement time for both par and distressed loans can take substantially longer during times of heightened market volatility.

The bank loan market does not have an established repo market to enable short selling of bank loans. Unlike with cash bonds, there is currently no method to enable the short selling of cash loans.

The bank loan market can be categorized into two rating segments: investment grade and sub-investment grade or high yield loans. Sub-investment grade or high yield loans are defined as loans rated BBB–/Baa3 or lower. Figure 4.2 compares the two segments. In the high yield segment, issuers carry higher levels of debt on their balance sheets. Leveraged loans refer to bank loans issued by issuers who carry higher levels of debt on their balance sheets relative to investment grade issuers. Credit hedge funds are typically focused on this

---

INVESTMENT GRADE LOAN MARKET

- Issued by investment grade companies (i.e., BBB–/Baa3 rated firms or better)
- Relatively low spread to LIBOR
- Primarily revolvers[8] (364-day and multiyear facility) used as backstop to commercial paper
- Generally held by commercial banks

SUB-INVESTMENT GRADE / HIGH YIELD LOAN MARKET

- Issued by sub-investment grade companies (i.e., firms rated lower than BBB–/Baa3)
- Higher spread to LIBOR
- Comprises revolvers, amortizing, and nonamortizing term loans
- Generally held by commercial and investment banks, mutual funds, hedge funds, pension funds, insurance companies, and collateralized loan obligations (CLOs)

Figure 4.2 The bank loan market by rating
Source: PAAMCO

segment of the loan market. The term *pro rata segment* refers to the piece of the loan facility that is held by banks.

As a result of the combination of seniority, collateralization, and more restrictive covenants relative to bonds, leveraged bank loans have historically exhibited lower loss given default relative to high yield bonds. Figure 4.3 shows the difference in default loss rates between institutional leveraged loans and high yield bonds.

Investors in Bank Loans

In the early days of the bank loan market, bank loans were simply what their name implies: loans made to companies by commercial banks. The loans were primarily held as part of the lending bank's balance sheet. However, over time, banks kept only part of the loan on their books and parceled out another tranche to institutional investors such as specialty finance companies, loan mutual funds, and hedge funds. As a result of the ability to tailor part of the loan facility to meet requirements of institutional investors, a more active market for bank loans

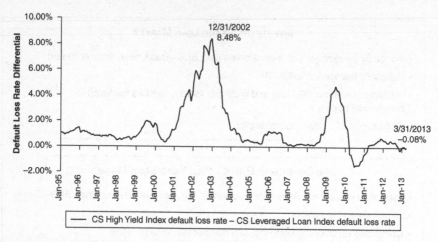

Figure 4.3   Difference in default loss rate between high yield bonds and leveraged loans
Source: Credit Suisse

was created and a broad spectrum of investors began providing capital into the sector. Around the same time, investment banks started to add loan syndication capabilities to their array of services, and thus the bank loan market was born.

Many institutional investors obtain their exposure to the loan asset class via collateralized loan obligations (CLOs), which are structured vehicles investing primarily in loans. The CLO structure enables institutional investors to obtain exposure to a diversified portfolio of bank loans under a specific set of risk characteristics. The rapid growth of the CLO market between 2003 and 2006 translated into increased demand for loans and the creation of more new loans. At the end of 2006, CLOs constituted more than 50 percent of the demand in the sub-investment grade loan market. Because the primary market is privately negotiated, there is flexibility in how the loan package is structured to meet the needs of different constituents. For example, in early 2012, Infor carved out a portion of their Term Loan B issuance with shorter maturity (4.5 versus 6 years) to meet the need of CLO investors who need shorter-dated loans to stay in compliance with their weighted average life (WAL) test.

There are two types of CLOs with fundamentally different structures: market value and cash flow CLOs. Market value CLOs have liquidation triggers that depend on the market value of the underlying investments. As a result, the deterioration in the price of bank loans in early 2008 triggered the liquidation of most market value CLOs. This was structured to protect the senior CLO note holders from significant impairment.

COLLATERALIZED LOAN OBLIGATION

In a collateralized loan obligation structure, investors can gain exposures with different risk and return characteristics to a diversified portfolio of bank loans. For example, a hypothetical portfolio has two investors. Investor A requires an investment grade rated investment with positive cash flow and wants any early prepayment of principal to go to him. Investor B has a longer-term perspective, higher risk tolerance, and is willing to trade positive cash flow for a higher return expectation. The portfolio of loans would be put into a vehicle and two different claims would be issued using the loans in the vehicle as collateral. Investor A receives an investment grade note that pays period coupons and has priority claim on all the prepayments from the underlying bank loans until the note is paid off in full. Investor B does not expect a periodic coupon payment but benefits from any excess cash flow from the underlying loans after investor A has been paid. The tranching of cash flow (Investor A is ahead of Investor B in the line for cash from the underlying bank loans) is often referred to as a payment or cash flow waterfall. Investor B benefits from increased value of the underlying bank loans; however, Investor B absorbs any loan losses until his claims are exhausted before the losses start to impair the claims of Investor A. Investor A benefits from the structure, which was created to provide some protection against significant impairment, while Investor B benefits from potential upside in exchange for taking additional risk.

Cash flow CLOs are less affected by the deterioration in the market value of the loans because unlike market value CLOs, a decline in market value of the loans alone will not trigger an event of default. The structure of a cash flow CLO is less sensitive to mark-to-market volatility in loan prices. That said, during the peak of the credit crisis, cash flow CLOs saw their limits tested. Still, most of the cash flow structures managed to avoid triggering the event of default clause. This is because cash flow from the underlying loans, the allowable amount for lower rated and defaulted assets, as well as the degree of portfolio diversification together play a role in determining the overcollateralization test for the structure: multiple breaches have to take place before an event of default[7] is triggered. As of the time of the writing, virtually all CLOs still in existence are cash flow CLOs.

 Key Takeaways on CLO Event of Default

Collateralized loan obligations are not all created equal. The likelihood of an event of default (EOD) leading to the unwinding of the structure depends on two key factors: first, whether the EOD is dependent on a single factor being breached (such as a drop in market value of the assets) or on multiple factors, and second, whether there is a cure provision should a breach takes place.

CLOs are very important for the hedge fund investor. First, it is important to track the pipeline of future CLOs, as they are large buyers of loans who from time to time can be price indiscriminate to a certain extent. Thus, their actions can have a significant effect both on short-term loan pricing and trading liquidity. Second, some hedge fund managers use the CLO vehicle as way to structure their investments. The equity and mezzanine pieces of a CLO are highly levered investments in loans; beware the hedge fund manager who then leverages the CLO residual.

KEY DEVELOPMENTS IN THE LEVERAGED BANK LOAN MARKET

The leveraged loan market grew from $317 billion in 1989 to its peak of $1.6 trillion[8] in 2009, a 400 percent increase (Figure 4.4). Demand for the institutional segment increased from being virtually nonexistent in 1993 to $856 billion in 2008 (Figure 4.5), or nearly half of

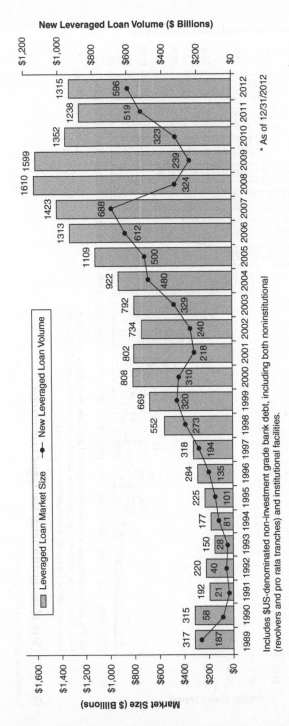

Figure 4.4 Size of the leveraged loan market

Source: Credit Suisse, Loan Pricing Corporation

Includes $US-denominated non-investment grade bank debt, including both noninstitutional
(revolvers and pro rata tranches) and institutional facilities.

* As of 12/31/2012

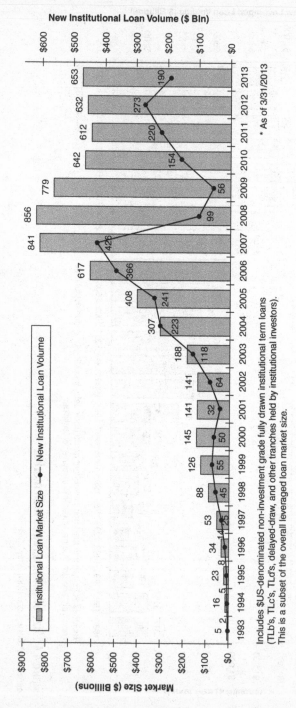

Figure 4.5 Size of the institutional leveraged loan market

Source: Credit Suisse, Loan Pricing Corporation

the total leveraged loan market. The development of a viable secondary market for loans was a key factor and was aided by the creation of the Loan Syndications and Trading Association (LSTA) in 1995.[9] The creation of the secondary market gave lending banks access to a broader pool of investors. Lending was no longer limited to the size of the banks' balance sheets. According to the LSTA, the secondary trading volume of loans grew from $50 billion in the first quarter of 2005 to $110 billion in the first quarter of 2010.[10] The opening of an active secondary trading market was a welcome development to an asset class that had been long perceived as illiquid. In addition, insurance companies and commercial banks wanted to invest in the highly rated tranches of CLOs.[11] The presence of CLOs as a robust source of demand for loans compressed the cost of borrowing in the loan market. Figure 4.6 shows annual loan volume related to merger activities, split into LBO and non-LBO deals. As secondary market trading developed, institutional investors came to the bank loan market. Their motivations varied as some sought to diversify their existing portfolios, others aimed to take advantage of select periods of price displacement in the loan market, while others sought to benefit from the balance sheet arbitrage trade.[12]

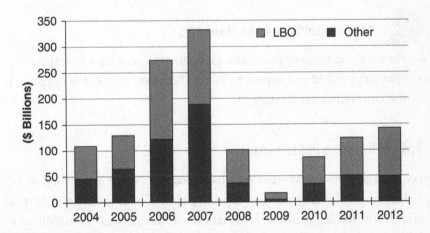

Figure 4.6 **Annual leveraged loan volume related to M&A activities**
Source: S&P Capital IQ LCD

Trading in the Secondary Market

There is currently no public market for loans. However, the birth of the LSTA in 1995 as a governing industry body that created a set of standardized market practices brought institutional investors into the secondary market. Institutions (CLOs, insurance companies, and hedge funds) have come to play a larger role in secondary market activities. In the secondary market, the transfer of economic interests related to loans takes place via assignment or participation. Assignment gives the buyer the economic benefit of loan exposure and the buyer becomes the lender of record, which confers negotiation, legal, and full voting rights during credit events. In the participation method, the loan buyer enters into a swap with the seller, essentially receiving the economic benefit of long loan exposure, but only limited voting rights. The seller remains as the lender of record. Some loan documents prohibit the transfer of ownership, which explains why the participation method exists. Additionally, investors with small exposure (typically less than $1 million) may opt to participate due to the cost of transfer associated with the assignment process. Counterparty default is an added risk to the participation method because the swap counterparty could default.

 Key Questions on Loan Managers

- How are you holding your loans (assignments versus participations)?
- How long would you expect to take to liquidate your entire portfolio in the current market scenario?

Risks of Investing in Bank Loans

As with all credit investments, bank loans involve a number of key risks, namely both credit and liquidity risk. The liquidity risk is more significant for loans issued by smaller borrowers, such as middle market companies. *Middle market* is an industry term and has no legal definition, and as such, the exact definition of the term can vary by speaker. Typically, the term refers to loans issued by companies between $50 million and $250 million in revenue, or up to $1 billion in capital structure. The larger, more liquid bank loans ("flow names") usually have fairly deep liquidity. For example, the size of the institutional segment of Hospital Corporation of America's (HCA) November 2006 loan issuance was $8.8 billion. In comparison, the average equity capitalization of a name in the Russell 1000 equity index (which is considered liquid) is approximately $10 billion.[13] HCA is one of the more liquid names in the bank loan market, but it is certainly not alone in terms of the liquidity it enjoys. Examples of other bank loans with high liquidity include EFH (previously TXU), Charter Communications, Wrigley's, and Ford.

There is also settlement risk in bank loans. Because of the more complex nature of bank loan documents relative to other securities, bank loans take substantially longer to settle than bonds and equities. Distressed loan trades, which are still largely paper based, involve a more complex set of documents and take longer to settle than par loans. Longer settlement time increases counterparty risk. The additional operational complexities related to bank loans necessitate a knowledgeable and experienced back office for timely completion of the trade. Firms often outsource the back office work for distressed loans to specialists.

 ## Key Takeaway on Settlement Risk

There is larger settlement risk for loans, particularly distressed loans, than for high yield bonds. Having the right trading and back office expertise are crucial parts of the investment thesis.

Unlike bonds, a bank loan trade (the loan assignment process) requires consent from the agent banks and possibly from the borrower. An unresponsive agent bank, a possible retraction of previously given consent, an absence of a standard assignment agreement, and the need to obtain physical signatures can add further delays to the settlement time. Furthermore, internal procedures for the assignment process vary across agent banks.

Given that bank loans may be held using total return swaps (TRS) or through participation swap, mark-to-market risk may be substantial. When there are periods of substantial illiquidity, such as in 2008, the underlying bank loans can effectively be "marked" at very low non-trading prices as the derivatives dealers attempt to protect themselves from further price declines. So, for example, a loan that has slowly traded down from the 90s to the 80s may suddenly be marked at 60 when the derivatives contract is marked to market. When adding leverage to the mix, the results may be lethal. During the height of volatility in the loan market in 2008, many of these market value triggers were hit, prompting a vicious cycle of selling and price decline.

Finally, for nontaxable investors one needs to be careful of unintended tax consequences. Investing in loans via the origination process (as part of a syndicate), participation, or exposure to a revolver could subject the investor to effectively connected income (ECI).[14] As with all tax-related matters, investors are advised to seek advice from tax counsel.

Loan Origination and Syndication Process

A brief review of the loan origination and syndication process may be helpful. A company interested in entering the bank loan market interviews commercial and investment banks to serve as arrangers. The arrangers present their proposed terms and pricing as well as strategy. A lead arranger ("book runner") is selected to carry out the deal.

The lead arranger puts together an information memo (IM) for potential investors. Key information in the IM includes proposed terms and pricing of various parts of the loan package and the borrower's financial information. Potential investors must select whether to have access to the borrower's private financial information including internal projections. If they choose to have such access, the investors are considered to be "over the wall" (in possession of material nonpublic information) and are restricted from trading in the borrower's public securities. For large issuers with multiple prior issuances of publicly traded securities and broad availability of publicly available information, investors often choose to forgo access to private information in order to remain unrestricted.

In the United States, most deals are done on a best efforts basis. Another type of deal is the "club deal." Popular in Europe with European regional banks[15] and with smaller deals in the United States ($100 million and under), the loan is premarketed to a small group of lenders. As the mobility of capital continues to improve across the globe, larger and more seasoned loan issuers can take advantage of different pricing across the globe. Ineos Finance's cross-border loan deal in April 2012 is an example. The issuer upsized its USD-denominated term loan, did "covenant-lite"[16] on the entire $3.025 billion loan package, cancelled the Euro-tranche of its bond deal, and was not required to offer higher yield for the larger, covenant-lite loan deal. This deal reflects Ineos's ability to take advantage of investor demand in the United States relative to the moribund European loan market.

INVESTMENT STRATEGIES IN BANK LOANS

While investment grade loans in and of themselves have become standard investment tools with many large asset management companies offering them in mutual fund format. Both the lower quality leveraged loans and leverage remain much less utilized in the traditional asset management space. This section begins with a discussion of the traditional loan hedge fund strategy followed by several variants on it.

Standard Leveraged Loan Strategy

As there are no fundamental long/short loan only credit hedge funds (at the time of the writing, one cannot short cash bank loans), the standard leveraged loan strategy is effectively long only. It should be noted that synthetic short exposure can be obtained through loan credit default swaps (LCDS).[17] However, it is worth noting that this market was still in its infancy when the 2008 credit crisis took place,[18] and as a result, the liquidity of single name LCDS has been limited.

The standard leveraged loan strategy may be described as purchasing a well-diversified portfolio of leveraged loans using leverage through a total return swap. The basic balance sheet arbitrage behind this strategy profits by using lower cost financing to invest in higher yielding assets. Loan investors can obtain leveraged exposure to the asset class through a TRS. A TRS is a bilateral agreement that allows counterparties to swap the total return of a single asset or a basket of reference assets in exchange for a floating rate (typically LIBOR) plus a swap spread. A TRS is similar to a plain vanilla swap, except in a TRS the total return of the asset (cash flows and price appreciation and depreciation) is swapped as opposed to just the cash flows.

Another form of this balance sheet arbitrage is the LIBOR arbitrage. This opportunity arises when a LIBOR-based TRS line is used to finance a loan with a LIBOR base set at a minimum higher than the current actual LIBOR. This, along with the original issue discount, provides borrowers with the flexibility to increase the attractiveness of their papers to investors. The investor profits when LIBOR is lower than the LIBOR floor on the asset.

Because the loans are floating rate instruments, direct interest rate risk is typically ignored. However, there is a realization that a significantly rapid rising interest rate environment induces, on a practical basis, at least a mild credit crunch. Thus, one more commonly sees broad market hedges (e.g., via credit indices, equity index puts) applied against the long side. In some cases, one might see a popular relative value trade that involves going long a bank loan and shorting a more junior part of the capital structure (of the same or different issuer) such as the subordinated bond or equity.

 ## Key Takeaway on Investment Grade Bank Loans

Investing in investment grade par or near-par loans, on a long-only or predominantly long basis, particularly if using low leverage or unlevered, should be done via traditional mandates and not hedge funds (investors should not pay hedge fund fees).

Finally, the widespread global issuance of loans translates into a potentially much more international portfolio. Unlike distressed debt, which requires a significant level of country-specific knowledge, and unlike high yield, which is often not issued in many countries, almost all the major capital markets have an active bank loan market. However, investors need to keep in mind that for loan markets outside the United States, liquidity profile can be significantly different than in the United States since many of the investors are largely buy-and-hold investors.

Edge Being Captured

This standard leveraged loan strategy seeks to capitalize upon the manager's credit research skills and ability to understand loan covenants and capital structures. The manager's view is then magnified through the use of leverage.

In particular, the leveraged loan market has some structural inefficiencies compared to the more traditional investment grade loan market. It is estimated that more than 80 percent of issuers in the leveraged loan market are privately owned: there are no public financials and very limited (if any) other information regarding the issuer.

 Key Investment Questions for Standard Leveraged Loan Strategy

The key here is to gauge the quality of the manager's research and trading process.

- Who is responsible for idea generation?
- What is the key driver of performance: Fundamental research? Distressed loans? Trading? Hedging?
- Describe the short side of the portfolio. How actively traded are the shorts?
- What is the average price and typical annual carry of your loan portfolio?

The high percentage of leveraged loans issued by small and private issuers leads to greater information asymmetry, and often they are underfollowed by the sell-side analyst community. Common situations one finds in a hedge fund portfolio include (1) orphaned issues by larger borrowers, (2) off-the-run issues of smaller or middle market issuers, and (3) situations involving complex capital structures.

Risks

Given that the standard leveraged loan strategy is typically implemented through a total return swap, this strategy generally works best in periods of economic recovery and expansion where both credit and derivative exposure are not under pressure.

This investment strategy has the risk of leverage and liquidity. Leverage magnifies both positive and negative return, and it exposes one to the counterparty risk. Leverage can also subject investors to the scenarios where they are subject to the principal/agent problem. During periods of price dislocation in the market, levered investors can be subject to margin calls and the default trigger on total return swap is deemed to be hit. If the investors are unable to meet the margin call in a prescribed time frame, the leverage provider has the right to liquidate the investments to satisfy the margin requirement. Having to liquidate the positions at noneconomic terms means that levered investors may be subject to situations where they are not masters of their own destiny.

In addition, if the funding is short term and the proceeds are invested on a longer-term asset, there is an asset/liability mismatch. In the case of Bear Stearns and Lehman, this risk became apparent as the availability of short-term financing evaporated within a short period upon jitters in the funding market. Credit hedge fund managers can manage their leverage and counterparty risk by limiting the amount of leverage used in the portfolio, understanding of the term of the funding agreement, and close day-to-day monitoring of the status of their financing lines.

Key Financing Questions for Standard Leveraged Loan Strategy

- What are the terms of your financing?
- Under what circumstances can the financing be revoked? Describe the process to monitor and manage the financing lines.
- How much of the attribution is due to LIBOR arbitrage?
- What happens when the LIBOR floor goes away?

Stressed and Distressed Loan Strategy

The stressed and distressed loan strategy appeals to distressed debt investors who typically look to invest in the fulcrum security within a company's capital structure. A fulcrum security is the security that is most likely to convert to equity in the reorganization process. The 2003–2006 LBO boom placed unprecedented amounts of leverage on companies' balance sheets. Much of the added leverage was in the form of bank loans, which has the impact of pushing the fulcrum security further up the capital structure. This means that in certain situations the bank loan can be the fulcrum security.

 Key Takeaways on the Cyclicality of Distress in the Loan Market

The supply of distressed loans is cyclical. The cycle typically looks like this: increased volume of issuance corresponding with looser lending standards leads to higher default, which leads to restructuring and recovery—rinse and repeat.

An example of this trade involves a company that is currently undergoing restructuring under the Chapter 11 process. Assume that the company's book liabilities are $100 million in bank loans and $100 million in unsecured bonds. Around the announcement of the Chapter 11 filing, a distressed investor may be able to purchase the loan at depressed prices, which reflects the heightened market risk premium from the uncertainties surrounding the bankruptcy process.

Let us consider two basic scenarios: a short-term profit opportunity and a loan-to-own opportunity. In the first scenario, assume the firm is valued at $150 million. In this scenario, the claims of the loan investors are fully covered at par, pre-Chapter 11 equity holders see their claims extinguished, and $50 million remains for unsecured bondholders. This trade profits when the loan price appreciates to par. In the second scenario, the firm is valued at $90 million. The loan holders receive $90 million and all of the company's equity for their $100 million claim, while the claims of the bondholders and equity holders are extinguished. If the company emerges from the bankruptcy process as a viable entity, this trade profits as loan holders become the sole owner of the postbankruptcy entity. Furthermore, during the restructuring process, the loan holders can expect to receive default interest, which can add 1–2 percent above the nondefault spread level.

Key Takeaway on Loans as the Fulcrum Security

As a higher proportion of indebtedness on a company's balance sheet comes in the form of bank loans, it is more likely that the loan, not the bond, is the fulcrum security in a restructuring.

There is usually another significant aspect to the stressed and distressed loan strategy, and that is the game theory behind it. Given the extensive use of the leveraged loan market by the large leveraged buyout groups, investors in distressed loans often have to negotiate with private equity and buyout firms. Unlike the common stock holders in a traditional bankruptcy where a particular stock position typically represents a very small fraction of their portfolio, in a private equity LBO-driven leveraged loan situation, the portfolio company often represents a significant fraction of that specific private equity pool. Thus the behavior of the equity holders in these two situations is usually quite different. In the traditional bankruptcy situation, the stockholder usually walks away and considers the situation a loss. With the exception of a holdout nuisance value, the prefiling equity holders are minimal players. However, in the LBO-driven deal, the private equity firm will often intervene prior to filing in order to protect the original private equity investment. The private equity firm may play hardball by attempting to force the loan holders' hand through legal interpretation of covenants and other aspects of the deal. In some cases, the private equity firm may even attempt to purchase the loan for a small markup in order to keep control of the deal. Therefore, it is important that the hedge fund that follows the stressed and distressed loan strategy understands how important the portfolio company is to the private equity sponsor and how the private equity sponsor is likely to intervene.

Edge Being Captured

The complexity, process risk, liquidity risk, silos and limitations of other investors, and investor fatigue involved in stressed and distressed situations can all present opportunities to investors with proper resources to conduct in-depth due diligence. Given the limited types and numbers of players in the leveraged loan market, unlike traditional distressed investing, the stressed and distressed loan strategy requires a much more thorough understanding of the motivations of each of the players in addition to the standard tool kit for distressed investing.

In larger companies, loans are often part of a highly complex capital structure where the covenants and legal protections are likely to be very different from those of standard bonds. For example, the Lehman Brothers bankruptcy has presented interesting opportunities for investors who can embrace complexity. Not only are there a myriad of subentities under the umbrella of the holding company, but the global nature of the enterprise also required deep expertise of various bankruptcy laws in various legal jurisdictions.

Risks

The main risk of this strategy lies in the navigation of the bankruptcy and restructuring processes. Determining the valuation of a company in bankruptcy is challenging. Various interest groups (shareholders, company management, and creditors) with competing interests will advance valuations that maximize their expected economic outcome. Cross-class litigation is a real possibility, and timing risk can be significant, as some companies have gone through long, drawn-out restructuring processes that can take years. The trade requires strong legal and negotiation capabilities in addition to valuation and investing skills. Distressed investing may include involvement in creditors' and other committees, which are time and labor intensive. Members in the creditors' committee are also subject to certain trading restrictions.

Debtor-in-Possession Strategy

While there are a few funds that focus almost exclusively on DIP financing, more typically it is part of a bank loan or a distressed portfolio. As a DIP lender provides a loan to a company in the Chapter 11 restructuring process, the loan provides the company the needed liquidity to continue operating as a going concern. A DIP lender receives superpriority status via a lien that receives priority relative to the prebankruptcy bank loan lenders (a "priming lien"). DIP loans typically carry larger coupons than the prebankruptcy bank loans and will also include other sweeteners such as commitment and closing fees. Due to the difficulty of hedging a company in bankruptcy, supersenior status, and high coupon, this strategy is generally, like most of the bank loan strategies, left unhedged.

While the bankruptcy process is discussed in length in Chapter 3, this section briefly reviews what the DIP loan looks like. Most important, it is typically a nondivisible asset. This means that if you want to "redeem" from a credit hedge fund with substantial investment in DIP loans, the DIP loan may be less liquid than the contractual liquidity term of the fund.

Edge Being Captured

Lending to a company in distress is a specialty area due to the complexities of the strategy and uncertainties stemming from the restructuring process. One of the challenges to being a DIP lender is sourcing the opportunity; if existing lenders can participate, they would prefer to provide the DIP themselves. This prevents the existing lenders from being primed as well as allowing them to participate in an investment that offers both supersenior lien status and very high yield.

A priming lien can only be granted with the consent of the primed prebankruptcy bank loan holders (prepetition lenders in bankruptcy jargon) or if the court decides that the claims of the prepetition lenders are sufficiently protected by the value of the company's assets despite the priming lien. The prepetition lenders would consent to being primed because the company (and thus the assets that collateralize their claim) is worth more as a going concern than it would be if forced to liquidate due to a lack of funds to maintain day-to-day operations.

To prevent priming, prepetition lenders can provide DIP financing, which is referred to as a "defensive DIP" in bankruptcy jargon. If a new set of lenders provide DIP financing, this is referred to as "new money DIP" or "offensive DIP." Coupon and fees tend to be lower for a defensive DIP and higher for an offensive DIP.

Risks

In addition to the risk of lending to a company in restructuring, a DIP lender faces extension and exit risk. The increasingly complex capital structures of issuers combined with a wide range of interests in the creditor groups can lead to a protracted and contentious restructuring process. A hedge fund manager trying to present a post-reorganization plan to a bankruptcy judge may face additional challenges during an economic environment where companies face uncertain economic outlook, making valuation difficult. In addition, if the company exhausts its DIP facility, a second, more senior DIP facility may be put in place, thereby lowering the original DIP priority. Last, a DIP lender needs an open and functioning capital market to ensure availability of exit financing.

 Key Questions for the DIP Strategy

- Describe your sourcing of the DIP opportunities.
- If the manager is starting a new DIP fund and sourcing comes from an existing loan position largely held by an existing fund, how do you allocate DIP between the existing and new fund?
- What is the sweet spot for the size of this fund?

New Issue Trade

While the new issue trade is not a strategy, there are a few technical details that should be addressed. A new issue trade results in a profit when an investor purchases a newly issued bank loan at a discount to par value and receives up-front fees, then resells the loan into the secondary market at par a few days after. The discount is referred to as original issue discount (OID), and it is part of the "market flex" language that arrangers can use to make a new issue bank loan more attractive to investors. In select deals, investors also receive up-front fees from the issuer at the close of the syndication process. Larger commitments tend to receive larger up-front fees, which are typically expressed as a percentage of commitment size. Having established relationships with loan syndicate desks plays an important part in a hedge fund manager's ability to access the new issue loan market. Access to major underwriter banks is particularly important in Europe, where club deals are more popular than in the United States.

Edge Being Captured

Hedge funds may participate in this trade on an opportunistic basis, but it is worth noting that this trade is typically not a dominant return generator for hedge funds. This trade generally works best in periods where the loan market enjoys a healthy balance of new issue supply and demand. During periods of economic contraction, low investor appetite for bank loans may result in select new loan issues offering higher OID and up-front fees. Investors who are able to participate in the new issuance can benefit from the "pull to par."

Risks

The initial investor may not be able to turn around and "flip" the new issuance if the deal is undersubscribed or not well received by the market. It is not a given that every new issue trades well; if it does not clear the market, the new issue may trade significantly lower. There may also be an issue with adverse selection. In the underwriting process, interested participants put in their orders and the underwriter assigns the allocation to each participant. However, participants may get full allocation in the event of an undersubscribed deal, leading to the winner's curse.

CONCLUSION

- The bank loan market has undergone significant changes since its early days. Standardized market practices, particularly in regard to trading, settlement, and documentation, have gone a long way toward creating an actively functioning secondary market, improving liquidity, and expanding the number and type of market participants.
- Bank loans are not securities. Thus, the loan market is subject to different trading dynamics and has different market practices than the high yield bond market.
- The private nature of the loan market adds an additional layer of complexity in terms of trading (due to potential ownership of material nonpublic information) and taxation.
- During the credit crisis of 2007–2008, the loan market saw unprecedented volatility, which was exacerbated by excessive leverage in the system. Much of the excessively leveraged bank loan vehicles have left the market.
- The loan market continues to heal as banks are slowly offering new financing for bank loans, albeit at more conservative terms.
- Existing CLOs continue to provide a level of support to the secondary bank loan market. There is potential for newly issued CLO vehicles, albeit with lower levels of leverage and simpler structures.
- Outside the CLO market, investors with favorable rates of funding can still benefit from the arbitrage opportunities while stressed and distressed credit hedge funds look to generate attractive returns on an unlevered basis.

Bank loans and the loan market will continue to provide leveraged issuers with an attractive financing method while presenting opportunities for institutional investors. Nonetheless, institutional loan investors need to be cognizant of potential risks such as financing, liquidity, and settlement risk.

CHAPTER 5

Convertible Bonds

A convertible bond describes a hybrid security that combines both the coupon feature of a bond and the upside participation of equity. Similar to a "straight" (nonconvertible) bond, a convertible bond typically pays periodic coupon, has a stated maturity date, receives ratings from the rating agencies, and has par value of $1,000. The upside participation comes through the conversion feature, which enables the bondholder to convert the bond into a fixed number of common stock. The terms and conditions of conversion usually are set at issuance. The conversion feature added embedded optionality to the bond, and in a given scenario, the convertible bond pricing behavior may be very different from the price behavior of a straight bond of the same issuer.

WHY INVESTORS BUY CONVERTIBLE BONDS

Convertible bond investors are generally split into two separate groups, those who invest on a long-only basis or on an arbitrage basis. Depending on where the common stock is trading, the convertible bond may behave like common stock or more like a bond. Convertible bonds are particularly suited for investing on a hedged or arbitrage basis because the bonds can incorporate a very wide range of risk factors ranging from credit to equity and volatility risks. A skilled investor can seek to profit from one or a few specific risk factors and hedge the exposure to other risk factors. The typical risk factors that hedge funds focus on include equity price, expected equity volatility, and credit spread.

Figure 5.1 shows the price of a convertible bond relative to the price of the underlying common stock. The relationship between the price of the convertible bond and the price of the underlying stock can be broken into four different zones. When stock price is high and the warrant is "in the money," the price of the convertible bond is greatly correlated with the price of the underlying stock and has little sensitivity to credit spread. If the warrant is deeply in the money, the price of the convertible bond may move in a one-to-one ratio with the price of the underlying stock.

When the convertible bond is said to be "at the money," price reflects its "hybrid" feature—it is influenced by both credit spread and stock price. Convertible bonds trading in this area are candidates for

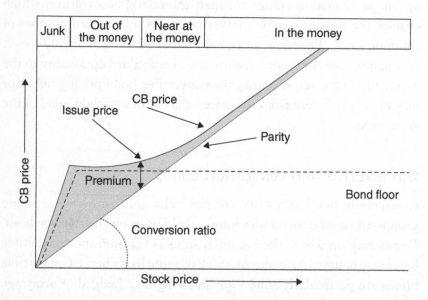

Figure 5.1 Convertible bond price relative to stock price
Source: PAAMCO

convertible bond arbitrage, because rapidly changing delta gives the arbitrageur many opportunities for trading profit.

Convertible bonds that are far "out of the money" or are in "junk" territory trade according to credit spread rather than stock price. At this point, pricing reflects the market's concern about credit issues of the bond issuer. For convertible bonds that are near at or in the money, the bond component gives the convertible bond a "bond floor" or "investment value." For far "out of the money" or "junk" convertible bonds, the warrant is far out of the money and the warrant value is worthless (or virtually worthless). The convertible bond price is very sensitive to changes in credit spread and tends to show negative convexity to stock price—a slight improvement in stock price may slightly improve the bond price in contrast to a slight decline in stock price, which may result in a dramatic drop to the bond price. Negative convexity also means that as the stock price declines, the convertible bond price declines by greater and greater amounts for every dollar decline in stock price.

Key Investment Strategies in Convertible Bonds

"Junk": Distressed investing, similar to investing in any distressed assets. Likely to be done on a long-only basis.

Far "Out of the Money": "Busted" converts, option value is positive but low. May overhedge by using equity shorts. Ideal scenario is "Goldilocks" scenario—situation is bad enough that the equity value falls close to zero, but not so bad that the bond goes from "busted" to distressed.

Near or "At the Money": Convertible bond arbitrage. Arbitrageur adds value via trading and rehedging his position. Generally hedged position, can be done on a delta neutral basis or on a slight long or short basis. Delta neutrality implies that a very small change in the value of the long position in a convertible bond is offset by a corresponding amount of change in the value of the short position in the stock.

> **"In the Money":** Hedge funds are rarely found in this area.
> Here, the convertible bond has a very high sensitivity to the
> change in stock price. When the option value is said to be
> very deep in the money, the ratio could be one-to-one. For
> every dollar change in the stock price, the convertible bond
> price rises by a corresponding dollar. There is very little
> arbitrage or distressed opportunity.

The long convertible bond position is essentially a long option
or long volatility position. The "premium" of the convertible bond,
the option value attached to the warrant, depends on the market view
of the expected volatility of the underlying instrument (its "implied"
volatility). In a long option position, the trade earns a profit if realized
volatility exceeds implied volatility. All else equal, one buys a convertible bond position if the implied volatility of the bond is lower than the
expected volatility of the underlying stock. However, a decline in either
implied or realized volatility may lead to a loss to the trade.

WHY COMPANIES ISSUE CONVERTIBLE BONDS

Companies who make the best candidates for convertible bond issuers are growth-oriented companies with significant upside optionality
in the value of their common stock. Many of these companies also
tend to either be young and/or have volatile earnings. If this type
of company wished to finance itself by tapping the high yield bond
market, it is likely that the company would have to offer a high coupon, making bond financing cost prohibitive. 144A investors (many
hedge funds fit in this category) provide a source of ready capital for
companies with poor credit who need capital in a hurry. By issuing
convertible bonds, the company can offer much lower coupon, and in
exchange, through the conversion factor, the investor receives a warrant on the equity. Simply put, the convertible bond is a forward sale
on the issuer's equity.

In addition, there are features of convertible securities that offer regulatory or tax benefits to the issuers. Certain hybrid securities offer the best of both worlds as they are considered as equity for the purposes of rating agencies as well as for regulatory capital while the coupon (interest) payment is tax deductible. Features such as exchangeability also give issuers additional flexibility in managing their capital structure.

Issuance by banks post the global credit crisis provides a good example of how preferred shares' flexibility can be used by issuers. In expectation of Basel III, banks looking to boost their capital holding did so by issuing preferred shares. Basel III required that banks hold common equity (including capital conservation buffer) equivalent to at least 7 percent of their risk-weighted assets and that banks hold at least an additional 1.5 percent of "tier 1 capital." Tier 1 capital can include common equity as well as preferred shares, which pay a fixed dividend and are senior to common shares but do not have voting rights. In a low interest rate environment, preferred shares provide both investors and issuers with a valuable option. Investors benefit from access to a yield bearing instrument, and the banks are able to continue to repair their balance sheet while benefiting from low cost of borrowing.[1]

THE SIZE OF THE CONVERTIBLE BOND MARKET

The size of the convertible bond market waxes and wanes as issuers and investors continuously evaluate the relative attractiveness of the convertible instruments relative to high yield bonds and equities. Figure 5.2 shows the size of the convertible bond market over time. When the high yield bond market sees a large amount of demand and the coupon difference between a straight high yield bond versus a convertible bond narrows, many issuers see straight bonds as more attractive because they don't have to give up the upside potential. Because a convertible bond is essentially an embedded warrant attached to a bond, all else equal, issuers tend to choose to issue convertible bonds in periods when the equity market is strong and/or the issuer feels that its equity is fairly priced or better.

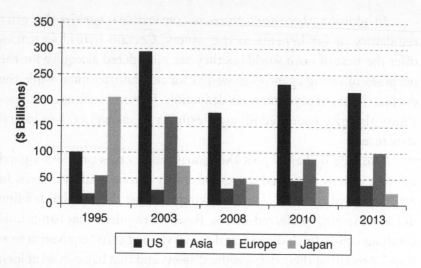

Figure 5.2 Size of the convertible bond market over time
Source: BofA Merrill Lynch Convertibles Research

TYPES OF HYBRID OR CONVERTIBLE SECURITIES

The most commonly seen convertible structure, especially in the United States, is a convertible bond that is issued at par and matures at par. This bond typically pays semiannual coupon in the United States and Japan, and annual coupon in Europe and ex-Japan Asia. This bond would have a certain preset conversion price. Figure 5.3 illustrates the basic set of information used to describe the features of a particular convertible bond.

Another common convertible structure is convertible preferred stocks, which pay dividends (interest), are convertible into common stock at a prespecified ratio, and are ahead of common stock in terms of seniority in the capital structure. Unlike a convertible bond, convertible preferred stocks do not have a specific maturity date. Also, unlike a convertible bond, dividend payment may be deferred without triggering default. Convertible preferred stocks are considered equity by rating agencies, and their interest payment is not tax deductible. Certain convertible bonds also come with features such as resets or make-whole provision. These features provide convertible bond

Issuer Information			Identifiers	
Name	PEABODY ENERGY CORP		BB Number	EG0532200
Industry	Exploration & Production		CUSIP	704549AG9
Convertible Information			ISIN	US704549AG98
Mkt of Issue	US Domestic	Convertible	**Bond Ratings**	
Country	US	Currency USD	Moody's	Ba3
Rank	Jr Subordinated	Series	S&P	B+
Conv Ratio	17.2563	Conv Price 57.9499	Fitch	BB –
Stock Tkr	BTU US	Stock Price 20.0600	DBRS	NR
Parity	34.62	Premium 136.1615	**Issuance & Trading**	
Coupon	4.75	Init Prem 20.00	Amt Issued/Outstanding	
Type	Fixed	Freq S/A	USD	732,500.00 (M) /
SOFTCALL CALL 12/20/36@100.00			USD	732,500.00 (M)
Calc Type	(49)CONVERTIBLE		Min Piece/Increment	
Announcement Date		12/15/2006		1,000.00 / 1,000.00
1st Coupon Date		06/15/2007	Par Amount	1,000.00
Convertible Until		12/15/2041	Book Runner	CITI,LEH,MS
Maturity		12/15/2041	Reporting	TRACE

PRX/SHR = $57.9498. INIT CVR PREM = 40%. GREENSHOE = $75MM. POISON PUT @101%. FINAL LEGAL MAT DATE: 12/15/66.

Figure 5.3   Example of basic information on a convertible bond
Source: Bloomberg

investors with additional protection by protecting the value of the bond or preserving the premium paid by the investor at issuance. Mandatory convertible securities (MCS) are the most equity-like out of all the hybrid securities. Investors should consider these as equities with higher dividend payment. For this reason, during periods of strong equity market, this structure tends to be popular with both issuers and investors.

Puttable convertible bonds allow the bondholders to redeem ("put") the bond from the issuer in exchange for a preset price (can be at par or at a premium above par) and time, typically within several years after bond issuance. Keep in mind that this concept may be more appealing in principal than in practice. As the issuer runs into financial troubles (which would be the time when the bondholder is most likely to want to "put" the bond back), this is exactly the time when the issuer is least likely to be able to meet its obligations to the bondholders. The puttable feature, however, does have positive value to investors. For example, a hedge fund focusing on credit event–driven trades may seek to invest in a convertible bond with an upcoming put date that is earlier than the straight bond in the capital structure. Although the straight bond is structurally more senior than the convertible, the earlier maturity gives the convertible bondholder leverage over the holders of the straight bond.

 Key Takeaways on Convertible Bond Features

Convertible bonds come with a wide range of features, some of which can add significant complexity to the bond. Specific features relating to takeover protection such as ratchet clauses or make-whole provision are often key parts of the investment thesis for hedge funds, which are able to benefit by taking either a long or short position depending on the situation.

PRICING OF A CONVERTIBLE BOND AND "THE GREEKS"

A convertible bond is essentially a straight bond plus a warrant on the underlying stock. As such, the pricing of a convertible bond consists of the value of the bond (the "investment value") and the value of the warrant (the "option value"). The investment value of the bond is driven by risk factors that influence the value of a bond, such as default risk and recovery rate. The option value, which can be priced by option pricing models such as the Black-Scholes option model or binomial trees, depends on things such as the price of the underlying equity, conversion price (akin to strike), and expected equity volatility. Other risks of a convertible bond include dividend risk, interest rate risk, event risk (e.g., takeover), and timing to maturity. The "Greeks" measure the sensitivity in the price of a convertible bond relative to the movement in the underlying risk factor.

The first Greek is delta, which measures the sensitivity of the convertible bond price relative to the underlying stock price. In Figure 5.1, a "junk" convertible bond would have a delta close to zero. The embedded call option has little value for this bond, and the instrument pricing should largely be dictated by the investment value of the bond. A deeply "in the money" convert would have a delta near 1: for every percentage change of the stock price movement, the convertible bond price changes by a percent or close to it. Around the middle, where the delta of the convertible bond is 0.5, the convert is "at the money."

DEFINITION OF DELTA – A BASIC GREEK

Delta is the sensitivity of the convertible bond price relative to the underlying stock price. A convertible bond with a delta of 0.5 implies that at that point, for every percent of the stock movement, the convertible bond price will move by approximately 0.5 percent.

The second derivative of convertible bond price relative to the underlying stock price is gamma. Delta does not change at a constant rate, and gamma measures the sensitivity of the convertible bond price relative to the rate of change of delta. Delta rises and falls as the stock price changes. As stock price and parity rises, the influence of the stock price on the convertible bond price rises. In other words, when parity is high, the convertible bond behaves more like a stock, and the opposite is also true—when parity is low, the convertible bond is less affected by the change in stock price and behaves more like a bond. For convertible bonds with short or medium term to maturity, gamma is highest (delta rises at the fastest rate) when the option is near at the money. In other words, when the convertible bond is at the money (or about), it is most sensitive to the change in delta. This makes sense because, for example, if a convertible bond is deeply in the money, delta may not change much with a slight change in parity. The option value of the convertible bond does not vary much with the underlying stock price—a small increase in price does not increase the likelihood of the option being in the money, and a small drop in price is not likely to put the option out of the money.

Key Takeaway on Gamma

Positive gamma can be interpreted as delta increasing at an increasing rate and decreasing at a decreasing rate. Gamma is highest for short-term, at-the-money options.

Another risk factor is implied volatility, which affects the price of the embedded warrant in the convertible bond. Vega measures the sensitivity of the convertible bond price to the change in implied volatility. The more volatile the stock price, the more likely that the warrant will expire in the money. If the underlying stock price is highly volatile, the warrant value and, consequently, the value of the convertible bond rises. A long convertible bond position is a long option and long volatility position. The purchase price of a convertible bond contains the current market view on the implied forward-looking volatility of the underlying stock. Vega is highest for long-term, at-the-money convertible bonds.

 Key Takeaway on Implied Volatility

Think about implied volatility as the "going rate" for option price. All else equal, option price goes up as implied volatility rises.

Convertible bonds are also affected by changes in interest rate. Rho measures the sensitivity of the convertible bond to changes in interest rate. A call option is akin to owning a leveraged position in the stock—thus, the higher the interest rate, the more valuable the option.

Another Greek that is worth mentioning briefly is theta. When convertible bond traders talk about theta decay, they are referring to the fact that an option becomes less valuable with the passing of time. Theta, also known as time decay, is not a risk factor[2] because theta is measurable at any point in time until the option matures. Theta is greatest for at-the-money options with a short term to maturity—the option loses value quickly when time to maturity is near. For convertible bonds, the warrant is akin to an American option (the owner of an option can exercise at any time before maturity), and having more time to expiration is valuable because there is greater possibility to sell to someone with higher expectation of implied volatility.

CONVERTIBLE BOND INVESTMENT STRATEGIES

Credit hedge funds are among the natural players in the convertible bond arbitrage space. Many of the issuers of convertible bonds are smaller or growth-oriented companies that typically cannot access the high yield bond market. These issuers often are not well covered by sell-side sales and research desks, and certain investors with deep analytical capabilities can have an informational edge relative to others. Many convertible bonds also have put and call features, which can lead to specific events (e.g., the bond being called) and present opportunities for event-driven investors. Credit hedge funds can also add value by concentrating their research expertise on off-the-run or niche bonds that are overlooked by traditional asset managers. Hedge funds can invest in convertible bonds either in a hedged way (engage in convertible bond arbitrage) or by investing in distressed convertibles. Credit hedge funds with trading orientation and ability to add alpha on the short side can also invest in convertibles on an arbitrage (hedged) basis. Credit hedge funds can benefit from their credit expertise when the price of the bond goes up (long exposure) as well as when the price of the bond falls (from shorting). For many credit hedge funds, their short portfolio acts as a profit center in addition to providing a hedge to their long portfolio.

Many credit hedge funds also have the flexibility to select the instrument with the most attractive risk-adjusted return in a particular capital structure. These credit hedge funds benefit from the ability to invest in convertible bonds on an opportunistic basis. This means they are neither specifically mandated to maintain an allocation to convertible bonds nor prohibited or limited from taking on a meaningful exposure to the space when there is outsized expected reward arising from a dislocation.

The put and call features found in many convertible bonds make these instruments suitable candidates for event-driven trades. For example, assume there is an issuer with both a high yield bond and a convertible bond outstanding. The convertible bond is puttable in the next month, and the high yield bond matures in a year. If the convertible bond investors put the bond back to the issuer for cash payment and the issuer is unable to meet this obligation, the issuer is going to be in default in regard to the convertible bond. Many bonds, however, have a cross-default provision. This means if an issuer is in default on a particular issuance, this may give the bondholders of other issues by the same issuer the right to "accelerate" their claim by requiring partial or full payment on the bond issuance they hold. If the company is unable to make the required payout to the convertible bondholders, it is not likely to meet the spike in additional required payment caused by the cross-default provision, potentially causing the company to have to file for bankruptcy. In this case, the impending put date on the convertible bond gives its holder a lever in negotiation with other bondholders. In exchange for extending the puttable date, for example, the convertible bond may receive a step-up in coupon and/or a higher put price at a later date.

Key Takeaways on the Seniority of Convertible Bonds in a Corporate Capital Structure

Structurally a convertible bond may be more junior than a senior unsecured bond. However, if the convertible bond has a puttable date earlier than the maturity date of the bond, the contractual ability to demand payment before others gives the convertible bond an advantage over the structurally more senior bond. Just like dinner time at the family table, in order to claim the most desirable parts of the roast, seniority helps but is not a guarantee. One also needs to get to the table quickly.

Credit hedge funds with expertise in distressed investing are well suited to invest in "busted" (distressed) convertibles due to the deep fundamental research and legal expertise often associated with distress investing. These credit hedge funds are likely to have a lower liquidity profile to reflect the lower liquidity and longer investment horizon of the fund investments.

Gamma Trading/Delta Hedged Strategy

This trade typically involves a long position on the convertible bond paired with a short position on the underlying equity. The basic concept is a "delta neutral" position—put the long and the short position together, and the pair has little exposure to movement in the underlying stock. The position is not dollar neutral. The ratio of the hedge, or the amount of the stock to short for every long bond position, is determined by the delta. For example, if the convertible bond has a delta of 0.6, the delta neutral hedge ratio would be 60 percent. For every $100 long exposure to the convertible bond, short $60 worth of the underlying stock.

Basic assumptions: assume immediate change in equity price—this example ignores coupon accrued on the bond and stock dividend. No transaction costs, cost of borrow, and margin interest. This example is given for one bond, and it assumes that it is possible to buy a fraction of a stock. Figure 5.4 shows the initial setup of the trade, an assumed 1 percent target increase in the underlying stock price and the P&L of the trade.

Stock Price/Parity Moves up by 1%

	Initial	Target	P&L
Long Convertible Bond	$1,000	$1,006.50	6.50
Convertible Bond Delta	0.6	0.75	
Equity Price	$100	$101.00	
Number of Equity Shorted	−6		
Short Equity	−$600	−$606	−6.00
Trade P&L			$0.50

Figure 5.4 **P&L for a delta neutral hedged position, assuming small increase in stock price**
Source: PAAMCO

Stock Price/Parity Moves Down Back to $100

	Initial	Target	P&L
Long Convertible Bond	$1,006.50	$1,000	−$6.50
Convertible Bond Delta	0.75		
Equity Price	$101	$100.00	
Number of Equity Shorted	−7.47		
Short Equity	−$755	−$747	$7.47
Trade P&L			$0.97

Figure 5.5 P&L for a delta neutral hedged position, assuming small decrease in stock price
Source: PAAMCO

When the 1 percent target stock price increase is reached, the manager will readjust the hedge. At the target bond price, the new delta of the convertible bond is 0.75. At that point, in order to maintain delta neutrality, the manager will need to increase the size of the short equity position. The number of equity short needed to retain delta neutrality is 0.75 * $1,006.50 / $101 = 7.47.

Figure 5.5 shows the P&L generated with the rehedged position as the initial position and what happens if the stock price falls back from $101 to $100.

Variations of this trade include a biased hedge and a reverse (or "Chinese") hedge. In a biased hedge, the arbitrageur is intentionally over- or underhedged to reflect a bearish or bullish view on the underlying stock. In a reverse ("Chinese") hedge, the arbitrageur is long the underlying stock against a short position in the convertible bond.

Edge Being Captured

This strategy works on convertible bonds that are at or slightly in the money. Delta neutral implies that the position is intended to profit regardless of the direction of the movement in the stock price. In Figure 5.1, delta hedging strategy tends to be most profitable for convertible bonds that are trading "at the money." This strategy is also referred to as "gamma trading" because it benefits from positive gamma of a convertible. An arbitrageur seeks convertible bonds with high gamma, which means that delta changes rapidly, giving the arbitrageur more opportunity to generate profit through rebalancing the hedge. Sticking to the example given above, if the stock price moves up and the delta rises from 0.6 to 0.75, the position is underhedged. The gain from the long convertible bond position exceeds the loss from the equity short, resulting in a profit. Assume the arbitrageur readjusts the hedge and increased the short exposure. If the delta falls back from 0.75 to 0.6, the position is overhedged. The loss from the long convertible bond position is more than compensated from the gain from the equity short, resulting in a profit.

 Key Takeaway on Convertible Arbitrage

In a delta neutral convertible arbitrage, the credit hedge fund manager is less concerned about whether the underlying equity price moves up or down. As long as the underlying equity price moves (i.e., shows some volatility) the manager is happy.

Another edge that experienced arbitrageurs add is in deciding how often they rehedge their position. There is a trade-off between the frequency of the rebalancing and the trading profit expected in each rebalancing. One strategy is to seek to capture small incremental movements in the underlying stock price, readjusting the hedge frequently. In this strategy, the profit generated for each rebalancing is small and the turnover is high. Another strategy is to capture larger movements in the underlying stock price. In this strategy, if there is a small amount of movement in the underlying stock price, the trader will not rebalance the hedge. The trader expects to capture greater profit from a bigger movement in the underlying stock price. The turnover is lower, and the trader faces the risk of the stock price reversing while waiting for the target price to be reached.

In a biased hedge, an arbitrageur with particular insight on the pricing of the underlying stocks can profit from that insight. For example, for the convertible bond with delta of 0.7, the arbitrageur can short $80 worth of underlying stock against a $100 long position in the bond. If the stock price declines as expected, this heavy hedge will result in a larger profit compared to a delta neutral hedge. However, if the stock price increases, the arbitrageur will see a larger loss from the heavy hedge relative to a delta neutral hedge. In a reverse ("Chinese") hedge, the arbitrageur may benefit from an overpriced convertible bond (i.e., one where the risk premium or implied volatility in the warrant is far too high).

Risk

Delta neutral, however, does not imply that the position is risk neutral. There are risks involved in a delta hedging strategy, particularly because the trade requires good liquidity condition for it to work. The trade is "delta neutral" only with respect to a small movement in the stock price. In order to keep the trade delta neutral, the trade assumes that the arbitrageur is able to adjust the delta ratio as the convertible bond moves deeper into or out of the money. Should the arbitrageur find himself in a market where liquidity of the convertible bonds or underlying equities is severely reduced, losses may be incurred due to the inability to rebalance or exit positions, not to mention opportunity costs from the inability to enter trades.

For a profitable trade, the arbitrageur needs to be able to enter, readjust, and exit short equity positions. If the arbitrageur is forced to cover shorts at an inopportune time due to factors such as the underlying equity borrow being called or a sudden ban on shorting, this may result in a loss to the arbitrageur.

 ### Key Takeaways on The Risks of Shorting

The shorting ban in 2008 is a great example to illustrate this risk. The speed and ferocity of the shorting ban, in the middle of a very chaotic market environment with little clarity, hurt many convertible bond arbitrage managers as they were forced to cover their shorts at losses. To make matters worse, an arbitrageur who is unable to put on a short position is faced with either keeping an unhedged long position or liquidating the long convertible bond exposure. Many chose the latter, crystallizing loss at a very inopportune time in the market.

Another risk is credit risk. The arbitrageur engaging in a delta neutral/gamma trading investment strategy is implicitly betting that should the stock price or parity fall, the investment value of the bond will protect the value of the investment (there is a floor to the bond value). However, should the drop in the stock price or parity be caused by a dramatic decrease in creditworthiness such that the bond is in serious danger of defaulting, the investment value of the bond would not hold and the bond price is likely to drop alongside the stock price.

Event Risk

A takeover bid is a risky event to a convertible arbitrageur. A takeover may shorten the life of the convertible bond, eliminating the time value embedded in the call option (time value that the investor paid for). This risk is highest for cash bids on convertible bonds that are trading above par. In this scenario, the arbitrageur may see losses on both the long and short side of the portfolio. The convertible bond premium collapses and its price declines. The short position experiences losses as the equity price rises. This risk is mitigated for an all-stock or partial-stock takeover offer. For a stock bid, the time value of the call option is not interrupted. The risk may also be mitigated if the change of control put is triggered (usually the case with a large stock bid) and the convertible bondholders are able to put the bond back to the issuer at a price substantially above par.

Distressed/Fulcrum Security Strategy

The phrase "busted" converts may imply outsize or unacceptable risks; however, these instruments can provide fertile hunting grounds in the hands of skilled investors. This investment strategy is focused on investing in the convertible bonds of companies that are nearing or in default (i.e., the investment value of the bond has fallen significantly). This strategy is essentially similar to buying a distressed high yield bond: the conversion option is far out of the money and has very little to no value. Depending on optionality embedded in the convertible bond such as a puttable feature, a distressed investor may find the bond attractive as it gives additional levers in negotiation with other creditors. A "junk" or "busted" convert typically trades on its bond characteristics, as the warrant is deeply out of the money. Unlike the arbitrage strategy described above, this strategy is largely done on a long-biased or long-only basis.

There are a few variants of this strategy. The first variant involves buying a distressed convertible bond under the expectation that a default will not occur and the equity option is severely undervalued. In this case, the investor would look for positive catalysts that would improve the creditworthiness of the company such as asset sale or additional equity infusion. These catalysts are expected to increase both the investment price and option value of the bond, resulting in a profit for the investor. Another variant is buying the distressed convertible bond when it is the fulcrum security with the expectation of receiving equity in exchange of bond payment. Unlike the prior strategy, this strategy involves working through the restructuring or Chapter 11 bankruptcy process and typically has a longer investment horizon. In this strategy, the investor swaps the debt claim for equity ownership of the new, reorganized company and expects to profit from the growth of a newly reorganized entity. A slight variation to this strategy involves buying the distressed convertible bond with the eye toward receiving liquidation value. Unlike the restructuring scenario, the investor is not expecting the company to exit the bankruptcy process as a going concern.

Edge Being Captured

Investing in a stressed or distressed convertible bond requires a significant amount of expertise in both credit and equity. Because the company has seen a decline in creditworthiness and is likely to be a candidate for default, credit analysis is a key part of the equation. An example of the ideal scenario in a stressed convertible bond is to buy an underpriced high yield bond combined with a free (or almost free) equity option. In many cases, the severely mispriced equity option may be a big part of the opportunity, and the ability to measure the equity upside is the other half of the equation. Many investors are well versed in either credit or equity, but not many investors can do both well. When a convertible bond becomes distressed, traditional convertible bond investors have typically left the space, as have equity investors who invest in convertible bonds as a dividend/yield pickup trade. Investors may choose to invest in a convertible bond to earn more income because the bond coupon is greater than the stock dividend, while the embedded warrant still gives the investor the ability to benefit from an increase in the stock price. These investors are not distressed investors and lack the skill set to evaluate the value of a distressed company. Credit hedge funds with the right combination of credit, equity, and legal skills can earn a handsome premium from these instruments.

Risks

One of the key risks in distressed investing is the illiquidity risk. When traditional convertible bond investors exit the name, there usually is a gap in the buyer base for the name. At a certain price and expected return level, distressed buyers will step in to capture the opportunity. However, similar to any type of distressed assets, in the early stage of distress there will be few marginal buyers in the name.

The illiquidity risk is compounded by the risk of further deterioration of creditworthiness. The expected positive catalysts may not take place as expected, and the company may continue to lose revenue and see margins deteriorate. Furthermore, a company in distress may also see its liquidity problem accelerate as suppliers demand to be paid in advance or it finds itself unable to access the financing market.

The risk of decline in creditworthiness is particularly high for convertible bonds due to their relatively junior status in the capital structure. The holders of convertible bonds stand further back in line relative to secured or senior debt when it comes to the restructuring and liquidation proceeds. In a situation where the distress is severe enough that the equity value is wiped out, the convertible bond or the preferred stock becomes the "first loss" piece, which may be wiped out if there is a next round of losses.

 Key Takeaways on "Busted" Converts

Negative gamma is a phenomenon often seen with "busted" converts. With negative gamma, the convertible bond price sensitivity to the stock price rises as the stock price falls and falls as the stock price goes up. In other words, the worse the stock price gets, the worse the impact of stock price on bond price gets.

CONCLUSION

- A convertible bond essentially is a bond with an embedded warrant. Depending on the value of the underlying equity, the price of a convertible bond may behave like a bond (or a distressed bond) or like the equity.
- A typical convertible bond is junior to the high yield bond and senior to common equities. The relative attractiveness of the high yield bond and common equities determine the opportunities in the convertible bond market.
- Convertible bonds come with a wide range of features, which adds significant complexity when evaluating the value of the instrument. Features such as ratchet clauses, make-whole provision, or putback feature can create events that can be explored by credit hedge funds.
- The price of a convertible bond can depend on many risk factors including the underlying stock price, interest rates, stock price implied and realized volatility, credit spread, and time. An investor can isolate one or several risk factors that she deems attractive while hedging the rest. Gamma trading (long position in the convertible bond, hedge with underlying equity) was one of the most common arbitrage strategy involving convertible bonds.

- During the 2008 credit crisis, the shorting ban highlighted the previously unexpected regulatory risk. At the time of this writing, the reduced volume of new issuance and the lower availability of leverage has changed the structural landscape of convertible bonds and reduced the scope of opportunities in the near term.

CHAPTER 6

Sovereign Debt

PIGS. Drachmageddon. Grexit. Many investors were ready to leave the ghosts of the 2008 U.S.-led credit crisis behind them when they found themselves facing yet another financial market storm, this time with a European flair. The fact that the acronyms are far catchier the second time around did nothing to soothe the pain from seeing more losses in the portfolio. Investors in hedge funds quickly found out that, despite their lack of exposure to European credit, their portfolio was not immune to the impact of the European credit crisis. The effects of the European sovereign crisis were felt globally across all asset classes, including credit hedge fund portfolios.

DEFINITION OF THE MARKET

Sovereign debt is generally defined as general debt obligations issued and backed by the full faith and creditworthiness of a sovereign nation, and not linked to any specific underlying assets or collateral. This includes IOUs issued by the sovereign government such as the German bund, U.K. Gilt, and U.S. Treasuries. Credit hedge fund managers with expertise in sovereign debt may also invest in IOUs of local municipalities, public projects, and quasi-governmental entities such as Fannie Mae, Freddie Mac, and Gazprom.

When a sovereign needs to raise capital, it can issue debt internally or externally. External debt typically is issued in hard currency (globally accepted currencies of trade such as the euro, the yen, or the dollar), and terms are governed by international law (i.e., issued in New York or United Kingdom courts). In countries other than the United States, European Union nations, and Japan, foreign participation in a sovereign's bond issuance tends to be focused on debt issued in a hard currency, although on the margin, hedge funds have now ventured into local currency debt. Domestic debt is typically issued in local currency, and terms are governed under the jurisdiction of local courts. We will later discuss the issues of concern should one find oneself as an investor in a credit hedge fund invested in domestic debt.

Size of the Market

The global size of the sovereign debt market is staggering—at the end of 2010 the global bond market grew to a record size of $95 trillion, with more than $75 trillion in the form of public domestic bonds.[1] More important, as leverage moves from corporate and consumer balance sheets onto sovereign balance sheets, credit risk and default probability are transferred in the same direction.

The size of the global sovereign debt market is immense. Figure 6.1 shows the domestic bond market by issuer. The relative creditworthiness of various sovereign issuers has also changed over time. In the 1990s and 2000s, if one asked investors about what came to mind when they heard the phrase "sovereign bond crisis," they were likely to cite the 1994 Mexican Tequila crisis, the 1998 Russian default, or the 2001 Argentinian default. In recent modern history, sovereign bond crises used to be the exclusive purview of emerging market countries, broadly defined as most or all countries in Latin America, Asia ex-Japan, Africa, Eastern Europe, and the Middle East. However, in today's market, many emerging market debtors have improved their balance sheets and have improved their ratings in the past two decades while some of the developed nations have seen their creditworthiness erode in the same period. Figure 6.2 shows the ratings of emerging sovereigns versus developed nations in the early 1990s versus 2013.

$ Billions Outstanding, 2010				
	Total		**......... of which ....**	
		Public	**Financial**	**Corporate**
U.S.	25,158	10,746	11,524	2,888
Japan	13,275	11,213	1,206	856
France	3,199	1,696	1,208	295
Italy	3,082	1,975	731	376
China	2,969	1,617	859	493
Germany	2,689	1,556	785	348
U.K.	1,687	1,344	322	21
Spain	1,466	606	837	23
Canada	1,389	971	262	156
Other	11,421	6,150	4,163	1,107
World	66,335	37,874	21,897	6,564

Figure 6.1 **Domestic bond market by issuer**
Source: World Federation of Exchanges

Emerging Countries		
Country	1992	2013
Mexico	BB+	BBB
Russia	BB–	BBB
Argentina	BB–	B–u
Venezuel	BB	B+
Brazil	B	BBB

Developed Countries		
Country	1992	2013
Greece	BBB–	B–
Italy	AA+	BBB+u
Ireland	AA	BBB+
Germany	AAA	AAAu
France	AAA	AA+u

Figure 6.2 **Comparative ratings of emerging sovereigns vs. developed nations, 1992 vs. 2013**
Source: PAAMCO, Bloomberg

Changing Macroeconomic Landscape: Rising Indebtedness of Developed Nations

After the 2008 credit crisis, the risks on the developed world's sovereign balance sheet and the risks of a systemic banking failure became more interconnected than ever. One of the most seminal changes that came out of the 2008 credit crisis was the nationalization of debt that occurred throughout most of the developed world. This took place as much of the leverage and risky assets were transferred from the financial system such as banks and insurance companies to governments' balance sheets. As leverage increased and tax revenue dwindled, many sovereign borrowers who were previously thought to have no or little credit risk began to take on a significant amount of credit risk at an astonishing pace.

In the United States, as the risk of a systemic banking system failure loomed over markets following the failures of Bear Stearns and Lehman Brothers, the U.S. government stepped in and pumped massive liquidity into the system. It provided liquidity backstop to the banks and created vehicles to take over toxic assets (TARP, Maiden Lane). Leverage and other risks moved from the financial system to the government's balance sheet. In Europe, the risk was also transferred from banks to the government balance sheet. Figure 6.3 shows the increase in the size of U.S. Fed, Bank of Japan (BOJ), and European Central Bank (ECB) balance sheets over the past decade.

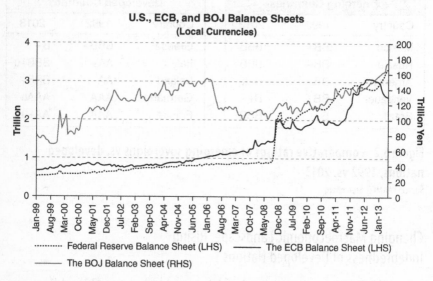

Figure 6.3 U.S., ECB, and BOJ balance sheets over time
Source: PAAMCO, Bloomberg

SOVEREIGN VS. CORPORATE DEBT

Similar to the corporate credit market, the sovereign bond market is also susceptible to cycles of easy credit, increasing leverage to unsustainable levels, and defaults. Nonetheless, there are several ways that sovereign borrowers differ from corporate borrowers.

First, willingness to pay may often matters more than the ability to pay. The government of a particular country may have the ability to repay the debt but choose to default instead. In November 2008, the Ecuadorean government declared a 30-day technical moratorium on the interest payment on part of its foreign debt for political reasons, despite its ample foreign currency reserves. The decision to default may be political or strategic; for example, the Ecuadorean government stated that this decision was due to some alleged irregularities during the bond sale process and not related to financial difficulties. Foreign creditors are exposed to the risk that the government may find broad political support in defaulting on financial obligations, especially when these obligations are more widely held by foreigners instead of domestic creditors. A sovereign debt moratorium takes place when a sovereign government delays the interest or principal payment of its debt.

Second, investors' ability to enforce their legal rights may vary as the borrower often holds sway over its own legal and judicial system. For example, regardless of the seniority described in the bond indentures, the claims of a domestic investor may not be deemed to be pari passu or junior to an international investor. If the court with jurisdiction on the bankruptcy proceeding is a local court, as will be the case for a domestic debt, there may be other investors who happen to wield powerful political influence on the local politicians and/or the court.[2] These local parties may influence the court into favoring their interests, which may be in conflict with foreign lenders.

Third, unlike corporations, in the case of a sovereign default, investors may not be able to put a lien on specific assets. With quasi-sovereigns (i.e., corporations with the implicit or explicit backing of the sovereign government) there are usually specific assets to lend against. In this case, the location of the asset collateralizing the debt obligation is of particular importance to the creditors. Even if foreign creditors are to win the court battle in a U.K. or U.S. jurisdiction, there are additional challenges that a foreign investor may face in enforcing the court's judgment in claiming locally domiciled and controlled assets.

Furthermore, sovereign borrowers have different levers to effectively reduce the value of creditors' claims without defaulting outright. For domestic debt denominated in local currency, the borrower has the ability to print money and can inflate its way out of debt. We'll discuss the opportunities and risks of sovereign debt using the European crisis to highlight the key points.

Case Study: Nakheel/Dubai World

Dubai World is a conglomerate owned by Dubai, an emirate within the United Arab Emirates (UAE). Dubai World owns Nakheel, a property developer behind The World, Palm Jumeirah, and Jumeirah Islands, which are multibillion-dollar property development projects.[3]

On November 25, 2009, bond markets were alarmed by the request of the Dubai government for a "standstill" and extension of maturities request for Nakheel bonds due in December 14, 2009, until at least May 30, 2010.[4] Investors had to consider the following risks:

- At the time, many bond market participants estimated default as almost a certainty. This would have been the first documented case of the default of a Sukuk bond.[5] Neither this type of structure nor the court system in Dubai had been tested before.
- Indenture for the structure is governed under U.K. law. However, the mortgages and leases behind the real estate collateral of the bonds are governed under Dubai law.
- Should investors prevail in the U.K. courts, there is risk in the investors' ability to enforce this judgment and foreclose on the company's assets, which are located in Dubai.

- Furthermore, to bring legal action against any government or government-owned entity in Dubai, one needs to get approval from the government. From the prospectus, "judicial precedents in Dubai have no binding effect on subsequent decisions," and court decisions in Dubai are "generally not recorded."
- Nakheel itself is the bond trustee.
- Nakheel 2009 bonds are guaranteed by Dubai World, which does not have to file any financials.

Some important lessons can be learned from Nakheel:

- Investors should pay attention to both the terms governing the bonds and the terms governing the collateral.
- The bodies deciding on creditors' rights may not be independent from the borrower.
- Newer structures and a wide range of jurisdictions mean that there may not be enough case law precedent on which investors can base their analysis.
- Winning in the bankruptcy court is only half the battle— controlling the collateral is the other half.
- It may be difficult to gauge the value of a sovereign or quasi-sovereign guarantee.

CASH SOVEREIGN DEBT VS. SOVEREIGN CDS

When talking about sovereign debt in the context of credit hedge funds, it is important to look at credit derivatives such as the sovereign CDS and CDX in addition to cash bonds. Many credit hedge funds used sovereign CDS to hedge the risks in the European credit crisis, and it is important to understand how sovereign CDS differs from corporate CDS, which may be more familiar to credit investors.

One of the key differences between sovereign and corporate CDS is what constitutes a credit event. For corporate CDS, bankruptcy filing of the borrower such as Chapter 11 filing in the United States and defaulting on interest payment or principal would constitute a credit event. For Western European sovereign CDS, failure to pay would constitute a credit event along with any restructuring, debt repudiation, or debt moratorium or standstill[6] event. Unlike a corporation, however, a sovereign cannot file for Chapter 11, and thus bankruptcy is not a credit event.

 Key Takeaway on Different Features Among Sovereign CDS

When investing via sovereign CDS, investors need to keep in mind that the structure of the CDS agreement varies for different sovereigns. For example, the Multiple Holder Obligation applies to Western European sovereign CDS but not emerging European or Middle Eastern sovereign CDS. The Multiple Holder Obligation states that in order for a restructuring to trigger a credit event, when the restructuring goes into effect, the debt obligation needs to be held by three or more debt holders that are unaffiliated with one another, and if it's a loan, at least two-thirds of holders (66.67 percent) need to consent to the event.

Case Study of Greek CDS: Lessons in Execution and Illustration of Cash vs. Synthetic Basis

Investors often think that the "secret sauce" to great investments is figuring out a unique, one-of-a-kind investment idea before everyone else does. Figuring out the idea is only part of the story: executing the idea is often just as, or even more, important.

At the beginning of the European credit crisis, sovereign CDS was used by credit hedge funds seeking to buy protection in the event that a Greek default would cause a domino effect over other weak peripheral European countries. Sovereign CDS was a more popular choice than outright shorting of cash bonds because CDS allows for a more efficient use of capital and there was often better liquidity in the CDS rather than cash market. Later, however, there was serious concern that, although economically Greek debt holders suffered significant losses in the restructuring, holders of protection through CDS would not be made whole because the terms of the restructuring would not constitute a credit event. Hedge fund managers who chose to hedge their portfolio using Greek sovereign CDS faced the risk that the hedge did not provide an effective hedge to the portfolio due to this ambiguity around the trigger for a credit event.

The key issue here is who decides whether a bond is in default or what constitutes a credit event. The cash bond default guidelines are fairly clear. Broadly defined, default happens when one of three situations take place: first, when payment to investors, both interest and/or principal, is not made in full and on time; second, when an issuer files for bankruptcy (in the United States, this usually means Chapter 11 restructuring or Chapter 7 liquidation) and its ability to meet its obligations becomes impaired; and third, when there is reduction of investor claim outside of the bankruptcy process. A common example of this is a distressed exchange. In a distressed exchange, a bondholder exchanges the original claim for another security such as another bond, but which has a lower value than the nominal amount of the original claim. The new security typically also would come with new terms such as lower coupon, extended maturity, or a payment-in-kind (PIK) feature.

In the case of Greece, both S&P and Fitch had opined that the voluntary exchange proposal for Greek sovereign debt would constitute a default. Per S&P, default takes place because investors receive less value than the original promised value of their investment. Second, the restructuring was done as a result of the borrower's distress and was not "opportunistic" (i.e., not a result of the borrower taking advantage of a frothy bond market by exchanging its existing debt for new instruments with different terms).

 Key Takeaway on Credit Event of CDS

When hedging the risk of a bond default using a credit derivative such as a CDS, keep in mind that a bond default in itself does not necessarily trigger a credit default event of the sovereign CDS.

In October 2011, the ISDA governing body stated that a voluntary exchange of debt would not trigger a credit event. According to ISDA, "There is no link between a rating agency declaration and a

CDS Credit Event. It is possible that the same set of facts might give rise to both, but it is also possible that one might occur but not the other."[7] The risk here is that the cash bonds for Greece could trade down to reflect the expected restructuring haircut, but at the same time the spread on the Greek sovereign CDS would narrow because the restructuring would not constitute a credit event. Some credit hedge fund managers I spoke to at the time, upon seeing increased likelihood of this scenario, decided to switch from CDS to shorting Greek cash sovereign bonds, others decided to unwind their CDS contract, and some have described it as "a nightmare."

Fast-forward from October 2011 to March 2012. After much turbulence in the market, on March 9, 2012, ISDA declared that due to the use of a "collective action clause" (CAC), a credit event was triggered in the Greek debt restructuring. A CAC means that if a majority of debt holders agreed to the distressed exchange, all debt holders including those who did not vote for the exchange are bound by the results. In the earlier voluntary debt exchange proposal, CAC was not invoked. The voluntary debt exchange required at least 90 percent of bondholders to agree to the distressed exchange for it to take place, and those who did not vote in favor of the exchange would not be subject to this.

Case Study: Government Intervention Risk in Sovereign Debt—ECB Monetary Policy of 2012

Unexpected changes in monetary policy constitute a key risk in sovereign debt markets. To highlight an example of monetary intervention risk, consider what happened to the sovereign debt of many peripheral European countries upon announcement of strong monetary support by the ECB in late 2012. Mario Draghi, the president of the ECB, stated that the ECB was ready to do "whatever it takes" to protect the euro. The ECB made a commitment to purchase any quantity of European sovereign debt in exchange for these issuers making a commitment to fiscal discipline. The cost of borrowing in many troubled European sovereigns, particularly Portugal, Italy, Greece, and Spain (the "PIGS," collectively), fell dramatically following Draghi's announcement and subsequent ECB action.

Key Questions On Sovereign Debt Exposure

- How do you size your sovereign debt positions?
- How do you measure the macroeconomic risk in your portfolio?
- How do you weigh the risk of policy intervention in your sovereign debt positions?
- What do you expect will happen to the portfolio if the government implements changes such as capital control or monetary intervention? What's your plan in this case?

Up to the announcement, European sovereign debt had been a popular hedge to global credit portfolios. It made sense given that the major risk to credit investors was driven by macroeconomic headwinds coming from Europe. However, this monetary support from the ECB was a game changer and illustrates a risk to short sellers of sovereign bonds. This commitment alone (the ECB had not come in and did what it said it would do) was sufficient to ease market concerns and dramatically reduced the tail risk of a euro breakup. Figure 6.4 shows

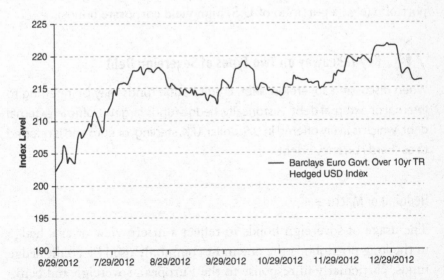

Figure 6.4 **Total return of European sovereign bonds in months following ECB announcement**

Source: PAAMCO, Bloomberg

the return for European government bonds surrounding the ECB announcement. Shortly after the ECB action, some hedge funds revisited their thesis on some of the more distressed sovereign debt (e.g., Greek, Portugal, Italy), and with the key risk of euro breakup being much reduced, took the opposite position (i.e., went long the sovereign bonds) and reaped handsome gains in the process.

INVESTMENT STRATEGIES IN SOVEREIGN DEBT

The sovereign debt market has historically been the playground of fixed-income relative value and global macro hedge funds. Until recently, with the exception of Treasuries short as an interest rate hedge, exposure to sovereign credit risk has not often been found in credit hedge fund portfolios. However, as the risk in the credit market increasingly became linked to the European macro risk, there has been an increased presence of sovereign debt in the toolbox of credit hedge fund managers. Whether in the form of cash bonds or CDS contracts, credit hedge fund managers may use sovereign debt to express a directional view such as likelihood of default as well as a hedge to the long portfolio (e.g., a portfolio of U.S. high yield corporate bonds).

 Key Takeaway on Two Types of Sovereign Debt

When discussing sovereign debt, credit hedge funds may be referring to internal or external debt. Historically, hedge funds largely traffic in external debt, which is likely offered in U.S. dollar, U.K. sterling, or euro and is referred to as "hard currency" debt.

Hedging or Macro

The usage of sovereign bonds to reflect a macro view or as a hedge to the long portfolio is the one most commonly used by credit hedge funds, particularly in response to the European sovereign and banking crisis of 2012. The strategy is most commonly seen on the short side of the credit portfolio to hedge the long exposure to corporate bonds and loans. This investment strategy reflects the manager's macroeconomic view on the world and how political or macro events may affect the portfolio. For example, if the credit hedge fund manager is expecting a highly volatile period due to the risk of euro breakup, he may decide that he does not have an edge in estimating the risk of a breakup taking place and decide to de-risk his portfolio. Part of this de-risking may include a reduction in long exposure by selling some of his long positions and reducing explicit leverage[8] combined with the use of sovereign debt shorts to hedge the macro risks to the portfolio. The manager can obtain the short exposure to sovereign credit via cash and synthetic instruments, as well as via single names or through credit indices such as the iTraxx SovX.[9]

If investors are rushing to buy protection via a credit default swap or a credit default index, the increased demand tends to push spread wider (the cost of buying protection is higher). The momentum will push spreads wider, which benefits a manager with an existing short exposure in his portfolio. In this case, a credit event (default) does not have to happen for the short protection to gain a profit. An increase in risk aversion to a particular country's debt will increase its spread, which will result in a positive mark-to-market to the short exposure.

Edge Being Captured

This strategy is popular during periods when macroeconomic risk is the overwhelming risk factor in many investment portfolios. During "risk-off" periods, pricing weakness is seen across various risk assets including the bonds of many borrowers with strong fundamentals. A credit hedge fund manager who aims to add value through credit selection can protect the portfolio from the day-to-day gyrations of the credit market using hedges and alpha shorts.

The manager can add alpha through active trading of the hedges as well as through selection of instruments used to hedge. Credit hedge fund managers can express their macro shorts by various instruments. Managers can express their bearish view by selecting among instruments such as cash sovereign bonds, sovereign CDS, or sovereign CDS index. The relative cost of hedging the portfolio varies depending on the instrument chosen, and the ultimate goal is to minimize the cost of "insuring" the portfolio while obtaining the best possible coverage.

Key Questions Regarding Hedging Sovereign Debt Risk

- What types of instruments are you using to hedge the portfolio? Why?
- How much is being spent in premium? How much is the maximum amount that can be spent?
- Will the hedges be actively traded?

Risks

Event Risk

The manager can match the notional size of the long and the short portfolio (i.e., have the book be "notionally neutral"). However, from a risk perspective, this does not automatically imply that the portfolio is fully hedged or, more important, that it has no risk exposure. For many credit hedge fund managers, there is basis risk in their portfolio, which comes in the form of quality mismatch. It is common to see a portfolio of long exposures to lower quality credit hedged with a synthetic credit index referencing higher quality sovereign debt. For example, a credit hedge fund portfolio that is expecting Germany to end up shouldering more of the debt burden of peripheral European countries may hedge $100 of long exposure to high yield bonds by shorting the cash on German sovereign bonds. On a dollar-for-dollar basis, the portfolio may look well hedged. However, there is a risk that this portfolio is exposed to the "flight to quality" risk. Should investors decide to sell risky assets and reallocate the capital into the Bund because of its perceived relative safety, the portfolio may suffer losses on both the long and the short side.

 Key Questions on Basis Risk

- What are the basis risks inherent in your investment strategy?
- How did you get comfortable with this basis risk?
- In the worst-case scenario where the basis moves against you, what is the expected loss in this portfolio?

Liquidity or Technical Risk

During the European sovereign crisis, one of the more popular hedges to express a bearish macro view on Europe was the iTraxx SovX Western Europe Index because of its relative liquidity and efficient use of capital. Hedging a less liquid portfolio with a highly liquid synthetic index comes with its own risk, however. The market for corporate credit assets, particularly the types that credit hedge funds tend to gravitate to (i.e., overlooked, unlikely to be found in large indices), tends to have a different investor base than synthetic credit indices. During challenging market environments, the two camps of investors may behave very differently. In a "risk-off" period when investors are rushing to hedge portfolios, a large, liquid index such as the iTraxx SovX Western Europe Index[10] is popular amongst investors who are looking to express a short macro view, and they often will "pile on" to this trade. There were periods when the shorts capitulated after a "pile on" period and the index was subject to a short covering rally where the index outperformed the cash bonds as investors rushed to take off their hedges.

Theta (Time Roll) Risk

When deciding to hedge the portfolio, managers have to make a decision on the size of the hedge. The managers can decide whether to match the dollar amount of exposure on the short portfolio to the long portfolio. The risk is that when the short exposure is expressed through credit derivatives or credit derivative indices, as the maturity of the credit derivative looms nearer, the DV01 of the short position gets smaller quickly. If the credit hedge fund managers are using shorter dated maturity credit derivatives relative to their longs, they may need to increase the size of their notional shorts as time rolls closer to maturity of the CDS or CDX. If they are unable or unwilling to do so, they may find themselves with an increasing net long credit exposure. In other words, a portfolio that might have seemed relatively hedged at the inception may become much less hedged over time due to maturity mismatch between the longs and the shorts.

Key Takeaway on Short Dated Credit Derivatives

The spread DV01, or the measure of sensitivity of the credit derivative to every basis point change in the credit spread of the underlying sovereign bond, may decline dramatically as the maturity of the sovereign CDS or CDX comes near.

Basis Risk

When hedging one's view against a broad macro risk, the instrument chosen to execute that view can be of vital importance. For example, managers could either short cash Greek sovereign bonds or buy protection via Greek sovereign CDS to express their macro view. Many used the Greek sovereign CDS. Some managers bought protection on CDS on the view that credit spreads would widen due to ongoing stress on the creditor, but not specifically with the view that Greece would default. For much of 2010, expectation of Greek default rose. This drove Greek sovereign CDS wider, resulting in a positive P&L for a credit hedge fund that had bought protection via the CDS.

However, the market would soon learn about the specific risk in the sovereign CDS market. The October 2011 Euro summit came out with a statement about a "voluntary" exchange of Greek debt where private investors would take a 50 percent haircut on the nominal value of their debt.[11] In the CDS market, there was a serious concern that although economically Greek debt holders suffered significant losses, this would not trigger a credit event on the CDS. If there is no credit event, the protection buyer of a CDS is not entitled to a payment. Upon a credit event, the payment due from swap seller to swap buyer is par minus the recovery amount.

Relative Value Strategy

A relative value strategy attempts to isolate a particular risk factor and profit from it while hedging the other risks in the trade. This strategy usually pairs a long and a short position, although in certain sovereign debt trades, there may be an additional short to hedge the currency component of the long exposure.

As an example of this strategy, one may be long a bond on one end of the sovereign credit curve while hedging some of the default risk with short exposure to shorter-maturity sovereign debt. A credit hedge fund manager may have the opinion that the long end of the sovereign yield curve for Spain is implying too high of a restructuring probability. The manager's investment thesis could be that a restructuring will take place and that the government is far more likely to restructure short-term rather than long-term debt. According to the manager's thesis, the market is overestimating the probability of restructuring on the long-term Spanish sovereign debt. However, the manager may not be willing to take a directional bet on spread narrowing on the long-term Spanish sovereign bond because he thinks there is too much risk that the spread may continue to get wider until resolution is reached. A relative value strategy to benefit from this mispricing includes going long the 30-year Spanish sovereign debt versus buying protection via 5-year Spanish sovereign CDS.

Should events unfold as per the manager's expectations, this strategy would yield profit both on the long and the short legs. The long exposure would benefit as the spread on the long end of the curve would compress as the market recognized that the 30-year debt would not be included in the restructuring. The short exposure would benefit as restructuring would trigger a credit event, which would benefit the short sovereign exposure via 5-year CDS.

Edge Being Captured

During periods of healthy or bullish credit market sentiment, investors may find value in active selection of sovereign bond investments. In a stable credit market, differences in spread and performance can be explained by fundamental drivers of creditworthiness such as amount of indebtedness, credit ratings, and trade deficit. However, during periods of crisis, credit hedge fund managers have observed that spread widening may be observed across the borrowers in a particular region regardless of fundamental creditworthiness. This provides an opportunity for investors who can spot attractive investment opportunities. The relative value approach allows investors to express a long exposure to underpriced securities while partially or fully hedging the risk of across-the-board price declines.

Risks
Event Risk

There are generally two types of event risk in a relative value trade. The event may not occur as the manager expected, or the manager's thesis may be correct but the event may not affect both legs of the trade as expected. The example given above is essentially a curve flattener trade: the trade is positioned to benefit if the sovereign yield curve flattens as the long end of the curve narrows and the front end of the curve widens on a relative basis.

An example of an event risk: if Germany were to acquiesce to providing greater support toward a pan-European banking and economic union, this may provide relief to all Spanish bonds, but the front end of the Spanish sovereign curve (where most of the risk aversion was concentrated) may see more spread tightening than the far end of the curve. In this scenario, the trade may end up with a loss because the positive P&L generated by the long end of the curve may not be sufficient to overcome the negative P&L due to the tightening on the short-term debt.

Timing Risk

A relative value trade involves a short trade, where usually there is a premium to maintain a position. As such, the timing of the event realization is of importance. The longer it takes for the event to materialize, the more it costs to maintain the position. Even in the scenario where there may be a positive profit from the long and/or short leg of the position, the profit may be completely wiped out or overcome by the cost to pay the premium of shorting the bond over time.

Basis Risk

One of the main risks in a relative value strategy is basis risk. This is the risk that the short trade does not move in the opposite direction and similar magnitude to the long leg of the trade. For example, if the trade pairs a 30-year cash sovereign bond long versus a 5-year cash sovereign bond short, there is basis risk. One of the potential sources for basis risk is different liquidity availability for short-term versus long-term sovereign debt. The longer-term sovereign debt may be less liquid; thus, the price may not change even as the more liquid 5-year sovereign bond rises in price. Another example is if the 30-year cash sovereign bond is paired with a 5-year sovereign CDS. There are different supply and demand factors at work for the synthetic credit market than for the cash bond market. There are also technical issues relevant to credit derivatives, such as when a default in the cash bond does not constitute a default in the credit derivatives world.

Directional Long/Short Strategy

Managers who have a strong view on a particular scenario playing out may take a directional position on a sovereign debt to express that view. For example, in the European sovereign crisis, one of the possible outcomes is a sharing of debt responsibility across the EU, for example, via Eurobonds.[12] This scenario is largely expected to have a positive impact on risky assets as it provides investors and markets with clarity and reassurance, at least on a short to medium term.

Credit hedge fund managers with high conviction of the likelihood of this event taking place are likely to position their portfolios to benefit from expected spread tightening and an increase in equity price, particularly in European stocks. The managers with this positive outlook added long exposure to highly distressed assets, including European sovereign bonds they perceived to be trading at spreads that were too wide.

Edge Being Captured

This investment strategy attempts to capture a manager's edge in discerning the likelihood of various macroeconomic events in the market. Credit hedge fund managers who have macro expertise and experience would be more likely to have a directional view on the market and consequently put a directional long/short sovereign bond trade. During the Eurozone crisis, attempting to discern which way the wind would blow for European politicians (and the corresponding market response) was no small feat. Many market participants, justifiably, did not feel comfortable exposing themselves to the risk of Eurozone political winds. Many simply wanted to rid themselves of European risk, whether by buying protection on European sovereign bonds or by simply getting rid of their existing European exposure. This has resulted in periods when certain sovereign bonds were oversold, presenting pockets of opportunities for discerning investors.

Risks

Fundamental Credit Risk

The main risk of this strategy is the fundamental credit risk. Should the manager's expected scenario not play out as expected, this strategy is expected to generate losses to the portfolio.

Key Takeaway on How Macro Winds Influence Fundamental Investment Strategy

The strong component of fundamental or default risk in a directional long/short strategy means that many credit hedge fund managers whose expertise is in analyzing corporate and not sovereign credit chose to stay away from this strategy during the European sovereign crisis.

Key Takeaway on Navigating a Macro-Driven Environment

Investors should be aware that for any given period, value added from fundamental research may be overcome by macro-driven fears. Credit hedge funds can mitigate this risk by adding value via trading and tactical shorts as well as active risk management.

Mark-to-Market Risk

Another risk factor is the mark-to-market risk. Although the manager's thesis may be proven right in the end, risk aversion may overcome the market and the portfolio suffer from a period of negative performance. Should the manager express a strong positive view by selling protection on the sovereign CDS, there is the additional risk that negative mark-to-market on the swap is likely to require the manager to come up with cash to pay the swap counterparty (unlike buying the sovereign bond cash, where the mark-to-market loss does not imply the need for additional cash). Should the manager fail to come up with the requisite cash amount in the appropriate amount of time, the manager can be deemed as having defaulted on the swap.

CONCLUSION

- Historically, credit hedge fund managers have not been active in the debt of sovereigns. However, as default risk is transferred from the private to the public sector, many credit hedge fund managers find themselves with unexpected sovereign risk in their portfolio.
- In addition to the complexities of analyzing the fundamentals of a public entity versus a corporation, politics and policy risk need to be considered.
- When analyzing value of collateral, winning in the bankruptcy court is only half the battle. Just because one has the right to foreclose does not mean one can foreclose, particularly if the collateral is controlled by the sovereign.

Hedging out one's sovereign risk exposure is challenging due to the basis risk between cash and synthetic sovereign debt. Understanding the terms of sovereign CDS and what triggers a credit event is key in successful hedging.

CHAPTER 7

Legal and Structuring

After the global credit crisis in 2008 followed by widespread gating and suspension of investor funds, large hedge fund frauds, and a sea change in the regulatory environment, investors place more and more emphasis on better legal and structuring aspects of their hedge fund investments. Many investors have experienced losses and headline risk due to lack of protection from weak legal rights or lack of proper fund governance. Due to the nature of the investment strategies and underlying instruments of credit hedge funds, there are additional complexities of these investments relative to long-only credit investments or equity-oriented hedge funds. Examples of the additional complexities include tax and structuring matters.

This chapter will begin with a discussion about the various structures used in hedge fund investing. The material will serve as a background to the vehicles commonly used, outline the legal rights and responsibilities of the parties involved, and include a discussion about the pros and cons of separately managed accounts. The discussion on legal concepts that uniquely affect credit hedge funds will follow, including the discussion about tax issues for U.S. nontaxable and offshore investors, as well as trading in the context of material nonpublic information. Last, the chapter will close with a discussion about liability management and investors' rights in the context of credit hedge funds.

This chapter is written from the perspective of a practitioner, with practitioners rather than their legal counsel in mind. It is intended to introduce some of the practical aspects of key legal and structural issues that an investor may encounter based on our experience as hedge fund investors. The key points presented are intended as starting points for case-specific discussion with legal counsel. Deeper understanding of these key issues hopefully will improve investors' ability to further raise the bar on standards of fiduciary duty and governance in the industry.

COMMONLY USED STRUCTURES FOR HEDGE FUND INVESTING

There are three basic structures most commonly used by investors in hedge funds: the side-by-side structure, the traditional master feeder structure, and the mini-master structure. Depending on the structure chosen, there are differences on where trading takes place, where the investments are held, and which documents are particularly relevant when assessing the rights of investors.

For the limited scope of our discussion, investors can be classified into two main groups—those who are subject to U.S. tax code and those who are not. Individual investors in hedge funds are subject to U.S. tax code. Pension plans (both public and corporate), foundation and endowments, and church plans are examples of U.S. nontaxable investors. Non-U.S. investors, both individual and institutional, are generally not subject to U.S. taxation, although they may be subject to the tax laws of their own country of origin.

U.S. nontaxable and non-U.S. investors invest in hedge funds through offshore funds. For U.S. nontaxable investors, the offshore fund structure provides a way to avoid unrelated business taxable income (UBTI).[1] The U.S. tax code allows for UBTI exemption under certain types of investment activities. However, investments that are debt financed and not heavily related to the stated tax-exempt purpose of the investor (e.g., charity work for a charitable organization) are not exempt from UBTI.

Acquisition indebtedness refers to borrowing to purchase an asset. The easiest and most obvious way to avoid UBTI is to avoid using leverage in the fund investment. However, this may not be practical given that many credit hedge funds utilize some form of leverage. In practice, U.S. nontaxable investors and non-U.S. investors can invest in an offshore structure to avoid incurring UBTI. The offshore fund acts as a "blocker," and unlike with limited partnership structure, the income is not "flow through" to the investor.

Offshore funds are located at jurisdictions with low or no income tax. For U.S.-based hedge fund managers, the most common locale for offshore funds is the Cayman Islands. Other venues include Bermuda and the British Virgin Islands. European-based hedge fund managers often choose Luxembourg and Ireland. Figure 7.1 shows the location of hedge fund managers and hedge funds across the world.

In the side-by-side fund structure, the investment and trading activities take place in the onshore and offshore funds, and the two funds would be run pari passu to the same investment mandate. The main benefit of this setup is the simplicity of the structure. Trade allocation can be a challenge to this setup, particularly for credit hedge funds, where certain assets may not be easily divisible between the onshore and offshore funds. This may lead to challenges of keeping the onshore and offshore funds truly pari passu. In this setup, investors need to keep an eye for the size of the tracking error between the onshore and offshore funds. Figure 7.2 shows the side-by-side fund structure.

Figure 7.3 shows another commonly used fund structure, the traditional master feeder structure. In this structure, the capital from onshore and offshore investors flow into the same types of vehicles as in the side-by-side structure. The difference is that in the master feeder arrangement, the offshore and onshore funds act only as feeder funds and the capital flows to a master fund. The management company of

Location of Hedge Fund Managers (% of All Funds)	
Cayman Islands	33%
United States	22%
Luxembourg	14%
Ireland	8%
British Virgin Islands	4%
Brazil	3%
Bermuda	3%
Guernsey	1%
Sweden	0.5%
Malta	0.4%
Others	11%

Percentage of Fund Managers Based on Location*	
New York	41%
London	19%
Connecticut	11%
Massachusetts	6%
Others	24%

*As of May 2011. Figures do not add up to 100% due to rounding

Figure 7.1 **Location of hedge funds across the world**
Source: PAAMCO, Bloomberg Magazine

the hedge fund is hired as the investment advisor to the master fund. Investment and trading activities are conducted at the master fund level under the discretion of the investment advisor. The master fund is typically organized as an offshore entity, whether as a limited partnership or a company.

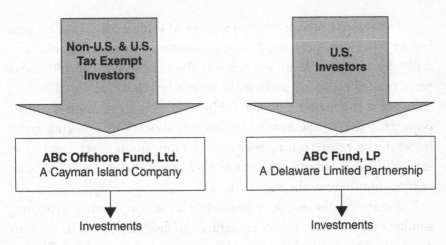

Figure 7.2 Side-by-side fund structure
Source: PAAMCO

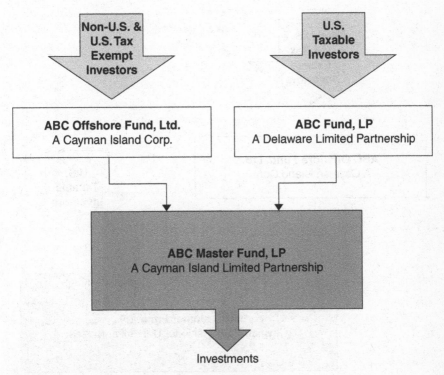

Figure 7.3 Traditional master feeder fund structure
Source: PAAMCO

In this structure, having an additional vehicle may translate into higher setup and operating costs for investors. The higher cost is partially due to higher legal fees (such as the need to have an additional set of fund documents), audit at the master fund level, and administrator work at the master fund level. However, this structure has gained popularity due to the ease of investment allocation. Tracking error between the return on onshore and offshore funds is removed or at least mitigated, as both feeder funds hold their pro rata ownership or partnership share in the master fund.

Figure 7.4 shows the mini-master structure. In this structure, similar to the master feeder structure, offshore investors invest into an offshore feeder, and the capital flows into the master fund. Similar to the master feeder structure, the offshore feeder fund and the master

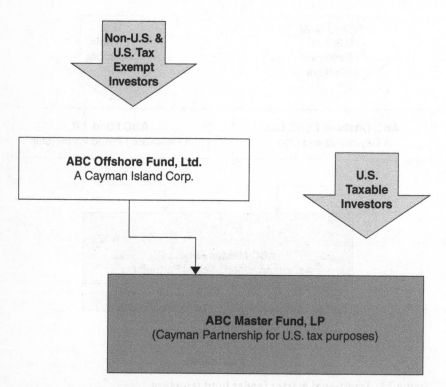

Figure 7.4 Mini-master structure
Source: PAAMCO

fund are organized as offshore entities, and trading and investment activities take place at the master fund. However, unlike in the master feeder structure, onshore investors invest directly into the master fund instead of via an onshore feeder fund. This simpler structure is more cost efficient for the onshore investors, because there is one fewer fund and set of documents to maintain.

 ## Key Takeaways on Commonly Used Investment Structures

The three most commonly used structures are side by side, master feeder, and mini master structures. The side-by-side structure is the simplest and least expensive to set up but tracking error can be an issue. The master feeder structure gives ease of allocation but involves additional costs. The mini master structure offers relative simplicity and cost benefit to the master feeder structure while mitigating tracking error.

Separately Managed Accounts

As part of investors' push to improve transparency, governance, and liquidity, separate accounts are often mentioned as a cure to all ills in hedge fund investing. Done correctly, separate accounts can offer ways to meet the objectives given above plus the flexibility to customize the investment mandate to meet the particular needs of the investor. Nonetheless, there are a few specific considerations regarding separate accounts that investors need to consider. The types of investment strategies and instruments used by credit hedge funds can add an additional layer of complexity to separate accounts.

The first thing to consider is the cost and economies of scale involved in starting and managing separate accounts. This is particularly true in the context of credit strategies, which may have greater trading and operational complexity. Expertise and experience in credit investing is required when investing via separate accounts. One of the threshold issues is the selection of service providers for the separate account. A separate account would require service providers such as prime brokers, administrator, and leverage providers. This means the investor may need to negotiate legal agreements with the prime brokers, International Swaps and Derivatives Association (ISDA) counterparties, and administrator.

Let's take the example of the appointment of an administrator. The investor may choose to use the same administrator for all of its separate accounts. This may be desired in order to receive aggregated reports and lower fees if the fee schedule is based on aggregated assets. However, a separate contract may need to be negotiated for each separate account, including if the investor has more than one account with an investment manager. The investor may need to set up and manage relationships with multiple administrators as different administrators may have different levels of expertise when it comes to investment strategy and asset types. Certain complex credit instruments such as structured products (collateralized debt and loan obligations) and synthetic credit instruments (credit default swaps and indices, swaptions) or distressed investments may require particular expertise.

Operational due diligence professionals interviewed for this book commented that the particular individuals and teams covering the account tend to be the drivers behind the level of service. The investor will also need to monitor personnel turnover with the service providers. From the credit hedge fund manager's perspective, additional resources including new hires in trading and operation may be necessary to manage separate accounts. Given these concerns, a separate account for credit hedge fund strategies is typically in the range of $50 million or higher.

Another key service provider to credit hedge funds is the financing providers. Many credit hedge funds run a levered portfolio, whether using explicit borrowing or through the usage of implicitly levered instruments such as credit default swaps and indices. Unless the separate account investor can exactly replicate the terms set forth in financing, prime brokerage, and swap agreements of the commingled funds, the difference in cost and terms of the financing arrangements will be reflected in the tracking error between the two portfolios. Clearly, the more expensive it is to borrow, the more financing cost eats away at the net return received by the investor. In a separately managed account, the investor benefits from the ability to control the selection and monitoring of service providers. However, in exchange for better control, there are certain factors to consider that may have an impact on the cost borne by the separate account investor.

For example, take an investor who wished to start a separate account for investing in a portfolio of high yield bonds and credit default swaps. The investor would need to establish a prime brokerage account (for leverage, custodial, borrowing for shorts) and ISDA agreements with swap counterparty. If the investor has strong existing relationships with the prime brokerage and the swap counterparty, the separate account may receive comparable pricing (comparable margin requirement, haircuts, or rebates) compared to the manager's prime brokerage account for its commingled fund.

There are also terms such as the cost of borrow, which fluctuates depending on the current market condition and availability of the bond in question. Prime brokerage terms are also subject to change on overnight notice by the prime brokerage. Although the initial terms may be comparable, ongoing monitoring by the separate account investor is required. In practical terms, the investor can conduct periodic surveys of the terms and borrowing cost of the separate account and compare them against the terms and borrowing cost received by the commingled fund (assuming the hedge fund manager is willing and able to disclose that information), although it can be a labor- and time-intensive effort.

It is also important for separate accounts to consider the margining provision in a bilateral swap. If the commingled fund's ISDA agreement calls for two-way margining while the separate account only requires the investor to post margin but not its swap counterparty, the commingled fund has better contractual protection because the margin posted by the swap counterparty provides some mitigation in the event of counterparty default.

Going forward, the Dodd-Frank Act–mandated clearing for swaps will be in effect. This requirement would mitigate much of the counterparty risk in bilateral swaps because the central counterparty (CCP) acts as "a seller for every buyer" and "a buyer for every seller."

Many swap types that are popular with credit hedge fund managers such as interest rate and European and North American credit default swap indices are covered by the central clearing requirement. Although this greatly mitigates counterparty risk, the new mandatory clearing requirement means there is another service provider for the separate account, the futures clearing merchant (FCM). The investor would need to evaluate and select an FCM as well as go through the on-boarding process, which can be extensive and time consuming, particularly surrounding the implementation date when many FCMs are backlogged. At this moment, select FCMs are not taking any new clients and smaller accounts may not get established until much of the backlog is cleared. The CCP also comes with margin requirement and daily collateral posting, which means the owner of the separate account should have the appropriate resources to manage cash, margin requirement, and do other Treasury functions in-house.

Other types of credit default swaps may not be subject to the mandatory clearing requirement; they will remain as bilateral swaps where each contract is uniquely negotiated by the parties involved. To illustrate the benefits of a central clearing system, let's work through an example with a commingled credit hedge fund and a separately managed account with a pari passu mandate. The commingled fund and the managed account have identical swap agreements with the same counterparty except for two key differences. The swap agreement for the commingled fund requires bilateral margining (both the fund and the counterparty required to post margin) and daily mark-to-market of the P&L. The swap agreement for the managed account only requires the account to post a 2 percent initial margin. No margin is required from the swap dealer, and the swap will be marked to market on a quarterly basis. A quarter minus one day has elapsed since the swap began, and the swap is deeply in the money. Alas, the swap dealer has declared bankruptcy. The separate account has a much larger amount at risk compared to the commingled fund, whose risk is mitigated by the margin posted by the counterparty and for having swept the proceeds from the swaps daily. The separate account is unable to realize its trading gain from the swap and finds itself in the bankruptcy process as an unsecured general creditor to the swap dealer, potentially receiving significantly less than a dollar for every dollar of trading gain.

 Key Takeaway on Minimum Size

Due to the additional setup, legal, back-office, and monitoring costs associated with a separate account, it does not make economic sense to have a separate account for less than $50 million. The amount may be higher for more complex strategies.

Limitation on exposure to a particular group of assets (the "restricted bucket") is another example of how the difference in a term of two different swap agreements can translate into meaningful impact in performance. For example, assume the swap agreements for both the commingled fund and the separate account specify a limit on how much bond below B rating can be in the portfolio. The commingled fund's limit is 10 percent, while the separate account's limit is 5 percent. In an event of widespread default, the separate account's lower limit may compel the separate account to sell the restricted assets at or near market lows.

 Key Takeaway on Replicating Service Provider Terms for the Commingled Fund

Replicating the terms of the commingled fund's service agreements for the separate account is practically impossible in most cases. This is due to several reasons, one of which is the confidential nature of the service agreements. Another reason is that service provider terms vary depending on current acceptable market level at the time of contract negotiation.

The next thing to consider on separate accounts for credit hedge funds is the issue of sourcing and trade allocation. Sourcing may be an issue when it comes to smaller or difficult to source assets. For example, take the case of a credit manager with an existing portfolio that has a significant exposure to corporate bonds that were issued on a "club" deal and have a small issuance size. The investment thesis is that these bonds were "orphaned" and overlooked, and although they have a similar claim on assets and seniority rank to a larger issuance, they are trading on a significant discount due to the lack of investor base. If a new investor is investing through a separate account with a pari passu mandate to the main fund, the manager will need to source additional allocations of these bonds. This may be very difficult to do because the opportunity may no longer be available or can be done only over a long period. In the meantime, there will be significant tracking error between the commingled fund and the separate account.

Another example would be for managers who invest via a direct lending strategy. The manager sources and originates loans directly to corporate borrowers, essentially acting as a merchant bank. In this scenario, not only may each existing loan not be replicable, but they are also indivisible. For these types of assets, replication of an existing portfolio in a new separate account with a pari passu mandate may present a real investment challenge for investors wishing to replicate an existing commingled fund in a separate account structure.

Another issue to consider regarding trade allocation is related to the minimum bite size required for certain investments. Investors can get exposure to bank loans via the assignment or participation method. An assignment, or buying the loan "on assignment," is something most people would consider as a true sale—the investor is considered as the lender of record and therefore has full voting rights. In a participation, the original owner of the loan transfers the economic benefit of owning the loan to the investor (the participant) via a swap. In this method, the investor may have only limited voting rights[2] and has exposure to the credit risk of its swap counterparty in addition to the loan issuer.

However, the assignment method may be problematic for separate accounts with smaller allocation sizes. For example, consider a credit hedge fund with a $1 billion commingled fund and a $25 million separate account. A 2 percent bank loan position in the commingled fund is $20 million, while a 2 percent position in the separate account is $500,000. The typical size for an assignment is typically $1 million, which is above the size of the position in the separate account.

The minimum size requirement applies to service providers in addition to the underlying investments. In the example, a $1 billion credit fund may have more than one prime brokerage account and multiple ISDA agreements with various counterparties. For the separate account in the example, it may not have sufficient size to have more than one prime brokerage. As such, the presence of multiple service providers may allow the commingled fund to receive better availability and pricing on shorts as well as better execution (trades executed more quickly and cheaply) relative to the separate account.

 ## Key Takeaway on Minimum Account Size

The minimum bite size for many credit instruments is another reason why a managed account does not make sense for accounts below a certain size. A managed account that's too small is also likely not to get the proper amount of attention from service providers.

One reason for investors to want separate accounts is typically to access better terms compared to the manager's commingled hedge fund, particularly on liquidity. However, the liquidity of the separate account may reflect the manager's need to avoid asset liability mismatch between the underlying investments and the separate account. Furthermore, managers may wish to avoid liquidity mismatch between the commingled fund and separate accounts, particularly if the investment programs are pari passu or fairly similar and involve less liquid investments, the improper liquidation of which may have negative impact on price. The liquidity profile on bonds can vary dramatically across different companies in the same industry or even between different bond issuances of the same issuer. Among other things, the size of the issuance, the makeup of the investor group, and whether the bond was publicly or privately issued can impact the liquidity profile of the investment. In the bond market, certain bonds that are fairly liquid during normal market conditions may see liquidity dry up when the credit market is undergoing significant volatility. Experienced credit hedge fund managers are aware of this and of the fact that investor redemptions, whether due to performance or other cash needs, may coincide with periods of increased volatility and decreased liquidity in the credit market.

The liquidity terms of commingled and separate accounts need to reflect the sensitivity toward the potential need for an orderly exit during times of lower liquidity. Investors looking to avoid side pockets or gates may be surprised to find out that separate accounts may not provide the liquidity panacea they are looking for. For business, investment, or operational reasons, some credit managers may not be willing to manage a "true" separate account (where the client has full control of the assets and effectively has daily liquidity). This tends to be a larger issue when the liquidity of the underlying investments is significantly mismatched with daily liquidity of the separate account. In a commingled credit hedge fund where a part of the portfolio is invested in less liquid assets, terms that limit the maximum redemption amount at any given time such as gates or side pockets may be appropriate.

If the commingled fund and the separate account have similar investment mandates and the assets are thinly traded, liquidation of assets in the separate account may have a negative impact on the pricing of the assets in the commingled fund, particularly if the market is in a fragile state. Given the liquidity profile for some credit instruments, some investment managers may manage separate accounts only if the liquidity terms are not significantly different from a commingled fund with a substantially similar investment mandate.

 Key Takeaways on Liquidity and Separate Accounts

When evaluating the liquidity profile of a hedge fund portfolio, be sure to include the investments made via the separate accounts in addition to the investments in the commingled fund.

TAX CONSIDERATIONS FOR CREDIT HEDGE FUND INVESTORS

There are a number of important tax considerations for credit hedge fund investors. The following material is written largely for the U.S. non-taxable investors and non-U.S. investors in mind. As with any tax-related matters, consultations with one's tax counsel about any particular situation is highly advised.

Effectively Connected Income

> "The hardest thing to understand in the world is the income tax"
>
> —*Albert Einstein*

The offshore structure alone is not a cure-all when it comes to making sure that a U.S. nontaxable investor or non-U.S. investor receives the appropriate tax exemption under the U.S. tax code. A foreign corporation (the offshore fund) is subject to U.S. tax on effectively connected income (ECI), defined as income from activities connected to a U.S. business. Generally, investing or trading in U.S. securities and other assets is not considered ECI.[3] Interest income from debt instruments is generally counted as portfolio interest and thus qualifies under the portfolio interest exemption. U.S. nontaxable investors and non-U.S. investors care about ECI because it is taxed at the U.S. income tax rate.

There are certain investment strategies, such as loan origination, that would trigger ECI. If an offshore credit fund participates in a new issue bank loan as part of the syndicate, the fund will be deemed as a loan originator and the gains from the investment will be subject to income taxes. One of the methods to avoid triggering ECI is "season and sell." A party other than the offshore fund will participate in the syndication process and hold ("season") the loan for a period of time and then sell the loan to the offshore fund after the seasoning period is over.

For credit hedge funds that engage in direct lending strategy, the onshore fund may originate the loan and hold the pro rata share of the offshore fund during the seasoning period. The offshore fund receives its share of the loan exposure after the seasoning period is over. Here, "season and sell" provides a good illustration how a legal issue can translate into additional operational complexity such as the need to manage the cash balance of the onshore fund and properly account for accrued interest.

The offshore fund will also be unable to claim portfolio interest exemption if the offshore fund holds 10 percent or more of the equity of the issuing entity as the fund is deemed to be actively engaging in the operations of a U.S. business. This may sound innocuous enough; however, it may present a tax complication for credit and distressed debt hedge funds. For these funds, one of the main investment strategies involves buying the debt of a company in financial distress and having part or the entire debt be converted to equity ownership. An offshore hedge fund owning more than 10 percent of the equity of the issuer or any interest in a limited liability corporation is deemed as actively being involved in a U.S. business; thus the gains from the interest ownership are subject to taxes. In both cases, the offshore fund typically owns the ECI-generating investment through a blocker.

Fixed, Determinable, Annual, Periodical Income

Another tax consideration for investors in offshore credit funds is the fixed, determinable, annual, periodical (FDAP) income. Income received by a foreign corporation from a U.S. source that is not classified as ECI may still be subject to a 30 percent withholding. This income is known as fixed, determinable, annual, periodical (FDAP) income.[4]

U.S. nontaxable investors and foreign investors in credit hedge funds that generate significant FDAP income should be aware of the impact of withholding on the returns of their investment. Onshore investors should take care that the blocker companies formed to shield offshore investors from FDAP withholding and ECI are created at the offshore feeder level instead of at the master level. If these vehicles are created at the master level, onshore investors unfairly bear the cost and expense of creating and maintaining the tax blockers that are created for the benefit of offshore investors. Investors in an offshore credit hedge fund should evaluate whether their credit hedge funds are sufficiently knowledgeable about whether the investment activity of the hedge fund manager would trigger either of the two types of taxable income.

Non-U.S. Sourced Income

U.S. investors should also take note of income from non-U.S. sources. Similar to the FDAP withholding in the United States, there may also be income tax or capital gains tax withholding in foreign jurisdictions. If your credit hedge fund invests a significant part of the portfolio in non-U.S. credit, take care to ensure that your investment has not been subjected to unnecessary foreign income tax or withholding.

TRADING CONSIDERATIONS FOR CREDIT HEDGE FUND INVESTORS

There are unique trading considerations related to credit hedge funds, which from time to time find themselves in possession of material non-public information (MNPI). Credit hedge funds are typically in possession of MNPI through a few different ways. For example, those that invest in bank loans may opt to be brought "inside the wall" (privy to MNPI), as may distressed investors who sit on creditors' committees.

In order to avoid running afoul of insider trading rules, a credit hedge fund in possession of MNPI from its bank loan or distressed debt exposure may be completely restricted from trading. Investors who are in possession of MNPI can trade among themselves with "big boy" letters. Big boy letters are typically bilateral agreements stating that one or both parties involved in the trade are in possession of MNPI and that the other party enters into the trade with knowledge of that fact.

 Key Questions On Steering Clear of Insider Trading Rules

- Do you commonly opt to receive private information? Why or why not?
- How do you mitigate the risk of trading positions for which you possess MNPI?
- How would your trader know what he can or cannot trade? Walk me through the process.

Restricted trading or trading only under big boy letters may mean reduced or no liquidity for that particular situation. This has an impact on the investors' liquidity profile and timing of exit. When a credit hedge fund manager possesses MNPI for a meaningful part of the portfolio and is restricted from trading, if there is significant redemption out of the fund, usage of liquidity management techniques such as side pocket or gates may be necessary.

LIQUIDITY MANAGEMENT TOOLS AND IMPLICATIONS

Liquidity management tools refer to terms that allow a hedge fund manager to manage the amount and timing of capital allowed to exit the fund at a given redemption period. These terms include side pockets, lock-ups, gating, and suspension, and they effectively reduce or delay the redemption of capital. There are situations where the use of the liquidity management tools are justified, such as in the case of a significant redemption out of an illiquid portfolio at a time of extreme market illiquidity. Nonetheless, investors are rarely pleased to find themselves unable to exit an investment. For investors in credit hedge funds, due to the liquidity profile of the investment strategies and instruments, there is a higher likelihood that during a crisis period, the fund manager may invoke at least one of these liquidity management terms. An understanding of these tools helps an investor in decision making prior to investment and in determining the course of action when these liquidity management tools are invoked.

Gates and Side Pockets

Managing the liquidity of hedge fund investment involves additional complexity when credit hedge funds are involved. Liquidity in certain parts of the credit market can switch from good to virtually nonexistent in a short period of time (market either "open" or "closed"). Due to the liquidity profile of certain credit instruments and strategies, credit hedge funds are more prone to invoke liquidity management moves such as gates or side pockets.

A gate limits the maximum amount an investor can redeem at any redemption period. There are two types of gates—fund-level gates and investor-level gates. A fund-level gate limits the maximum amount of redemption as a percentage of the fund size. For example, a 25 percent fund-level gate caps the maximum redemption amount out of the fund at 25 percent of the fund size at the effective redemption date. A full redemption by a $5 million investor in a $100 million credit hedge fund will not trigger a 25 percent fund-level gate if he is the only investor to redeem at that time. If total investor redemption at a particular redemption date exceeds 25 percent of the total fund size, investors would receive pro rata shares of the 25 percent maximum redemption amount. An investor-level gate sets the maximum amount an investor can redeem at any redemption date based on a percentage of the investment. For example, a 25 percent quarterly investor-level gate means a $5 million investor planning a full exit from a $100 million hedge fund can only take 25 percent of his total investment per quarter regardless of other redemptions from the fund that quarter. Keep in mind that the full redemption is subject to audit holdback: after four quarters the investor will receive the proceeds in excess of the audit holdback, which usually is available to the investor after fund audit.

Investors in credit hedge funds who lived through 2008 are familiar with the concept of side pockets. Technically, side pockets are share classes within the same fund with no redeemable shares. Credit hedge funds are more likely to need to use side pockets in times of market crisis when there is no liquidity for part of the portfolio. A side pocket is created and the illiquid assets are transferred into the side pocket (investors, including redeeming ones, hold on to their pro rata ownership of these assets), while the liquid assets remain in the fund. The fund manager will liquidate the redeeming investor's pro rata share of the liquid assets, and the redeeming investor's share of illiquid assets is usually liquidated over a longer time period.

A close cousin of the side pocket is the synthetic side pocket. Certain fund documents do not allow for creation of a side pocket in the fund. The original fund would move its illiquid assets to a new fund (the synthetic side pocket) with a nonredeemable share class created only to hold these assets.

On one end of the spectrum, the use of gates and side pockets by a hedge fund investing only in liquid public equities is clearly inappropriate. In some cases, even when the side-pocketed investments are illiquid, investors are concerned that the side pocket is used to house nonperforming investments and allows the manager to continue earning performance fees from the performing investments. One way to mitigate this risk is to have an offset feature where the performance of the side pocket at liquidation offsets the performance of the non-side-pocketed investments. If the side pocket is liquidated at a loss, it reduces the gains of the non-side-pocketed investment. Another provision is not to charge management fees or to charge reduced management fees for side-pocketed investments, or to have a private equity–like feature where the gains of the manager are back-ended (i.e., the manager is only compensated if the side pocket is liquidated at a gain to investors within a reasonable time frame).

Gates and side pockets may be used in select situations where not using them means disadvantaging a group of investors. The example here would be for less liquid credit assets, where having to sell a large position into a "closed" market to meet investor redemption would negatively affect the price of the position. This lower price would translate into a drawdown for the remaining investors in the fund. If a gate is invoked and the fund manager can liquidate the position in multiple quarters instead of a quarter, the gate can help to achieve an orderly liquidation and limit market impact of the sale.

Another example would be the use of side pocket for a special situation or distressed position. Assume there is a credit hedge fund with two positions. Bond A is a liquid high yield bond. Bond B trades by appointment only, and the issuer is in the middle of a restructuring. Bond B is marked at 90, but it has not traded recently (the mark may be "stale"). Bond B has been accruing noncash interest—if the bondholders are successful, they will receive full value of par plus accrued of 120. However, the downside case is that the bond may trade down to 60. Due to the infrequent trades, it is difficult to ascertain whether the current mark of 90 reflects current market price for Bond B. If an investor redeemed, the hedge fund manager faces the option whether to side-pocket Bond B or let the investor redeem his pro rata share of Bond B at 90. The hedge fund manager may decide to side-pocket bond B due to its illiquidity and the timing of impending events.

Key Takeaways on Liquidity Management Tools

Gates and Side Pockets have received plenty of negative press, some of it well deserved. There are particular situations and types of instruments where the use of gating and side pockets is not only justifiable but also necessary to protect remaining investors from the impact of exiting investors. Constant monitoring, deep understanding of the true nature of one's investment portfolio, and knowledge of market condition are crucial in determining whether gates and side pockets have been used and managed appropriately.

Lock-Ups

Lock-ups can be used to manage the liquidity of the fund as well as to control the manager's business risk, where lock-ups exist to ensure predictable fee income. Certain investors are willing to lock up their capital in exchange for lower fees. Lock-ups can be applied to the investor or to the investment. In other words, if there is a one-year lock-up, this lock-up can expire one year after the first day the investor comes into the fund, or every new dollar that comes into the fund may be subject to a one-year lock-up, even if the investment is made years after the initial investment.

Lock-ups can be hard or soft. A soft lock-up allows redemption for a fee, usually a few percentage points of the amount redeemed. An example of a soft-lock provision is a 3 percent penalty for redemptions made within two years of the initial investment. This penalty can be payable to the fund or to the management company. The former is done with the reasoning that when an investor exits a less liquid investment, there may be negative market impact on the remaining investors, and the penalty compensates remaining investors in the fund. The latter interpretation benefits the manager, not investors in the fund. For lock-ups to effectively function as a liquidity management tool, there is an assumption that at any given point in time, there is a balanced mix between locked-up and non-locked-up capital. During a liquidity crisis, if most of the investors are out of their lock-up period, the lock-up provision will not be of much help in managing orderly exit in a low liquidity environment.

Suspension

In 2008, when hedge fund managers faced redemptions they were unable to meet, they invoked their ability to suspend redemption. A suspension is supposed to be temporary, and it completely prohibits any investor redemption. Similar to the other liquidity management tools, hedge fund managers argued that the ability to suspend redemptions allowed the manager to avoid a fire sale of assets and possibly cause further market deterioration. However, investors were concerned that suspension may be used as a method to lock up investor capital, as managers continue to earn fees on these assets, potentially at overly optimistic marks. Prior to 2008, suspension was generally seen as a death knell to the fund, if not the manager. First, the suspension would cause the remaining investors to rush for the exit, causing a wave of redemption out of the fund. Second, the suspension would also put a stop to future fund-raising efforts; 2008 saw a lot of funds and fund managers go out of business after suspending redemptions. However, some funds managed to survive and continue fund-raising after the suspension was lifted. As a matter of practice, some fund managers restructured the investment terms of their funds. Investors were given the option to keep their redemption or to stay in the fund. Investors who elected to stay in the fund received lower fees in exchange for locking up their investment for a longer period of time. Also, investors were more accepting of cases where the fund manager reduced or eliminated fees on the suspended fund.

 Key Takeaway on Suspension

In cases where suspension was inevitable, managers who offered reduced or no management fee and/or gave investors the option to stay or redeem (with attractive terms for investors who elect to stay) tended to maintain goodwill with their investors throughout and after the liquidity crisis.

MANAGING THE EXIT PROCESS

When investors find themselves stuck in a fund that is no longer actively making new investments but without a clear plan for liquidity or exit (i.e., a "zombie" fund), there are a few avenues the investors can pursue. Investors should be cognizant about the potential conflict of interest between investors (some investors may face more urgent liquidation needs than others do). However, a restructuring that allows for a faster exit for investors who choose the option and a slower exit for longer-term investors may be an option. In this case, investors typically ask for fee reduction (a best practice is for the manager to offer a fee reduction instead of waiting for investors, dissatisfaction to peak) because one of the main concerns is that managers are perceived to be holding onto assets, possibly at inflated marks. Another common goal is to get the manager to commit to a liquidation plan that is both timely and allows for maximum liquidation value. However, these negotiated options assume that a significant portion of investors are aligned and that the manager is willing to negotiate. Often, in reality, both of these assumptions may not hold by the time investors are contemplating alternative exit options.

Investors' legal rights include the ability to change the investment manager as well as the makeup of the board of directors. Changing the investment manager is typically difficult to do; at least a supermajority is needed. In some cases, certain funds require unanimous vote by the investors to change the investment manager. In many cases, the existing directors of zombie funds have also abdicated their responsibility to the fund manager and have not acted in the best interest of the fund investors. Alternatively, many of the changes in the fund's terms can be effected by appointing new independent directors and/or replacing existing directors. There are also other alternatives such as filing a creditors' winding-up petition in the Cayman funds. For Cayman funds with suspended redemptions, a possible option for the redeeming investors is to file a creditors' winding-up petition and argue that the court takes over the liquidation process because the fund is no longer able to function in its original investment purpose.[5]

CONCLUSION

- Hedge fund investors can maximize the value of their hedge fund allocation by focusing their risk taking on the investment aspect while minimizing other risks. Proper structuring and control are important parts of "noninvestment alpha."
- Separately managed accounts, although key to resolving a lot of governance and control issues, are not silver bullets and are resource intensive. Often, there is a minimum account size and minimum amount of internal resources (manpower, knowledge, systems) required before the cost of managed accounts start to be outweighed by their benefits.
- Best structuring practices and standards of governance will continue to evolve—investors' involvement and understanding of portfolio is key. As there are trade-offs between more robust structures, cost of setting up and maintaining these structures, and maintaining the optimal version of investment flexibility, structuring cannot be done in a vacuum. Investors need a cohesive team where structuring and legal experts work hand in hand with investment, risk management, and operational experts.
- The credit landscape provides unique challenges to governance due to the variety, complexity, and lower degree of standardization (the very same features that bring additional risks are also sources of opportunities).

CHAPTER 8

Operational Due Diligence Program for Credit Hedge Fund Investing

Operational due diligence has long been a key part of the due diligence process for hedge fund investors. However, it has only increased in importance due to events that have evolved in the past few years. Losses stemming from counterparty failures such as Bear Stearns, Lehman Brothers, and MF Global, hedge fund fraud, and insider trading have all pointed to some of the real operational issues that can arise with hedge funds. Over time, as the hedge fund industry continues to grow and evolve, the operational complexities related to running a hedge fund will increase.

Historically, the lighter regulatory requirement and oversight on the hedge fund industry has required greater investor supervision and management of operational risk in addition to investment and portfolio risk. In 2008 and 2009, there were times when operational risk and investment risk were closely intertwined. In the post-Lehman world, new rules on hedge funds such as the SEC registration requirement are intended to provide additional transparency and protection for hedge fund investors. Nonetheless, investors still need to be cognizant of some of the operational complexities behind their hedge fund investments. The complete elimination of operational risk is neither a reasonable, cost-effective, nor realistic goal. Nonetheless, the goal of hedge fund investors should be to take on selective investment risk while minimizing operational risk.

PURPOSE AND PRINCIPLES OF AN OPERATIONAL DUE DILIGENCE PROGRAM

The fundamental purpose of an operational due diligence (ODD) program is to identify hedge funds that are operationally weak. Despite superior investment talent in some cases, operational weakness may result in a suboptimal investment result all the way to a fund shutdown due to regulatory breaches or fraud. In addition to the potential of significant loss of capital, there is also a substantial reputational risk related to having an operational failure or a fraud occur under one's watch. Being able to avoid investing in these types of funds is critical.

Institutions have been keenly aware of the need to avoid hedge fund "blowups," industry jargon that typically describes a disastrous failure of a hedge fund. The term could be used in relation to failure as caused by a long list of events, ranging from investment failure (typically combined with excessive leverage), fraud, overwhelming redemptions combined with asset/liability mismatch, business failure, and operational failure or any combination of the above.

According to the 2012 SEI investor survey, investors have only increased their focus on operational strength of hedge funds. Eighty percent of the respondents in the survey agreed with the statement, "Optsional strength is a hallmark of an institutional quality hedge fund."[1] The survey indicated that investors have also shown greater focus and insistence on seeing specific practices as part of a robust ODD program. The most sophisticated institutional investors of hedge funds have long seen the separation of duties between investment and operational professionals as key in preserving the authority and independence of the back office. Figure 8.1 shows that more than 50 percent of investors see separation of duties (previously often seen as optional) as "important" or "very important."

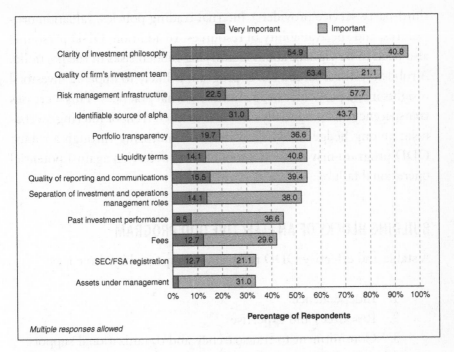

Figure 8.1   SEI investor survey: important factors in hedge fund manager selection
Source: SEI Hedge Fund Investor Survey

When it comes to fraud prevention in hedge funds, it is important to note that similar to crime prevention in general, it is very difficult to predict fraud ex-ante (before the event). Fraud still continues and will continue to exist despite the presence of extensive legal and judicial systems. However, a tight and rigorous set of internal policies governing middle and back office functions of a hedge fund can act as a deterrent and a potential warning sign should anything start to go wrong.

In addition, there is a set of third-party service providers such as hedge fund administrators, auditors, and custodians that serve as additional sets of eyes and act as "checks and balances" to the fund manager. Hedge fund managers that are "institutional quality" understand that there needs to be a demonstrable standard of care on how investors' assets are being managed.

The areas of examination covered in an operational due diligence review should include existence and quality of counterparties (including third-party service providers), internal trading policies, valuation procedures, and the availability of resources. In addition, ODD personnel also need to be vigilant about identifying hidden risks in the portfolio. A robust, well-resourced ODD program is likely to improve investors' insights into a particular hedge fund's internal practices. This increases transparency and potentially can serve as a deterrent or filtering mechanism among hedge funds. Continuous monitoring through a robust ODD program may serve as a tool of early detection against potential operational failure.

BUILDING BLOCKS OF AN EFFECTIVE ODD PROGRAM

A stable and effective ODD program is supported by three legs:

1. Independence
2. Resources and expertise
3. Commitment to transparency and organizational support

These elements need to exist for any organization committed to effectively managing the operational risks of its hedge fund program. The dynamic nature of hedge funds requires a commitment over time to keep up with the current best practices. Investors need to constantly evaluate whether the building blocks of their operational due diligence program remain in step with the most recent challenges of the industry.

 Key Takeaway on Creating a Stable and Effective Operational Due Diligence Program

Three legs to a stable and effective operational due diligence program are independence, proper resources, and organizational commitment.

Independence

First, the operational due diligence needs to be handled by a dedicated group for whom hedge fund operations are their main focus. This group is responsible for evaluating hedge fund managers solely from an operational perspective and is empowered to operate and make decisions independently from the portfolio team. In order to do so, the ODD group needs to report to a separate body other than the portfolio manager. This group could be a board or an investment committee.

In order to operate effectively, an ODD team needs to independently determine the breadth and depth of its operational review process, including testing mechanisms, as well as have a veto right in the due diligence process. If the ODD personnel feel that there are significant operational risks associated with a hedge fund, with veto power they will be able to stop the due diligence process. ODD personnel then have the discretion to ensure that the ODD process is not a formality. This encourages both empowerment and accountability of the ODD team. The team needs to balance the need to be independent and yet integrated into the whole due diligence process. Many of the decisions that rest on the ODD team involve a certain degree of judgment calls, and there may be multiple viewpoints that need to be considered. Decisions need to be made in the context of various risks and rewards of a particular investment and not in a silo. The goal is to create a healthy, productive tension where multiple perspectives can exist but the ODD team can make up its own mind given the facts.

There are a number of areas where the operational risk needs to be evaluated in context of the nature of the investment. For example, one issue that is pertinent for many credit managers is the issue of leverage. The portfolio manager may be focused on the fund's level of leverage used, whether it is appropriate given the strategy, and whether the risk profile with the use of leverage is acceptable from an investment perspective. The ODD team, on the other hand, looks at different aspects of leverage use, such as the specific clauses in the prime brokerage agreement that may grant the leverage provider the right under some circumstances to liquidate the portfolio. The ODD team may also interview the fund manager's back office personnel to evaluate the quality of resources being dedicated to monitor compliance with the leverage facilities.

In addition, the ODD team may review the fund's policy when it comes to managing unencumbered cash. There are many dimensions to the operational risks involved in a portfolio; therefore, it is critical that a group is focused on the monitoring and mitigation of these risks.

Resources and Expertise

Given the degree of independence and power of decision making in the hands of the group, the ODD team needs to have the proper amount of dedicated resources. One of the key resources needed is time to dedicate to the process. From discussions with experienced ODD professionals, the initial ODD process on a potential hedge fund investment typically takes at least 100 man hours of intense, focused effort. The process may take significantly longer depending on the investment strategy and the complexity associated with the fund.

At the minimum, the ODD personnel need to do at least one on-site visit to the manager to focus on testing the back and middle office systems and internal procedures. More complex investment strategies and newer or emerging managers may require more than one on-site visit or a multiday visit with the hedge fund manager. Additionally, if the hedge fund uses a third-party provider that is not familiar or has not been vetted, a visit to the third-party provider may also be appropriate. The usage of well-known service providers alone is not a guarantee that the fund will not suffer from operational mistakes (i.e., it is a "necessary but not sufficient" condition).

In order to maximize the usefulness of an on-site visit, the visiting ODD team members will need to familiarize themselves with the fund and the fund manager prior to the visit. A significant amount of time may be required to analyze and review the fund's legal documents, policy and procedure manual, compliance manual, and other requested documents such as forms ADV Parts 2a and 2b (if the manager is SEC registered) and the AIMA due diligence questionnaire prior to the visit.

Furthermore, once the initial due diligence phase has been completed and the hedge fund manager has been approved for investment, the work is hardly over. The continuous changes in the industry necessitate ongoing monitoring, which is also time and resource intensive. If the investment was approved contingent on the hedge fund manager's commitment to making some changes and improvements to internal policies, ODD personnel need to ensure that the changes actually take place. Continuous monitoring of a hedge fund manager's progress and development is needed to keep up with the industry's best practices as well as natural changes with the fund. When significant operational changes take place, a reassessment of the hedge fund manager's operational soundness needs to take place and the original evaluation needs to be updated. In financial frauds, for example, the fund manager may not start with the intent to defraud investors but may do so to conceal trading losses from investors. Red flags may not have shown up in the initial operational due diligence but may be spotted later. Examples of periodic follow-up reviews include reviews of audited financial statements of the fund, completion and reviews of periodic questionnaires, subsequent on-site visits and testing, periodic calls, and in-person discussion with middle and back office personnel of the hedge fund.

Another important resource in an ODD program is in the form of the proper operational expertise. The team needs to be staffed with individuals who have the right level of experience and sufficient depth of knowledge in a wide range of operational issues. The key operational areas include pricing and valuation, hedge fund accounting, trading and settlement of various security types, financing methodologies, cash and collateral management, hedge fund compliance and regulation, trading and accounting system, prime brokerage, asset custody, and audit. Furthermore, the global nature of many hedge fund portfolios requires expertise in various geographic regions. Common practices, in addition to regulatory regimes, can vary significantly across the United States, Europe, and Asia. This often means that having people on the ground in these geographical areas may be important.

There are additional complexities associated with the operational side of credit hedge funds. For example, many credit hedge funds use leverage, which can be accessed via their prime brokers or other means such as a total return swap. ODD personnel need to understand the fund manager's monitoring process and steps that exist to ensure the fund remains in compliance with its financing terms. Take, for example, a credit hedge fund that invests in bank loans. The ODD personnel need to understand the operational complexities of investing in bank loans such as industry practices for trading and settling bank loans. Another example is credit hedge funds that invest in less liquid areas of credit, where knowledge of industry best practices about pricing and valuation is important. Many credit hedge funds also invest using credit derivatives such as credit default swaps, credit default indices, and options on credit default swaps (swaptions). The ODD personnel need to have the proper expertise on the trading and valuation on CDS to evaluate whether the hedge fund manager's back office is sufficiently capable of handling these instruments.

Furthermore, the Dodd-Frank Act of 2010 brings significant changes to the trading and clearing of credit derivatives. Investors in credit hedge funds need to understand how credit hedge funds will be affected by the new rules and whether the middle and back offices are prepared to deal with the changes.

Individuals who are certified accountants (CPAs in the United States and chartered accountants in other jurisdictions) are often the candidates with the proper experience in audit and accounting needed for these types of analysis. However, after our discussion on specific complexities, it is important to note that these individuals should have actual experience in evaluating or working in hedge funds.

Commitment to Transparency and Organizational Support

Strong due diligence programs operate on the maxim "Trust but verify." The ODD is no exception. Some of the largest frauds have gone unnoticed for a long time because investors have placed their trust in the hedge fund manager without verifying the information they were given, starting from the simple fact of verifying the existence of the assets in the fund. For example, in the Madoff fraud, an investor who contacted the auditor of the fund as part of an operational inquiry could have spotted several big red flags. First, an experienced ODD professional would have noticed that the auditor was virtually unheard of, and calls to a network of experienced operations professionals could have confirmed this. Furthermore, a call to the auditor would have revealed him as highly unqualified for the job, particularly given the size of the fund.

Another detailed point where transparency can give some insight into the fund is about the issue of expenses. Fund expenses are charged to the fund in addition to the management and incentive fees. The range of fund expenses can vary dramatically from fund to fund. There is currently no law or rule that defines acceptable versus unacceptable charges. However, without a detailed review of the documents, investors may be surprised to find out what they have been charged for. Some fund expense policies include employee salary to travel and entertainment expenses related to the marketing of the fund. Reading the fund's offering memorandum and the financial statements of the fund can give an idea as to what type of expenses are allowed to be charged to the fund and what are actually being charged to investors. To understand the full story behind fund expenses, the ODD personnel will need to request detailed expense information to tie out to the financial statement line items. Recently, the SEC announced that it is taking a closer look at the fees and expenses that hedge and private equity funds are charging to their investors.[2]

The ODD personnel's commitment to transparency has to be fully supported by their organization. This means that in some instances, the investor needs to be willing to walk away if there are serious disagreements on material issues. This is related to the earlier point about veto power, where the ODD team can vote to end the due diligence process if they are not able to have sufficient transparency to address serious operational concerns. It is also important to be sensitive to the hedge fund manager's need for confidentiality, and certain hedge fund managers may be sensitive about sharing information about their processes. At the very minimum, the ODD personnel need to be able to view certain documents and written procedures on-site and in person. That way, the existence of these documents can be verified and the ODD team can confirm certain claims made in the offering documentation. Some documents that should be transparent to the ODD team include fund agreements, reconciliation paperwork, trade documentation, valuation details and supporting documents, board minutes, and compliance manuals.

However, reading the written documents alone is not sufficient. Over time, the written manuals can also get outdated and need to be rewritten to better reflect changing practices of the hedge fund. In order to review the process and evaluate how the policies and procedures are put into practice, it is crucial that the ODD program incorporates testing as part of its pre- and postinvestment due diligence.

 Key Takeaway on the Importance of Testing

In order to "peel the onion," ODD personnel need to test the processes that the manager has put in place to understand how they are being put to work in the day-to-day activity of running the fund.

CURRENT HOT TOPICS IN OPERATIONAL DUE DILIGENCE
Pricing and Valuation

Investors rely on managers to calculate the value and performance of their investments. The fees that investors pay, mainly management and incentive fees, are charged based on the net asset value (NAV) of the investor capital. Many credit instruments are not exchange traded and trade only by appointment. Due to the lower liquidity in the credit market, it is even more important that the credit hedge fund manager have a well-documented and reasonable pricing valuation.

Pricing and valuation methodologies for exchange traded instruments are the most straightforward. Equities, equity options, index options, and other exchange traded options should be valued using this methodology, and third-party pricing is commonly obtained from data providers such as Bloomberg or Reuters. Over-the-counter (OTC) traded instruments such as many high yield bonds are typically priced using third-party data services such as Interactive Data Corp (IDC).

Credit derivatives such as swaps and swap indices (CDS and CDX) as well as bank loans are also typically priced using third-party data service such as Markit or Thomson Reuters Loan Pricing Corporation. When there is no recent trade, the manager may decide that the last closing price is "stale" and use more recent pricing information such as broker quotes. Bonds and loans that are not priced by third-party pricing services but are traded by broker-dealer desks typically are marked by broker quotes. Obtaining two to three broker quotes and taking the average is an example of a common practice. Common practices in the industry include marking long positions at the bid and marking short positions at the ask or marking long and short positions at the midpoint between the bid and ask. The latter is less conservative than the former; however, both are acceptable industry practices.

What investors should focus on is that the manager has a well-thought-out written pricing and valuation policy that is consistent with acceptable accounting standards (U.S. GAAP or IFRS) and that the policy is followed consistently. Beyond having a well-written policy, investors should also review the process to check that the policy is being followed. As part of their operational due diligence, investors should test how certain positions and trades are marked in the portfolio and review the pricing support of select trades. Over time, investors should conduct periodic follow-up price testing on positions as part of ongoing monitoring after the investment has been made. The best practice for a credit hedge fund manager is to have internal pricing and valuation procedures that reflect changes in the organization and investment strategies as the hedge fund evolves.

Some of the least liquid and most challenging instruments to value are post-reorganization equities, which distressed debt hedge funds typically receive as a result of their investment in fulcrum securities. Prior to the listing on the Pink Sheets or an IPO, the equity position is likely to be priced using the manager's internal models. In this case, typically managers will also periodically use a third-party valuation expert to assist them in evaluating the equity position. For these positions, there can be a wide range of reasonable valuation as a slight difference in performance assumptions and/or multiples used can translate into significant difference in value. For these positions, the emphasis on having a clear written valuation method that's followed consistently is particularly important.

 ## Key Takeaway on Valuation

The administrator may not provide valuation on all the positions in the fund. Ask your manager for situations where the administrator's pricing has been overridden and for supporting documents.

At each month end, the valuation for each position and the NAV of the fund as well as the supporting documents are received by the administrator for review and verification. The process for price verification for exchange traded positions such as equities or equity options and indices as well as futures is straightforward. The administrator can obtain pricing from third parties such as Bloomberg or Reuters. For positions that are valued via broker quotes or the manager's internal models, the administrator may rely on the documentation and pricing support provided by the manager.

 ## Key Takeaway on the Role of Administrator

Common pricing practice in the industry is for the administrator to follow the policy outlined in the fund documents. Two funds with the same administrator owning the same level 3 asset may have different pricing if the funds have different pricing policies per the fund offering memorandum.

Managing Counterparty Risk

Much of the assets that hedge fund managers invest on behalf of their investors are under the control of the fund's trading counterparties, such as prime brokers. After the Lehman 2008 bankruptcy and MF Global 2011 bankruptcy, investors are rightly placing much higher scrutiny on managers' counterparty risk mitigation and monitoring of their counterparty exposures. Having proper procedures to monitor and manage the fund's exposure to its counterparties is important to better safeguard clients' assets.

For credit hedge fund managers, the use of credit default swaps and total return swaps means that monitoring of swap counterparties is key in addition to monitoring prime brokers. One way that credit hedge fund managers try to mitigate exposure to a particular counterparty is by having multiple prime brokers and swap counterparties. Nonetheless, should one entity fail, investors may still be subjected to significant losses. There is no "right" number of prime brokers or swap counterparts. In practice, there is a business reality regarding the minimum account or usage required for a counterparty and the cost in time and labor required in having and monitoring multiple counterparties. At some point, there may be a declining marginal utility to having an additional counterparty due to the additional complexity and time required to monitor the counterparty relationship. Investors should focus on how managers are monitoring their various counterparty exposures, such as whether an operations professional can easily access the key terms of swap agreements instead of having to go through multiple ISDA agreements one by one. Additionally, an example of strong operational practice in this area requires an ex-ante plan by the manager should their counterparties be in imminent danger of failure. Another area to review is the manager's exposure relative to different divisions within the prime broker's overall organizational structure. For example, some managers who run a low leverage or unlevered portfolio may specifically choose to go with the U.S. prime brokerage instead of the U.K. unit.

Case Study: Centralized Clearing[3]

One of the important recent developments in the credit market is the regulatory push toward more transparency in the area of OTC derivatives trading. Market participants have pointed out that in the time surrounding Lehman, one of the greatest risks was the risk that arises from "gap risk," loss stemming the failure of a counterparty. Part of the system-wide panic rose from the difficulty in assessing Lehman's net liability to various counterparties in the banking system, and consequently, the amount of exposure of different banks to a Lehman failure.

The Dodd-Frank Act, which was passed by the U.S. Congress in 2009, mandated that more OTC derivatives trade on electronic venues (swap execution facilities, SEFs) and cleared through a clearinghouse (central counterparties, CCPs). This change will mandate that instead of having multiple counterparties in the OTC derivatives market, a CCP serves as the counterparty facing every trade—the seller for every buyer and the buyer to every seller.

The mandate to have derivative contracts be cleared by a well-capitalized entity (similar to existing practice in the futures industry) mitigates the risk of overall loss in the system should a trading counterparty fail to deliver on its swap obligation.[4] Some operational due diligence experts have pointed out that leading into the implementation phase of the new rules, there was a wide variation in hedge fund managers' estimation of the impact of these rules.[5] The impact will be in areas of how managers obtain leverage and manage collateral, where they trade, and the trading counterparties used as intermediaries in the process.

 Key Takeaways on Central Counterparties

There are multiple CCPs for different geographies, and they are competing entities with different coverage for different assets. Different asset coverage and margin requirement across CCPs add complexity to how a credit hedge fund manager manages cash.

Hedge fund managers need to consider how their day-to-day back office operations will be affected by the new regulations on central clearing. The additional complexity to trade flow is likely to add to operational risk unless the manager has a robust process in place. The manager may need to change internal workflow and processes to adapt to new clearing requirements. Implementation of mandatory clearing will be done in multiple stages starting in March 2013 ("Category 1") with broad-based credit default swap indices in North America and Europe as well as interest rate swaps for banks and active funds. Category 2 is in June 2013 for participants such as commodity pools and private funds. Category 3 is in September 2013 for entities that fall outside entities specified in Categories 1 and 2.[6]

Credit hedge fund managers need to make several important decisions regarding centralized clearing. First, they need to create the list of traded instruments eligible for central clearing. Credit hedge funds often trade a significant amount of credit derivatives, both synthetic credit indices, tranches of these indices, and single-name credit default swaps as well as some interest rate derivatives. Next, they would have to evaluate and select the appropriate intermediaries, the clearing broker or futures clearing merchant (FCM). After the selection is made, there is usually an extensive on-boarding process before live trading can commence. With each clearing broker, there will be a negotiation of terms and a set of documentation would need to be executed. Last, investors' operational due diligence would need to review the compatibility of the manager's systems (e.g., trade capture, accounting, risk, and portfolio management) with the various clearing brokers, FCMs, CCPs, and SEFs.

 Key Takeaway on Different Clearing Rules for Different Jurisdictions

Another complexity associated with central clearing is the differences in the rules adopted by different jurisdictions. For example, the U.S. and European regulators used different starting points as the basis of the new rules surrounding the central clearing of derivatives.

Managing and Controlling Cash

Cash management and control is tightly related to the posting and managing of collateral against trading counterparties. For credit hedge funds, ensuring that the fund has enough cash to meet margin requirements for swaps or prime brokerage (PB) margin call is an important part of sound investment policy. Furthermore, given the cyclical nature of the credit market, there will be times when credit hedge fund managers want to ensure that they have sufficient purchasing power ("dry powder") to capture market opportunities during periods of distress.

Additionally, cases of fraud often involve inappropriate or unauthorized transfer of client cash to an outside account. Managers should have a well-documented cash transfer and cash management policy. Cash wires should be approved by more than one signatory—for example, one can be a senior operation professional while the other is another senior member of the firm. In order to provide safeguard measures of cash while minimizing delays in sending wires, the number of authorized signatories should exceed the number of required signatures to release a wire. The administrator and prime brokers of the fund should be provided with a list of authorized signatories and preapproved counterparties.

Selection of Third-Party Providers

Similar to the discussion about prime brokers and trading counterparties, investors also are affected by the fund manager's selection of other service providers to the fund. The list of important service providers includes administrator, legal counsel, and fund auditors.

From comments given by various credit hedge funds, the quality of service from the top largest administrators tends to be comparable. The only caveat is that the quality of service with administrators in practice tends to vary widely with the person and team assigned to the fund at the administrator firm. If the hedge fund manager has strong operations personnel, it is highly likely that the CFO/COO or the controller would have significant experience working with hedge fund administrators and have very specific opinions as far as who they like to work with and why. Some reasonable questions from investors can include quality and timeliness of reports, responsiveness of the service team, and overall service quality. Given the breadth and complexity of the range of instruments utilized by some credit hedge fund managers, investors should ask the fund's operations professionals details on the administrator's expertise on credit instruments.

Furthermore, investors should inquire about the manager's selection process for third-party service providers. The most selective managers would narrow down the field into the top tier providers and systematically collect information on the quality of coverage and service by each service provider. Managers may do so via interviews or questionnaires. For example, they may test a PB by submitting a few randomly selected cash shorts and review the availability and cost of borrow of various PBs as well as the timeliness of the response.

 Key Questions on Service Providers

- Ask your manager about the selection process for the fund's service providers.
- Have they worked with this firm before?
- Have they worked with the specific professionals that will be servicing the account?
- What are some of the criteria that the manager used to make the selection?
- Can the manager show you their documentation of the interviews with the various service providers, which may include a questionnaire or a "scoring sheet" on various metrics.

Another important factor is having built-in redundancy when it comes to individuals responsible for specific steps. If there is only one trader, there needs to be a backup to cover trading responsibilities should the trader be out of the office due to vacation or illness. In certain strategies, if the portfolio manager has a trading background, he or she may be the backup person.

Another point about redundancy is whether the manager is replicating the work that's being done by the administrator. Some managers choose to go with the "gold standard"—the operations team of the manager performs daily reconciliation of the list of positions, realized and unrealized gains and losses, interest income and expense, as well as cash balances between the portfolio accounting system and the various trading counterparties. Here, it is important to use a portfolio accounting system that has the capabilities to allow the operations team to perform these reconciliations and is compatible with the portfolio accounting system used by the administrator.

 Key Takeaway on Systems

If the manager uses a system that is not widely compatible with those of trading counterparties or administrators, it may result in discrepancies and opens the door to human oversight or error. For example, some credit managers are trying to "fit a square peg into a round hole" by using equity-based systems on their credit portfolio, which may necessitate constant manual adjustments.

Regulatory Compliance

Compliance is defined as the manager's ability to operate within the set of rules and guidelines that have been set by the relevant regulatory bodies. It is one of the cornerstones of an effective ODD program. Financial service providers including hedge fund managers assume a tremendous number of responsibilities and duties when their investors decide to entrust them with the management of their capital. There is an important need for a set of rules and regulations to guide the manager's conduct and provide oversight on behalf of investors.

From investors' perspective, managers who can show that they are properly complying with the regulatory requirements provide investors with some degree of comfort that the managers are providing appropriate disclosure on their business practices and/or not behaving in ways that are reckless or unfair to investors.[7] Furthermore, when managers have a strong compliance culture, there is a reduced probability of headline risk. Headline risk may arise from news of compliance breach or problems that arise from managers trying to sweep a compliance breach "under the rug."

Key Questions on Compliance

- Who are the relevant regulators?
- Who are the individuals responsible for compliance? Whom do they report to?
- Is there an external compliance consultant? What is the extent of the external consultant involvement in day-to-day compliance monitoring? Is it appropriate?

Managers should have a clear and detailed compliance manual for their staff. This manual should include policies and procedures on important compliance areas including trade allocation, best execution, soft commissions, personal account dealing, and trade errors. This manual should provide enough guidance for the decision-making process of fund staff in day-to-day investing and fund management activities. However, a compliance manual alone is not enough. The manager also needs to show that there is a compliance monitoring program in place. Investors should see that internal procedures are being followed and that the controls put in place are sufficient and effective in protecting investors' interests.

Key Takeaways on Trade Allocation

A fair trade allocation process is key, particularly in capacity-constrained trades. A concern of investors, for example, is that the manager may allocate more of the opportunity to accounts where the trade has a higher probability of earning incentive fees for the manager.

Key Questions on Trade Allocation

- Ask managers for a written trade allocation procedure.
- Select a few trades and ask the operations personnel how these trades were allocated across accounts.

As part of the due diligence, investors should also ask the manager about significant contact and communications that manager has had with regulators as well as whether the fund has been subject to any formal inspections or investigations. Similarly, ask the manager if the fund has been required to make nonstandard disclosures to any regulatory body. As "trust but verify" is an important maxim for operational due diligence, a review of the correspondence and any other documents between the manager and the regulator is important to complete the picture.

 ### Key Takeaway on Regulatory Breaches

Any significant regulatory breach is generally part of public record. Investors should take care to review the firm's disciplinary history on regulators' websites as well as general searches for stories in the financial press.

Case Study: Expert Networks

An important aspect of compliance is ensuring that hedge fund managers have proper procedures and controls surrounding their use of expert networks. The idea is that managers should take proper care in avoiding the use of material nonpublic information in their trading and investing activities. In October 2009, insider trading became a front and center issue for regulators with the high-profile events related to the allegations aimed at the Galleon Group.[8] The SEC followed by issuing a series of subpoenas in November 2010 that put a deeper degree of scrutiny on the use of expert networks, consultants, and boutiques (collectively, "experts").[9]

There are a few things that hedge fund managers need to have in order to properly monitor their usage of experts. At a minimum, the manager should have a detailed set of written policies and procedures regarding use of experts and how to handle material nonpublic information. There should be a person or a group—a chief compliance officer (CCO) or compliance team—specifically tasked with approval and monitoring of experts used by the firm. This group or person should also review the contracts with the experts and the information received from the experts. As of the time of this writing, these practices (and beyond) have already been in place for many of the hedge fund managers who place value high compliance standards.

 Key Takeaways on Use of Expert Networks

Review of the information received from experts can include having the CCO or the compliance officer being present during conversations with experts. Alternatively, the conversations should be documented or recorded and the record should be available to the CCO or compliance officer for his or her review.

CONCLUSION

- As institutions entrust a larger slice of their collective capital in hedge funds, the concern about mitigating fraud and operational risk becomes of larger importance.
- The main goal of an operational due diligence program is to identify funds that are operationally weak.
- A high percentage of hedge fund failures were caused by operational factors, and investors are focused on minimizing the probability of investing in an operationally unsound hedge fund.
- Hedge fund investing is a resource-intensive effort, and detailed preinvestment due diligence and postinvestment monitoring are equally important.
- An effective operational due diligence program is supported by three key elements: independence, resources, and commitment to transparency.

CHAPTER 9

Risk Management

Risk management has taken on an increasingly important role for hedge fund investors, particularly after recent episodes of crisis where significant losses took place. After these events, investors are placing ever-greater emphasis on risk management and for very good reasons. Nonetheless, risk taking is a necessity and a fact of life for any investor who wishes to earn expected returns above the risk-free rate. A risk management approach that balances control and appropriate risk taking is the key.

Investors' risk management approach should focus on understanding the risks being taken in the portfolio, deciding whether the risks being taken are commensurate with the expected reward from taking such risks, and managing or hedging unacceptable risks. Investors in a credit hedge fund are exposed to risks stemming from the underlying investments and at the portfolio level. Risks stemming from the individual investment include default and mark-to-market risk, while the portfolio level is exposed to counterparty, leverage, and concentration risk. Compared to a long-only investment, investment in a credit hedge fund is less likely to be exposed to mainstream risk factors. Therefore, traditional risk measures such as duration and spread duration are less effective in capturing the true risk in a credit hedge fund. Investors in credit hedge funds should broaden their risk analysis to include particular risks in credit hedge funds.

This chapter will start with looking at how the risks in a credit hedge fund are different from the risks in an equity-oriented hedge fund or from the risks in a long-only credit portfolio. Next, we will discuss why the most popular analysis for evaluating any investment is particularly unsuitable for evaluating credit hedge funds. A discussion on the three different types of risks, "known known," "known unknown," and "unknown unknown," follows, and the chapter will close with discussions about some of the current topics in risk management.

RISK IN CREDIT HEDGE FUNDS VS. EQUITY HEDGE FUNDS AND LONG-ONLY CREDIT FUNDS

Many investors' introduction into hedge fund investing starts with long/short equity or equity-oriented hedge funds. Compared to equity-based hedge funds, credit hedge funds employ a wider array of instruments including a variety of credit and interest rate derivatives. Credit hedge funds often trade instruments that are traded over-the-counter or bespoke in nature, which present additional dimensions of risk to the investors. Analysis that can be done on equity return typically relies on the assumption of a lognormal distribution. The nonlinear nature of the payoff of credit instruments and the nonnormality of return distribution (mean and median are both positive, with a fat left tail) add another layer of complexity to the analysis.

Compared to long-only credit funds, credit hedge funds share a similarity in that they are both exposed to credit and default risk. However, by the virtue of not being tied to a particular benchmark, credit hedge funds have greater flexibility to venture into situations or borrowers that are more complex, less liquid, or smaller (both in size of issuer and issuance). This flexibility allows credit hedge funds to venture into situations that are overlooked by traditional credit investors. In addition, credit hedge funds also have the ability to employ both cash and derivatives to add short exposure to their portfolio. However, similar to a powerful engine, the flexible mandate has to be carefully monitored and managed to ensure that hedge fund managers are not investing in strategies that are outside their skill set or taking outsized risk in the "flavor of the month" trade (or both!).

Compared to long-only credit funds, the potential for higher leverage by credit hedge funds can magnify both the risk and return in the hedge fund portfolio. During economic downturns, fundamental deterioration increases, forward-looking default expectations increase, and there are lower recovery rates in the event of default. At the same time, risk appetite tends to decrease during the same period and investors demand much higher risk premium to bear the risk of holding risky assets. It is important to differentiate mark-to-market losses from actual losses. For bonds and loans that are "money good," selling the instrument during market lows will crystallize mark-to-market losses into real losses. It is worth noting, however, that leverage not only magnifies mark-to-market losses (as it magnifies mark-to-market gains) but may also increase the risk that the mark-to-market losses will be translated into actual or realized losses due to price-based triggers.

 Key Takeaways on Mark-to-Market Risk vs. Permanent Loss

When discussing risks with a credit hedge fund manager, investors should be specific whether it refers to permanent impairment of capital or mark-to-market risk. Be aware that in a volatile credit market, efforts to minimize mark-to-market risk can result in selling at or near market bottom, turning a mark-to-market loss into a permanent loss.

WHY TRADITIONAL RETURN-BASED ANALYSIS IS INSUFFICIENT

Traditionally, investors have placed significant reliance on historical returns. The returns are used to calculate correlation among funds and between each fund and broad benchmarks. The returns are also used to calculate historical return and risk, as measured by the standard deviation of return. These measures have been a large part of risk analysis for a long time, and they are popular for good reasons. After all, a return series is essentially what investors get when they entrust their assets to a hedge fund manager.

Investors have strongly demanded that returns be calculated by an independent administrator and audited by a reputable auditor. Return series are third-party verified numbers that investors can use to compare performance across managers and over time. Furthermore, in the past, return information has been more readily available to investors than other types of portfolio information. The analysis based on return is also simple to conduct, tends not to require expensive or complex risk systems, and most important, is intuitively easy to understand as well as to explain.

With return-based analysis, investors are using backward-looking information to make forward-looking expectations about the performance and risk profile of the fund. Hedge funds change their positioning over time, and the degree of the change can vary widely between funds or over time. One of the most attractive features of hedge funds is the flexibility and the freedom from some of the constraints of the traditional asset management world. For many investors, a flexible mandate to weather different market cycles is exactly what investors are looking for in hedge funds. Many credit hedge fund managers have the ability to invest in a wide range of asset classes up and down the capital structure, enabling them to benefit from wherever the opportunity lies. The managers may describe themselves as "event-driven" or "multistrategy credit." Regardless of the description in the marketing material, these hedge fund managers may have significant exposure to noncredit instruments. As these managers change their portfolio exposure over various market cycles, investors need to rely on more than historical returns alone to assess a fund's risk because the current risks in a hedge fund may be significantly different from the risks in the fund a year ago.

 Key Questions on Portfolio Risk

- How has the risk changed in the portfolio over the past few years?
- What are the most attractive opportunities currently, both on the long and the short side?
- What have you learned from the credit crisis of 2008?

Investors who have access to information beyond historical return analysis can access valuable additional information regarding the portfolio that may not be reflected in returns. With return-based analysis, it may be difficult to tease out the impact of separate risk factors in the portfolio because performance of different trades may cancel each other out. Return-based analysis is also often insufficient to separate luck from skill. Investors need further information such as detailed exposure or position-level information to gain additional insight when trying to form forward-looking risk expectations.

 ## Key Takeaways on Historical Return

Solely using historical return to make forward-looking investment decision is akin to driving forward while looking at the rear view mirror. It is also important to analyze how the portfolio is expected to perform going forward based on current risks in the portfolio.

Return-based analysis also tends to be insufficient for capturing idiosyncratic or event risk that many credit hedge fund managers are trying to capture. For example, a credit hedge fund manager may take a long position on a bond priced below par with the expectation that the issuer will shortly announce that it is about to be taken over and that this will trigger a change-of-control put. The bond would be taken out at par plus a premium. This trade relies on a hard catalyst to generate positive profit for the hedge fund manager. The main risk in this trade is the risk that the takeover will fail. The historical performance of the fund may have predictive quality of the success of this trade only if the past performance of the fund was generated based on similar strategy.

A long credit exposure has a payoff that is similar to selling a put. In the Merton model, bondholders have sold a put option to the firm. Investors in a firm's bank debt or bond receive coupon (akin to premium received by option sellers) in exchange for bearing the risk of loss should the value of the firm fall below its debt. Given the cyclical nature of default, the historical return stream may show steady positive numbers for an extended period of time, leading investors to underestimate

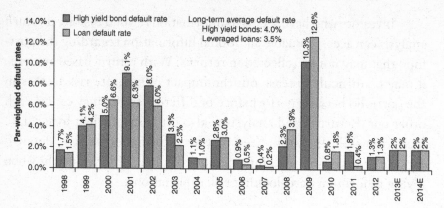

Figure 9.1 High yield bond and loan default rates
Source: JP Morgan

the risk of the investment. However, upon a dramatic move in credit spreads, either a very large spread widening or tightening, the fund may suffer a large amount of loss.

For credit hedge funds, past return can be highly misleading because default tends to be cyclical and there can be a long period of calm before another storm. Figure 9.1 shows the historical default rates for high yield bonds and bank loans. Credit hedge funds with a track record starting in 2003, for example, would have benefited from a long period when the default rate was either stable or declining. Based on historical return only, in 2006, an investor evaluating the credit hedge fund's three-year track record might have concluded that it was an extremely attractive investment, especially if the fund was highly levered and the short portfolio very small or nonexistent. However, historical return alone would not have reflected the extent of risk contained in this portfolio. Assuming the typical 6 to 12 months due diligence and on-boarding period, the investor would have bought into the fund only to shortly experience one of the worst crises in the history of the credit market.

The risk of using backward-looking historical return data to make forward-looking investment decisions is further heightened when there is significant concentration in the portfolio of lower quality credits with high coupon. Leading to the global credit crisis in 2008, many investors had been lulled by years of low default and easy credit availability. As a response to lower yield on credit, some credit hedge fund portfolios reached for yield by adding leverage to the portfolio or by having concentrated exposure in lower quality and less liquid credit. When the crisis hit, the lowest quality and less liquid credit were hit the hardest and investors saw losses beyond what they would have expected based on the historical track record.

Relative concentration and a show of conviction, up to a certain level, is desirable in hedge funds. However, understanding of the true nature of drivers of risk and return in the portfolio beyond simple return analysis can add tremendous value to investors in better managing their hedge fund investment.

 Key Questions on Concentration Risk

- How large are the top 5 or top 10 positions in the portfolio?
- What's the largest issuer in the portfolio, and how has the position size changed over time?
- Are there hard caps or guidelines on position or issuer size?

"KNOWN KNOWNS" AND "KNOWN UNKNOWNS"

> "There are known knowns; there are things we know we know. We also know there are known unknowns; that is to say we know there are some things we do not know. But there are also unknown unknowns—the ones we don't know we don't know."
>
> —*Donald Rumsfeld,*
> *DOD News Briefing, February 12, 2002*

There are three broad types of risks in a portfolio: "known knowns," "known unknowns," and "unknown unknowns."[1] The goal of a robust risk management program is to orient the portfolio's risk taking, not to completely eliminate risk from a portfolio. Known knowns are identifiable, measurable risks in the portfolio. These include common risk factors such as the risk of credit spread widening for small local moves. Known unknowns are identifiable risks with imperfect measurement due to an imperfect data set, the nature of the instrument, or human error. In this case, the error in measurement adds a degree of uncertainty. Examples would include credit risk in the event of large market moves and risk of illiquidity in a crisis. Unknown unknowns are risks that are not yet identified and are thus not measurable. An example of this would be how all the money printing by global central banks will affect the global credit market.

"Known Knowns"—Common Risk Factors in a Credit Hedge Fund

Credit hedge funds and long-only credit funds share common risk factors such as sensitivity to credit spread, interest rates, and equity market movement. Investors should expect their hedge fund investment to exhibit better return asymmetry (participate on the upside while limiting loss from default) and lower beta to both credit and equity market compared to the long-only portfolio.

The exposures to these risk factors are typically represented by credit spread duration, interest rate duration, and equity beta. As a quick reminder, modified duration is defined as the percentage change in the value of the instrument for a percentage change in interest rate or credit spread. A credit spread duration of 3.5 implies that for every basis point increase in credit spread, the value of the bond decreases by 3.5 basis points. Similarly, an interest rate duration of 3 implies that for every basis point increase in interest rate, the value of the bond decreases by 3 basis points. In some cases, for example with simple bonds with fixed coupon payments, duration can be computed using closed-form solution. Figure 9.2 shows the formulas for calculating duration.

 Key Questions on Measuring Credit Risk in the Portfolio

- Do you think spread or interest rate duration is useful to measure the risk in your credit portfolio?
- If not, why not?
- What is the current spread duration and rate duration of your portfolio?

$$Modified\ Duration = \dfrac{Macaulay\ Duration}{1 + \dfrac{Yield\ to\ Maturity}{Number\ of\ Coupon\ Periods\ per\ Year}}$$

$$Macaulay\ Duration = \sum_{t=1}^{n} \dfrac{(PV)(CF_t) \times t}{Market\ Price\ of\ Bond}$$

Figure 9.2 Duration formulas

Source: PAAMCO

Definitions:

$(PV)(CF_t)$ = Present value of coupon at period t

t = Time to each cash flow (in years)

n = Number of periods to maturity

 Key Takeaways on the Risk of Rising Rates

The portfolio manager of a long-only or long-biased credit portfolio used to focus on managing credit risk rather than interest rate risk. However, given rates at or near an all-time low, interest rate risk has now moved from secondary to primary importance. The longer the duration of the portfolio, the higher the interest rate risk.

The interest rate and credit spread duration for a portfolio of credit instruments is the weighted average of the duration of the individual instruments in the portfolio. Investors should keep in mind that the default option for many off-the-shelf risk tools is to assume parallel shift in the interest rate and credit curve when shocking the portfolio for losses. During periods of dramatic spread widening, the bonds with lower quality and longer tenor are likely to see greater negative impact than the high quality bonds with short time to maturity. Because duration is a linear measure that works best for small changes in interest rate and credit spread, scenario analysis may be more helpful to guide investors' expectation during dramatic spread widening environment.

Key Takeaways on Nonlinearity of Credit Instruments

Although linear risk factors such as equity beta capture the sensitivity of the portfolio for small market moves, investors should be cautious of extrapolating these numbers for large market moves given the nonlinear nature of the expected return of many credit instruments. During extreme market volatility, stress tests may be more helpful in illustrating the risks to the portfolio.

For many investors, the main risk in their portfolio is equity market risk. In order to diversify away from this risk, they turn to alternatives (including credit hedge funds) to generate return that is uncorrelated to the broader equity market. Given the increased interconnectivity between markets, the equity beta of a credit hedge fund portfolio is a basic, yet important, risk metric. However, equity beta alone is not a sufficient measure of risk in a credit hedge fund portfolio.

The beta between corporate credit instruments and the broad equity market, usually measured by the S&P 500, can increase dramatically during market dislocation. Right after a market dislocation, the beta of risky assets to the equity market may look alarmingly high. Taking an example of a high yield bond whose volatility relative to the S&P 500 does not change in a market dislocation compared to during a normal market, an increase in the bond's correlation to the equity market will lead to a 1-for–1 increase in its beta.

During market downturns, this phenomenon may be driven by an orthogonal factor such as investors' overall "risk-off" mentality. For example, during the credit crisis of 2008, there were days when the loan market moved almost on a lockstep basis with the equity market. Figure 9.3 shows the performance of the loan index (LSTA Total Return Index) versus the broad equity market (SP500 Total Return Index) in 2008.

2008 was widely regarded as a "black swan" event in the loan market. Figure 9.4 shows the historical short-term beta of the loan market to the equity market. The beta, previously zero, spiked up as correlation of risky assets went to one and there was nowhere to hide unless one sold risky assets and went whole hog into U.S. Treasuries. In

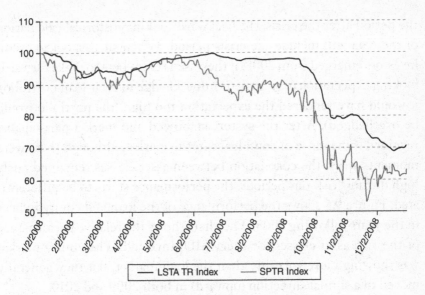

Figure 9.3   **Performance of loan vs. equity indices in 2008**
Source: PAAMCO, Bloomberg

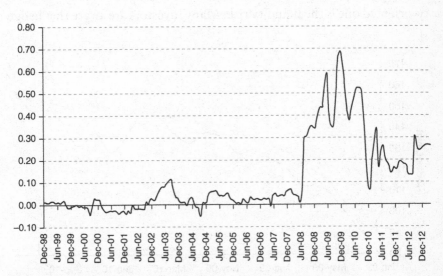

Figure 9.4   **Historical beta of the loan market to the equity market**
Source: PAAMCO, Bloomberg

the period after the crisis, the backward-looking historical calculation of the beta will include the crisis period. When shell-shocked credit investors emerged from 2008, if they used recent beta to make forward-looking expectation (e.g., to determine a hedge to their loan portfolio), it would have rendered the expectation too high (the portfolio would be overhedged). After the system stabilized and market participants regained some sense of confidence in the market, although there were moments when the correlation between asset classes remained fairly high during "risk-on" periods, the performance starts to be differentiated. Figure 9.5 shows the performance of the loan and equity indices in the years following 2008. The chart shows the relative performance of the two asset classes for every $100 invested. The equity market was showing more volatility than the loan market, but they generally moved in a similar direction (upward) in both 2009 and 2010.

"Known Unknowns"—Liquidity Risk

One of the key risks that differentiate a credit hedge fund from an equity-oriented one is the liquidity risk. Many investors are aware that hedge

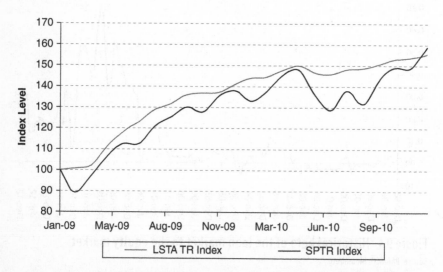

Figure 9.5 Performance of the loan and equity markets in 2009 and 2010
Source: PAAMCO, Bloomberg

funds may invest in off-the-run bonds or other opportunities that tend to be less liquid than public equity, government bonds, or large liquid bonds. However, the extent of the difference in liquidity between good and bad market is difficult to measure, making it a "known unknown." The market structure in the corporate credit market affects the liquidity of many high yield bonds and loans. Unlike exchange-traded public equities, many corporate credit instruments are privately traded on the over-the-counter (OTC) market. Exchanges provide a centralized place for buyers and sellers to meet, as opposed to having dispersed meeting points leading to a more fragmented market. The lack of a centralized marketplace where buyers and sellers come together makes it difficult to measure liquidity. The fact that most of the secondary trading occurs on the OTC market also means that liquidity in the corporate credit market, particularly the sub-investment grade market, is fairly fragmented with specialized pockets of liquidity. Credit hedge funds also may extensively use credit derivatives, which until recently have not been cleared on a clearinghouse. Post Dodd-Frank reform, the majority of credit derivatives swap indices will be cleared on clearinghouses. Also known as central counterparties (CCP), clearinghouses serve as a counterparty to every trader, which, combined with netting and margining requirement, greatly mitigates counterparty risk and improves liquidity.

Historically, dealer desks provided significant liquidity in secondary trading of credit instruments. However, the significant shrinking of sell-side balance sheets that followed the 2008 credit crisis combined with regulatory changes as part of the Dodd-Frank rule meant that banks' role had dramatically changed from risk-taker to agent. The lack of trading and research sponsorship from investment banks combined with an absence of marginal buyers during "risk-off" periods can translate into a secondary market with greater liquidity and volatility risk. Figure 9.6 shows the drop in capital committed by dealers over time. Combine this reduction in the amount of dealer balance sheet (the "shock absorber" in the market) and the increase in the size of the leveraged corporate bond market over time, and investors can expect increased volatility in corporate bond spreads.

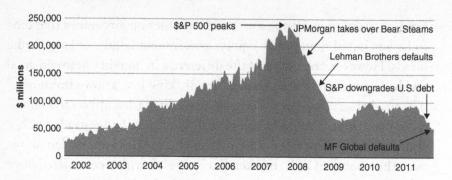

Figure 9.6 Dealer corporate bond holdings with greater than one-year maturity
Source: Bloomberg

For any hedge fund, the liquidity profile of the fund needs to reflect the liquidity profile of the underlying investments. Many credit hedge funds tend to have a less frequent redemption period or longer notice period relative to public equity-based strategies (long/short equity or statistical arbitrage). Investors are also more likely to find investor- or fund-level gates with credit hedge funds. Simple ways to manage liquidity risk include guidelines on maximum size at position level as a percentage of the issuance or limiting exposure to smaller issuances and smaller issues (for example, some hedge funds limit themselves only to issuers with capital structure larger than $500 million). The liquidity in the credit market tends to be good when the market is on its way up and poor to nonexistent on the way down.

 Key Takeaway on Liquidity Risk

Investors should consider the trade-off between flexibility to invest in smaller, less liquid or niche opportunities and the liquidity risk in a portfolio.

 Key Questions on Liquidity Risk

- How long do you expect to take to liquidate the entire portfolio under normal circumstances? Under stressed scenarios?
- What measures do you use to monitor the liquidity of your portfolio?

During periods of market dislocation, which often coincide with a spike in investor redemption, it may be necessary for funds to separate illiquid assets into side pockets and/or to spread the sale of assets across multiple periods. In this scenario, redeeming investors may find themselves with lower or less immediate proceeds than expected. In this sense, liquidity is one aspect where credit hedge funds significantly differ from hedge funds that traffic in public equities (with perhaps only the exception of micro-cap equities) where the liquidity in the secondary market for equities is largely reliable, even if it comes at a price. The liquidity profile of the secondary market for credit has been described by credit professionals as "it's there until it's not" or "only there when you don't need it."

 ## Key Takeaways on Modeling Liquidity Risk

Liquidity for credit instruments is notoriously difficult to model before the fact (ex-ante). The OTC market translates into a liquidity that can be defined as "it's there until it's not." Size of issuance, ownership as percent of issuance, and the number of active dealers trafficking in the name are some of the liquidity proxies commonly used. Investors should also ask their credit manager about the time required to liquidate the portfolio during normal and stress scenarios.

 ## Key Takeaways on Stop Losses as a Risk Management Technique

Stop losses are more difficult to implement and less effective as a risk management tool for less liquid credit due to higher mark-to-market volatility and wider bid-ask spread.

"Known Unknowns"—Event Risk

Credit hedge funds are often thought of as a specific subset of event-driven investing because identifying a specific catalyst such as bond-for-loan takeout or expected default is a key part of the investment thesis for many credit hedge fund managers. However, the risk is that the event does not materialize and that, at one end of the spectrum, there is opportunity cost to capital (the investment is "dead money"). On another end of the risk spectrum, there is the risk that a negative credit event (such as default) that was unforeseen by the manager may take place.

Hedge funds are best suited to take idiosyncratic rather than systematic risk—alpha, not beta. By definition, idiosyncratic risks of a particular investment, such as complexity or process risk, are unique and largely situational. The extent of these risks is highly dependent on current market condition. In a bullish credit market, everything moves up in price, and credit hedge funds that have short position based on particular events may see losses regardless of being right on the event. Investors need to be cognizant that event risk is difficult to model and that the results are highly dependent on the assumptions used in the model.

At the far end of the event spectrum is distressed debt investing. By definition, hedge funds that invest in borrowers who are entering into or are in the restructuring process are heavily exposed to event risk. Developments such as a decision of the bankruptcy court or the ability to obtain financing greatly influence the potential outcome of the investment. The idiosyncratic risks such as an adverse ruling by the court or the financing market shutting down are not going to be captured by a risk model. Estimating the size of the directional risk in a distressed debt portfolio is also particularly challenging. Investors may experience a "kink" in the beta of a distressed debt position. A distressed company's performance may show only moderate equity market beta in a bull market but high equity market beta in a bear market. Although in medium-term distressed debt investors benefit from a healthy equity market, company-specific factors (e.g., the need to replace management) are likely to be the key drivers of performance in the short term. In a bearish equity market, capital may flee from complex situations or less than pristine borrowers (both of which can be found aplenty in distressed situations), resulting in disproportional losses compared to the overall market.

Key Questions on Modeling the Risks of a Distressed Portfolio

- How do you model the distressed positions in your portfolio? Distressed managers are, by definition, investing in idiosyncratic risks, which are difficult to map.
- Are there any positions that are modeled using a proxy in the risk model?
- When the fulcrum security is turned into equities, what is your view on the directional equity risk of this exposure? Do you think it makes sense to hedge that risk?

Furthermore, when the credit quality of the investment deteriorates, there is also the risk of increased illiquidity for the name. Credit hedge funds, particularly those with a value-oriented approach, face the risk that should they find themselves on the wrong side of the trade when an expected event does not take place, exiting the position may be difficult or very costly. For example, say the credit hedge fund manager entered into a bond at 90, expecting the bond to be called at par. However, new negative information regarding the borrower has surfaced, and not only has the market shut down the possibility of rolling the bond into a new issuance (and enabling calling the bond at par) but the price of the bond is quickly slipping into the 40s. A loan or bond trading at 90 trades very differently than the same instrument when it is trading at 40. Liquidity will be lower at 40, which translates into wider bid-ask, and possibly the bond may only trade by appointment at 40.

 Key Takeaway on the Volatility of Lower Priced Credit Instruments

Lower priced corporate loans and bonds are usually more volatile. When evaluating the portfolio of a credit hedge fund, ask for the weighted average price of instruments for both the long and short portfolio.

"Known Unknowns"—Basis Risk

Using the size of the exposure to various risk buckets, investors in a credit hedge fund can determine the risk factors to which they are likely to be exposed. A second step is to model the risks in the portfolio. For a credit hedge fund, this can be quite complex given the range of the instruments and the difficulty in modeling basis risk. Basis risk is the risk that the price of a short position designed as hedge does not move as expected when the long position declines in value.

Basis risk can arise because of the inherent positioning of the portfolio (it's always been in the portfolio, but the investor was not aware of it), or because of technical factors. An example of the first scenario is that when the short credit portfolio is similar in market value to the long credit portfolio, an investor looking at the portfolio may falsely conclude that the portfolio is neutrally positioned against credit spread widening. A simplistic risk analysis assuming a parallel spread increase (i.e., the same amount of spread increase [e.g., 100 bps] for both investment grade and high yield credit) would further support this false conclusion. Nonetheless, if the short portfolio consists of investment grade shorts while the long portfolio consists of high yield bonds, the portfolio will suffer losses in a spread widening event because the spread widening is not likely to be parallel across the credit curve. In other words, lower quality bonds such as high yield bonds will experience greater spread widening than high quality or investment grade bonds.

Even when investors are well aware of this risk, it is difficult to predict accurately how much high yield spread will rise for every basis point rise in investment grade spread. It is made more complex by the fact that the beta of high yield spread to investment grade spread is likely not to be linear. This is to say, in a normal market condition, the spread of high yield bonds may rise and fall along with the spread of investment grade bonds. However, in a market downturn, high yield bond spread is likely to rise at a multiple to the rise in investment grade bonds. In a "flight-to-safety" scenario, high yield bonds may see a rise in spreads as investment grade bonds see spread tightening. This scenario will result in losses in both the long and short portfolios of a credit hedge fund that hedges its long high yield portfolio with investment grade short positions.

Key Takeaway on False "Risk Neutral" Claims

A portfolio with risky long positions hedged with an investment grade index may look neutral on net exposure basis, but it is not neutral to credit spread risk—it will lose money when credit spread widens.

An example of the second scenario is when the CDX HY index is used to hedge a long portfolio of high yield cash bonds. Even when the long portfolio consists of cash bonds of every issuer in the CDX HY index, a credit hedge fund is still exposed to the risk of incurring losses in both its long and short portfolio. This is known as the cash-synthetic basis. This is calculated as the spread of the credit derivatives (CDS, CDX) minus the spread of the cash bonds. When credit derivatives spread stays flat or narrows while the spread cash widens, the basis "widens" (becomes more negative).[2] This can be caused by technical factors, such as if there is selling pressure on the cash bonds accompanied by the sellers taking off their CDS hedge.

Another type of basis risk exists when a long portfolio of cash bonds is hedged with CDS or CDX.[3] The price fluctuation in cash bonds can come from both the fluctuation in risk-free rates and credit spread. In contrast, the pricing of credit derivatives is based on credit spread, not risk-free rates. In the past, credit hedge fund managers spent most of their time worrying about their exposure to credit risk, not interest rate. In an environment with very low interest rates and yield, however, credit hedge fund managers are now also exposed to rate risk on their long portfolio. A credit hedge fund hedging its cash longs with buying protection via CDS on equal notional amount is not neutrally positioned to interest rate moves but has a long exposure to interest rate instead.

 ## Key Portfolio on Hedging Interest Rate Risk

A credit portfolio where the long side consists of cash instruments and the short side consists of synthetic instruments is taking interest rate risk. Just because the net exposure of the credit is neutral or low, do not assume that the portfolio is hedged against interest rate risk.

IMPROVING THE MODELING OF THE "KNOWN KNOWNS"

There are several ways to improve the modeling of the "known knowns" of risk in credit hedge fund investment.

Accounting for the Short Portfolio

The first measurement an investor should look at is the sizes of the long and short portfolios separately, and measure them as a percentage of net asset value (NAV). For many cash instruments such as loans, bonds, and equities, the measurement of exposure is fairly straightforward: by the market value of the instruments. For long positions in certain derivatives such as futures, forwards, swaps (including credit default swaps), and contracts for differences (CFDs), the common market practice is to report the market value adjusted notional. This is defined as notional amount of the contract, adjusted for the mark-to-market value of the contract. For example, an investor bought $1 million notional worth of T-bill futures. When the interest rate falls and T-bill price rises, the investor sees $10,000 mark-to-market profit on the swap. The market value adjusted notional amount is $1,010,000 ($1,000,000 + $10,000). Here, the logic is similar to that of the exposure measurement for cash instruments; the market value adjusted notional amount represents the true economic exposure of the contracts. The theoretical maximum that an investor who bought the futures could have lost is the sum of the notional amount adjusted by the mark-to-market gains or losses.[4]

Synthetic hedges tend to be measured by mark-to-market adjusted notionals because the measurement is easy to understand and is the more conservative way of reporting the exposure. However, it tends to overstate the amount of the short exposure. For example, let's assume Investor A wants to obtain short exposure to the credit market and chooses to do so by buying five-year protection on the CDX IG. The index is currently trading at par, and the annual coupon is 1 percent. If Investor A is buying protection on $100 million of the index, then Investor A is said to have $100 million worth of "notional." If no credit event happens during the five-year period of the CDX contract, then this investor's maximum expected loss at any given point is the present value of the future premium payments.

This point is an important one, because when an investor has $100 million long exposure to an index, the maximum loss is $100 million. However, in the example given above, having $100 million short exposure to the index does not imply that the maximum loss is $100 million. At the beginning of the contract, his largest risk is that nothing happens and his maximum loss is the future sum of unpaid premium, discounted using a LIBOR/swap curve for the applicable currency.[5] The maximum loss is the present value of $1 million annual coupon times five years. However, during the life of the contract, the investor bears mark-to-market risk; if the market yield for the index goes below 1 percent ("tightens" below 100 bps in market parlance), then there will be a mark-to-market that the short investor needs to meet, and this potential cash requirement needs to be accounted for.[6]

Payment-in-Kind Feature

When a bond has a payment-in-kind feature, investors may see the price of the bond increase to reflect the accrued coupon. Certain models may interpret this as an increase in value; the investment seems less risky (because it went up in price), but it's actually riskier because there is more capital at risk.

 Key Questions on Instruments With Payment-in-Kind Feature

- How much of the exposure in the portfolio is to bonds with payment-in-kind (PIK) feature?
- How much of the NAV is from PIK interest?
- How are PIKs accounted for in the portfolio, and is the PIK amount included in calculating fees paid by investors?

"UNKNOWN UNKNOWNS"—DEALING WITH THE EXTRAORDINARY

When dealing with "unknown unknowns," the first step is to understand the true purpose of your risk management program. A risk management system is not a panacea against all possible risks to investments in a credit hedge fund. Indeed, even for risks that are known and measurable, investors can still suffer losses if the manager decides to take that risk and the market moved against him or her.[7] When dealing with unknown and immeasurable risks ("unknown unknowns"), close and active monitoring of the market and the portfolio as well as astute management of leverage are some of the tools in the investors' toolbox.

Here, we will discuss some of the areas where certain assumptions that are necessary in risk modeling highlight the challenges in modeling the risks in particular parts of the credit market. For example, because of their maturity and callability profile, corporate bonds have finite lives (a particular bond is issued and eventually redeemed or called), unlike equity, which has a perpetual lifespan. Thus, when analyzing the sensitivity of a particular bond to changes in interest rate and credit spread over time, there may not be enough historical information on which to base this analysis. A common methodology used by many risk systems is to "map" each particular loan and bond to a particular bond curve. In short, the mapping process simply means that instead of using the past performance of that particular bond, it is proxied by a basket of instruments with similar features such as rating. The system then looks at the past performance of the proxy basket and tests this past performance against various risk factors.

 Key Takeaways on the Limits of Risk Models

A risk management exercise worth doing is to focus on how the manager expects these positions to behave "out of model"—how it will actually behave in a current crisis compared to predefined stress tests. Before coming to visit credit managers, spend a few days to research some of their niche or idiosyncratic positions.

The mapping process is important because the default curve of the risk management software may not be the correct one, and incorrect mapping can lead to overstating or understating of risk. For example, a typical mapping for a bank loan was by price—a loan would be mapped to either the par or the distressed curve. The distressed curve is made up of loans priced below 80 cents on the dollar. The typical default option for most bank loans prior to the credit crisis was to map their loan portfolio to the par curve. During the 2008 credit crisis, not many loans were priced above 80; in fact, at one point, anecdotally there were only three loans in the entire institutional loan universe priced above 80. Given the severity of the price decline of almost the entire loan universe, then the par curve was made up only of very few loans and therefore was not representative of the risks in a typical loan portfolio.

In fact, in the months leading to the peak of the crisis in 2008, despite the extreme volatility seen in late 2007, the par curve barely moved, implying that bank loans would not see much price change during the crisis, which was clearly incorrect. In order to fix this error, an investor would need to use a bespoke curve, one that would better represent the market volatility seen in the loan market. This implies that investors need to have the expertise to narrow down the potential curves, understand the risks contained in the portfolio on a forward-looking basis, and select one curve that best represents the risk in their loan portfolio. Whether the risk modeling and analytics is done by the investor or by the asset manager, proper selection of the curves and interpretation of the results needs to be based on knowledge of the underlying investments in the portfolio and an understanding of the real risk drivers of those investments.

 ## Key Takeaways on Shortcomings of Credit Risk Models

Watch out for basis risk between an instrument and its proxy. In order to get a long period of historical data, fixed-income instruments are usually mapped to a particular bucket. For example, the risk of a particular B-rated bond is mapped to a basket of B-rated bonds. However, if the issuer of the bond in the portfolio is smaller than the average bond in the basket, it may be affected more heavily in a scenario of economic downturn and the basket may not sufficiently capture the risk of the bond being modeled.

REAL-LIFE LESSONS FOR MANAGING THE RISKS IN CREDIT HEDGE FUND INVESTING

Following are some principles for dealing with risks in credit hedge fund investing.

No Risk Management Theory or System Can Replace Human Insight

The hedge fund structure targets alpha rather than market or beta risk, meaning that the structure emphasizes taking idiosyncratic risk by design. Overreliance on models and historical data should be avoided when looking at hedge fund portfolios. In hedge fund portfolios, many of the risk factors are difficult to quantify and predict with a high amount of certainty. The liquidity and risk/reward feature of corporate fixed-income instruments often compound this challenge. During periods of market crisis, investors were unpleasantly surprised to find larger exposures to risk as well as unexpected risks in the portfolio when large losses happened and/or they faced suspension due to the illiquidity of the underlying investments. In addition to quantitative analysis based on historical returns such as correlations and beta, investors are also asking more specific qualitative questions about the nature of the underlying positions in each credit hedge fund portfolio and the risks associated with these investments. Among other things, investors wish to know if they can detect signs of overconcentration of a particular type of risk or excessive leverage in the portfolio.

 Key Takeaways on Risk Models

Credit instruments are more difficult to model than equity instruments. Modeling the risk of credit instruments may involve a greater degree of complexity to capture features such as convexity. Investors should keep in mind that a complex, shiny risk engine should not distract from the intuitive understanding of what the models are trying to do and the limitations of modeling.

There Are Trade-offs Between Flexibility and Security

Much of the discussion has been focused on having proper procedures and adherence to procedures in practice. However, if investors believe that one of the most attractive features of the hedge fund structure is its investment flexibility, then the important question is, what is the appropriate balance of guidelines that allow for risk mitigation and sufficient flexibility to let the fund adapt to different market environments? Limits that may work with other strategies may not be appropriate for a credit hedge fund. For example, stop-losses work very well with CTAs and actually can limit the fund from incurring greater losses, thus benefiting the investors. With credit hedge funds, when liquidity in the market dries up, certain bonds and loans can see a big drop in value even when the creditworthiness of the borrower remains intact (the investor is still just as likely to receive interest and principal payment as before). In this scenario, a hard stop-loss limit may be a way to ensure that a mark-to-market loss is crystallized into an actual loss.

Buy vs. Make

Investors with a large amount of capital may find it economical to invest in a risk system. The next question becomes whether it makes more sense to buy or build such a system in-house. For most institutional investors, even the largest ones, buying an off-the-shelf system is a more attractive proposition from the cost perspective compared to having to build an in-house system from scratch. Nonetheless, software purchase cost is only one part of the total cost investors need to consider.

One of the options is for investors to request that their hedge fund managers upload their portfolios into an off-the-shelf system selected by the investor. When deciding which off-the-shelf systems provider to go with, it is important to keep compatibility in mind. Different asset managers will be requested to upload their portfolios to a system, and if the manager has a high degree of familiarity with a chosen system (whether because it's the system the manager uses in-house for its own risk management or because it has uploaded a portfolio to the same system for a different investor), the investors can expect a higher degree of adoption of the risk system across managers as well as potentially better, more refined modeling of the complexities in uploaded portfolios. In this case, the investors still need to ensure that the managers are providing the system with enough and accurate information, that the bucketing that the investors chose was appropriate for the types of underlying investments in their hedge fund portfolios, that positions are being modeled appropriately, and that the methodology and process are consistent over time.

Cross-sectionally, investors also need to ensure that definitions and methodology are being consistently followed by different fund managers in the portfolio. The monitoring process may require dedicated staff who are familiar with the funds' investments, as errors in data may be spotted through counterintuitive results produced by the risk system.

Counterintuitively, the cost of the software is not necessarily positively correlated with the usefulness of the software to the investor, and in certain cases, buying a big, complex risk system may have the opposite result than intended. First, large, sophisticated risk systems with a long list of bells and whistles tend to be more complex to learn and operate, and new users have to overcome a higher, steeper learning curve. Second, these systems may also be more complex to operate and may require staff with programming experience to maintain. Third, having access to a sophisticated system may create a false sense of security, which can be particularly dangerous especially when combined with the two previous factors. Complex systems, combined with a complex credit hedge fund portfolio, often require heavy user involvement and are unlikely to be simple plug-and-play systems. When considering the purchase of a risk system, investors should consider the costs beyond the purchase cost. The cost of an effective risk management program includes the cost of dedicated human resources and expertise necessary to monitor the input, operate the system, interpret the results, and recommend proper courses of action.

CONCLUSION

- Credit hedge funds are exposed to different risks than equity hedge funds and traditional long-only credit investments. Thus, the traditional risk modeling techniques that are effective for the latter are likely to be insufficient for the former.
- The cyclical nature of credit default means that investors need to take particular care when using historical data to make forward-looking investment decisions.
- In the past, credit (default) risk is the main risk in a credit hedge fund portfolio. After three decades of tightening of interest rates, we are entering a brave new world where many credit hedge fund portfolios have to contend with significant interest rate risk.
- When assessing the risk of a credit portfolio, nonlinearity of many risk parameters means that many risk measures need to come with significant caveats. This makes traditional risk management techniques such as hedging and stop losses less reliable for credit than for exchange traded instruments.
- Investors also need to be aware that the "degree of confidence" in models should be lower than that for publicly traded equities. Many risk parameters, such as liquidity risk, are difficult to model with reasonable accuracy.

CHAPTER 10

Financing

In this chapter, we will discuss the various options available to credit hedge funds to use leverage as part of their investment program. The practice of using leverage to enhance the return from various asset classes is a feature that has been popular with many investors in hedge funds. If one of the attractive features of a hedge fund structure is greater flexibility in the use of leverage, it is prudent to understand how this flexibility works not just in good but also in difficult times.

When asset prices fall, many investors are aware that the leverage will magnify the losses. However, that is not the only risk inherent in leverage. Whether the investor obtains leverage via explicit borrowing or through inherently levered instruments, a hedge fund is exposed to other risks such as the credit risk of its counterparty. Furthermore, in the scenario of borrowing funds to obtain leverage, a credit hedge fund, just like an individual investor who buys stock on margin, has a heightened risk of having to sell assets during a market downturn and thus crystallize losses.

A judicious use of leverage can help investors achieve better expected return if the tail risks inherent in the use of leverage are mitigated. Compared to their long-only brethren, credit hedge funds have the ability to use a greater amount of leverage and go short. Shorting, whether through a prime brokerage account or use of synthetic credit instruments, also introduces leverage to the portfolio. This chapter is intended to help credit hedge fund investors better understand the potential risks associated with the use of leverage in their credit hedge fund investment.

BASICS OF FINANCING

We will begin with the basics: the reasons for using financing and the reasons for providing leverage.

Reasons for Using Financing

Credit hedge funds utilize leverage to enhance their return profile. The broadest definition of leverage is when investors obtain risk exposure that's greater than the amount of capital they have at hand. In other words, if a credit hedge fund has $100 in net asset value but $220 of exposure to high yield bonds, the portfolio is levered by 2.2×.[1] In this example, investors can obtain leverage either by borrowing $120 ("explicit" leverage) or by using a structurally levered instrument ("implicit" leverage) such as taking a long position via an unfunded or partially funded swap with $220 of notional value and holding on to the excess cash.

   In practice, credit hedge fund managers use both explicit and implicit leverage on both the long and short portfolios. Hedge funds explicitly borrow funds from their prime brokers. The borrowing is collateralized by the assets in the prime brokerage accounts. Instruments such as credit default swaps allow credit hedge fund managers to obtain a short credit exposure by buying credit protection or a long credit exposure via selling protection. Repurchase agreements are another instrument for borrowing funds, while reverse repurchase agreements are used to short a bond.

 Key Takeaways on Financing

Many investors intuitively seek the cheapest financing. However, investors should not focus solely on managers with the least expensive financing. Financing providers may offer cheaper financing in exchange for stricter and less flexible covenants.

The following figure illustrates the principle that using leverage can both enhance returns and compound losses when returns do not exceed the cost of funding. In the first scenario in Figure 10.1, we assume a high yield bond portfolio that earns 5 percent return on an unlevered basis and 2 percent cost of financing per every dollar borrowed. In this scenario, the levered investor earns 8.6 percent return. Leverage, however, is a double-edged sword. In a second scenario, if the high yield bond portfolio earns 0 percent return (less than the cost of borrowing), the levered investor loses 2.4 percent. In this case, the levered portfolio underperforms an unlevered portfolio. As long as the return of the asset exceeds the cost of financing, a leveraged investment will earn a higher rate of return than an unlevered investment. Figure 10.1 compares the return of the levered versus unlevered portfolio for both scenarios.

	Unlevered	Levered
NAV	$100	$100
Long Exposure	$100	$220
Financed Amount	$0	$120
Leverage	1	2.2

Scenario 1: Asset Return > Cost of Financing

	Unlevered	Levered
Return on unlevered asset	5%	
Cost per $ of Financing	2%	

	Unlevered	Levered
Portfolio Return Gross of Financing Cost	5%	11%
Cost of Financing	0.0%	2.4%
Portfolio Return Net of Financing Cost	5.0%	8.6%

Scenario 2: Asset Return > Cost of Financing

	Unlevered	Levered
Return on unlevered asset	0%	
Cost per $ of Financing	2%	

	Unlevered	Levered
Portfolio Return Gross of Financing Cost	0%	0%
Cost of Financing	0.0%	2.4%
Portfolio Return Net of Financing Cost	0.0%	-2.4%

Figure 10.1 Comparison of levered and unlevered portfolios based on different asset returns

Source: PAAMCO

Figure 10.1 shows how leverage has a multiplier effect to investors' return. The basic rules about leverage apply regardless of the method used to obtain leverage. Effectively, leverage increases the portfolio's sensitivity to risk factors such as interest rate and credit spread risk by the factor of the leverage. In the example above, assume the high yield bond portfolio has a sensitivity to interest rate change (duration) of 3 on an unlevered basis. The levered portfolio has a duration of 6.6 (leverage amount multipled by the duration of the unlevered portfolio equals the duration of the levered portfolio). For every basis point increase in interest rate, the unlevered portfolio is expected to lose 3 bps (duration of 3 multiplied by 1 bp increase in interest rate) while the levered portfolio is expected to lose 6.6 bps (duration of 6.6 multiplied by 1 bp increase in interest rate).

 ### Key Takeaways on the "Right" Amount of Leverage

The right amount of leverage (which can be none) depends on the volatility of the instruments and the terms of the leverage, not the expected arbitrage profit. Increasing leverage when arbitrage profit narrows in order to reach a target return is a very risky strategy.

 ### Key Takeaways on How Mark-to-Market Loss Becomes Actual Loss

The risk of leverage is in its ability to turn mark-to-market loss into actual and permanent loss of capital. Term financing, cure provision, and non-mark-to-market are features that mitigate this risk.

Reasons for Providing Leverage

In the case of explicit borrowing, the providers of financing earn profit from the cost of funding arbitrage. Institutions with lower cost of funding such as commercial and investment banks can obtain cheaper financing in the market (typically at close to LIBOR or even at LIBOR minus basis) and then lend the funds out at LIBOR plus a spread. The difference in the spread is income for the bank, and lending to hedge funds is an important source of revenue for the banks. The spread earned by banks when lending to hedge funds is higher than what they can earn on similar collateralized loans to investment grade–rated institutions such as insurance companies and other banks, which reflects some of the risks of lending to hedge funds. The question of "how risky is a hedge fund" is the 64-million-dollar question (and the raison d'être for this book). Funding providers to hedge funds such as banks and swap dealers developed a process in measuring and mitigating the risks of their hedge fund exposure.

Some of the risk mitigation techniques that banks have adopted in their funding of hedge funds include margin requirement (a cap on leverage), periodic mark-to-market on the portfolio, and periodic margin call. The financing agreement has specific details on the types of assets allowed as collateral depending on certain metrics such as rating (proxy of credit quality) and size of issuance (proxy of liquidity). The financing providers also would specify a degree of diversification required in the portfolio of collaterals to avoid an oversized exposure to a particular issue, issuer, or sector. If the hedge fund is unable to meet a margin call or cure a breach within a certain period, the fund may be deemed to be in default of the financing agreement.

A commonly seen "event of default" is when a hedge fund portfolio is deemed to have become significantly riskier per certain measurable metrics, for example if the net asset value of the fund drops by more than a preset limit within a period of time. If the event of default trigger is hit, the fund is deemed to have defaulted on its financing, and this gives the funding provider the right to seize and liquidate the collateral. The terms of the risk mitigation techniques used by banks who lend to hedge funds are found in the documentation that governs prime brokerage accounts and repo and swap agreements. Today, the typical triggers are 20 percent monthly decline in net asset value (NAV) (excluding redemptions), 30 percent decline in NAV over a quarter, and 40 percent decline in NAV over the period of a year.

In the case of inherently levered instruments, no capital is explicitly being lent or borrowed. Both sides of the trade agree on an unfunded or partially funded swap and both benefit from levered exposure to a portfolio of assets. For example, for a single-name credit default swap, the protection seller has a long exposure to the credit risk of the underlying bond. Economically, this position is similar to having a long exposure on the bond without having to come up with the capital to purchase the bond. The protection buyer has a short exposure to the credit risk of the underlying bond and has a levered exposure.

For many credit hedge funds, the leverage on the long side typically is obtained via explicit borrowing through prime brokerage financing or total return swaps, while the short positions are levered as a result of usage of credit derivatives such as CDS or CDX. During a market environment when the soundness of various banks is in question, managers that typically run a well-hedged credit portfolio may face a higher risk of losing access to one leg of their trade. For example, say a credit hedge fund manager in summer 2008 owned a portfolio of bank loans financed via a total return swap with J.P. Morgan and bought protection on the CDX HY index from Lehman Brothers. As the market deteriorated, the manager might have thought that he was well hedged because the mark-to-market gains from his CDX HY shorts offset the losses from the long loan exposure. However, when Lehman Brothers filed for bankruptcy, the manager would have found himself holding an unsecured general claim against Lehman Brothers (worth less than a dollar for every dollar of his mark-to-market gains from the CDX HY shorts) instead of a hedge against the broad credit market.

 ## Key Takeaways on Financing "Basis" Risk

There is basis risk associated with different ways long and short portfolios are exposed to different financing lines. Managers who thought they were hedged by buying CDS protection from Bear and Lehman as counterparties found themselves with significant net long exposure when both firms went belly up in 2008.

PRIME BROKERAGE FINANCING

Prime brokerage (PB) financing is basically collateralized borrowing. It is the most commonly seen method of financing with hedge funds for high yield bonds and convertible bonds. PB financing is typically overnight financing. It is possible to have term PB financing (longer than overnight), but in practice, hedge funds often find long-term PB financing cost prohibitive and it is not commonly used. In very severe market situations such as 2008 where the entire financial system was in serious danger of collapsing, PBs exercised their right to withdraw financing overnight.[2] Under normal market condition, it is unlikely the PB will do this as it will jeopardize the business relationship. After Lehman, many credit hedge funds opt to have multiple PB accounts. This is not a free option—there is typically a minimum account size for opening a new PB account. Furthermore, there is a cost associated with maintaining the relationship and monitoring each PB account. The larger and more complex the credit hedge fund, the more likely it will have more than two PB relationships. Younger, smaller credit hedge funds tend to start with one PB relationship and add more relationships as their asset base grows.

Credit hedge funds, due to the nature of the instruments in their portfolio, face a unique set of circumstances when it comes to financing their portfolio. PB financing is no exception. Leverage for high yield corporate bonds tends to be less available and more expensive relative to publicly traded equities. Prime brokers are typically more willing to finance liquid, exchange-traded instruments such as public equities. This is also often reflected in a lower margin requirement and higher maximum leverage allowed. Prime brokers can post liquid, exchange-traded collateral in the repo market for financing even when market conditions are tumultuous. Furthermore, for this exchange-traded collateral, the market value is set every day at the close of the market. Knowing the value of the collateral makes it easier for the PB to measure and manage risk. The PB can recalculate margin payment and change margin if necessary.

The margin requirement for a long bond position is typically determined by the bond rating, while for a short position it is determined by rating and trading price. In addition, the financing is typically subject to a certain maximum trade size and minimum issue size outstanding. Investment in smaller issue size bonds, particularly larger exposure to smaller issue size bonds, tend not to be levered. This makes sense from the PB's perspective because limitation on issuance size and maximum financing size protects their interest. From the credit hedge fund manager's perspective, these smaller bonds tend to be less liquid and to see greater volatility accompanied by drastic reduction in liquidity during a bear market. Prudent credit hedge fund managers tend to use limited or no leverage on less liquid credit instruments.

Margin requirement is higher for naked long or short corporate debt positions compared to hedged or arbitrage strategies such as convertible bond arbitrage positions. For example, a hedge fund that holds the convertible bond for Amgen would need to post more margin if it held the bond as a long position compared to if it hedged the convertible bond either with a CDS position, another cash bond, or equity. Hedging a bond with interest rate hedges may also reduce the required margin on the position. The degree of the margin reduction depends on the extent that the short hedge matches the long position, as determined by factors such as whether the hedge (cash or reference obligation of the CDS) is senior, pari passu, or subordinated to the bond position.

 ### Key Takeaways on Financing Mechanisms for Credit Instruments

Investors tend to be most familiar with PB financing. Nonetheless, there are a variety of financing methods available for different credit instruments. For example, bank loans are typically levered through total return swaps (TRS) and not PB financing. As such, if investors ask to review a PB agreement, a credit hedge fund predominantly invested in bank loans may not be able to show this. Investors should ask to see the ISDA agreement instead.

Prime Brokerage Financing Post Lehman

The collapse of Lehman Brothers highlighted the main issues regarding the safeguarding of posted collateral in a PB account: asset segregation and rehypothecation. U.S. broker-dealers are subject to certain rules such as Regulation T that are intended to safeguard customer assets.[3] Hedge fund industry practices in relation to these rules are pertinent to how hedge fund investors were affected in the demise of Lehman Brothers. Out of these rules, in practice many U.S.-based hedge fund managers have PB accounts with U.K.-based broker dealers to access greater leverage. When establishing a PB relationship with Lehman, some hedge funds used Lehman Brothers International Europe (LBIE, the U.K. broker-dealer) rather than Lehman Brothers International (LBI, the U.S. broker-dealer arm). The broker-dealers outside the United States, including U.K. broker dealers, are not subject to the leverage limit of Regulation T[4] and therefore the potential leverage allowed in the brokerage account is higher.

In the United States, at the time of the asset purchase, Regulation T of the Federal Reserve Board defines the minimum amount of margin at 50 percent ("initial margin") (i.e., maximum leverage is set at 2×). Leverage is calculated as the market value of securities or equity capital. After the asset is purchased, Financial Industry Regulatory Authority (FINRA)[5] requires a minimum 25 percent of equity in the margin account ("maintenance margin") (i.e., maximum leverage is set at 4×). Some brokerage firms may ask for a higher amount of margin than required by Regulation T or FINRA, effectively reducing the maximum amount of possible leverage in the portfolio.

In the United States, broker-dealers are required to hold investors' assets in segregated fashion. This means that customers' assets are kept separately from the PB's proprietary assets. In most cases, the assets are still held in "street name," which means the holdings are registered in the name of the PB, but they are not commingled with the PB's actual assets. In the United Kingdom, assets of the PB's customers are not automatically segregated from the proprietary assets. This means that a credit hedge fund in the process of nego-tiating a potential new PB relationship has to "opt-in" and specifi-cally request that the fund's assets be held in a segregated manner. Otherwise, in the event that the PB goes insolvent, the hedge fund will be treated as a general unsecured creditor. This means that the hedge fund will not have sole claim on its assets. Rather, the assets will be part of a larger portfolio of assets owned by the prime broker. Out of the assets, value in excess of the secured creditors' claim will be distributed pro rata to its unsecured creditors. In the event of insolvency, the value of the assets is likely to be significantly less than the value of unsecured claims. The credit hedge fund (and the fund investors) will suffer losses because they will receive only part of the value of their assets.[6]

In addition to segregation of assets, hedge funds using margin financing (whether through non-U.S. PB accounts or U.S.-based prime brokers) also need to deal with the issue of rehypothecation. Rehypothecation is the idea that the prime broker or counterparty can take assets that the hedge fund has in custody or put up as collateral and loan these out to other entities. In the United States, due to Rule 15c3-3[7] the prime broker is only allowed to rehypothecate up to 140 percent of the customers' debit balance (the amount of margin loan given from the PB to the hedge fund manager). Simply stated, if you had a margin loan of $100,000 from your PB, it could rehypothecate (loan to others) $140,000 of your securities. One of the key concerns surrounding Lehman was treatment of rehypothecated securities. In the United States, if a credit hedge fund had the bonds it posted rehy-pothecated, in the event of insolvency for a U.S. PB, the claim on the rehypothecated assets belong to the fund. This is not believed to be the case in the United Kingdom. This means that those hedge funds that had Lehman as a prime broker in the United Kingdom are more likely to get back their assets if they had them in custody (assuming they had explicitly opted for segregation of assets) than if those assets had been rehypothecated.

Credit hedge funds have also moved toward having multiple counterparties (multiple PBs or multiple swap lines) to hedge their counterparty risk. However, there are certain trade-offs to the number of counterparties a hedge fund can have. As mentioned, having multiple PB accounts and swap lines are not free options. For example, total return swap lines often have a minimal usage fee. There are also legal fees associated with the negotiation process of PB and swap agreements. In addition, there are man-hour costs of having to negotiate, maintain, and monitor multiple counterparty relationships, not to mention the potential opportunity cost of the time and effort of the back office personnel. Having too many counterparties without understanding the real triggers and pressure points in the documentation may backfire and actually increase counterparty risk. If the back office is overwhelmed by the number of financing agreements in place, accidental triggering of a termination event for one agreement may trigger termination events across other PB and swap agreements due to cross-default provision.

TOTAL RETURN SWAPS

Much has been written about total return swaps; however, much of it has been written from the banks' perspective. As important as it is to understand the motivations, limitations, and other factors affecting the behavior of both parties in any bilateral agreement, many institutional investors seek to understand the TRS from the perspective of credit hedge funds and the potential impacts the swap may have on the portfolio.

In a total return swap, two parties enter into a bilateral contract to exchange the stream of return on an asset or portfolio of assets. The total return payer is the party who owns the assets and passes on the economic benefits of owning these assets to the total return receiver in exchange for the floating payment. Credit hedge funds are frequently the total return receivers and use TRS to finance their leveraged loans. Similar to the other types of financing we've discussed in this chapter, large financial institutions with low cost of funding such as investment and commercial banks are the natural financing providers (i.e., they are the total return payers in this case).

The reference obligations in a TRS can include various types of bonds (e.g., investment grade and high yield corporate bonds, asset-backed securities, sovereigns), bank loans (e.g., term loans and revolvers), and equities. In practice, one popular asset class that credit hedge funds often finance through TRS is bank loans (e.g., term loans and revolvers). From the perspective of credit hedge fund investors, a judicious amount of leverage can be justified for par bank loans to improve the attractiveness of the asset class. Furthermore, the historical low volatility of par loans makes them an attractive candidate for leverage. Nonetheless, after the market saw unprecedented volatility around the 2008 credit crisis, although the asset class retains relatively lower volatility compared to other asset classes such as public equities, the low volatility feature is no longer something that investors can take for granted.[8] Thus many credit hedge funds have taken a more muted and measured approach to using leverage, increased their back office capabilities, and actively worked to better manage their financing lines.

In practice, TRS are almost always based on a portfolio of assets rather than a single asset. From the total return (TR) payer perspective, a portfolio of assets provides a more diversified pool of collateral. From the perspective of TR receiver, having one swap against a mix of assets means administrative simplicity and lower administrative costs, as well as better investment flexibility. For example, having to redo the paperwork for every new asset to the fund may delay the purchase and is administratively cumbersome. The examples in this chapter are based on a single asset for illustration purposes. The term *reference obligations* refers to the specifically defined assets that underlie the TRS.

In a TRS, the TR payer transfers the mark-to-market and credit risk of the reference obligation to the TR receiver. At the end of the swap, the TR receiver has the right, but not the obligation, to buy the assets from the TR payer. In common practice, the credit hedge fund rolls the swap into a new swap, either with the same swap counterparty or a new swap counterparty, instead of buying the assets cash. In addition, by entering into a TRS as a receiver, a credit hedge fund is able to obtain long-levered synthetic exposure to a set of assets that cannot be financed via other popular financing methods such as PB or repo financing. The leverage feature of the swap is extremely important because that is why credit hedge funds enter into TRS. The typical range of leverage varies depending on the quality of the eligible reference obligations and the market conditions. In the pre-Lehman era, select TRS facilities had allowed for up to 10× leverage (for every $100 of notional exposure, a credit hedge fund is required to have $10 of capital). However, the range of leverage actually used by credit hedge funds was typically much lower, in the 2× to 5× range. A few years after Lehman, the typical range of maximum leverage available in total return swaps is usually at 3.5× or below.

Figure 10.2 shows an example of a TRS on $10 million of a bank loan trading at par that pays LIBOR plus 350 bps. The payer receives the swap spread of LIBOR plus 100 bps, for example, on a notional of $10 million and pays the TR on the loan. This TR consists of coupon payments, fees, amortization payments, and price appreciation and depreciation. Total return can be negative if the loan price falls.

The receiver also puts forth $2.5 million cash (25 percent margin rate) as collateral, which is invested in Treasuries. This lowers the

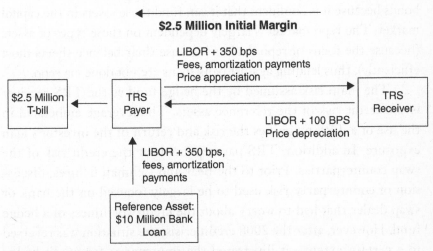

Figure 10.2 **Illustration of a total return swap**
Source: PAAMCO

counterparty credit risk in situations where the loan drops in value and the payer should receive a large payment. The collateral requirement changes as the market price of the loan fluctuates, and the TR payer usually has the right to change the margin rate with reasonable notice to the receiver.[9]

In the scenario described above, the receiver borrows at LIBOR plus 100 bps to obtain an asset that yields LIBOR plus 350 bps. The receiver only had to come up with $2.5 million worth of capital to obtain $10 million exposure to the bank loan (4× leverage).[10] This use of TRS as a funding mechanism renders it similar to a synthetic repo transaction. The cash repo market for bank loans is virtually nonexistent, for a few reasons. First, bank loans are not securities, and thus they are settled physically rather than electronically through a clearinghouse such as the Depository Trust Company (DTC). Second, bank loan contracts are often highly negotiated, and potentially with a myriad of bells and whistles that are deal specific. The intensive settlement process combined with the complexity and nonfungibility of the asset make bank loans difficult to rehypothecate. Rehypothecation is an important process in the borrowing and lending of funds between financial institutions. A PB is more willing to lend against rehypothecable assets such as Treasuries or liquid, high quality corporate bonds because it is confident that it can fund these assets in the capital market. The repo market is largely dependent on these types of assets (because the focus of repo dealers is to use their balance sheets most efficiently), thus lending against bank loans are not done via repo.

The main risk assumed by the hedge fund as the TRS receiver is the credit risk of the reference assets. The leverage embedded in the use of a TRS magnifies the risk and return of the investor's loan exposure. In addition, TRS participants bear the credit risk of the swap counterparties. Prior to the Bear and Lehman failures, discussion of counterparty risk used to be largely focused on the bank or swap dealer that had to worry about the creditworthiness of a hedge fund. However, after the 2008 credit crisis, the situation was reversed to a certain extent—it illustrated the importance for credit hedge funds and their investors to understand the extent of their exposure to the credit risk of the banks. The higher the credit risk of the swap payer, the lower the swap spread and/or margin charged to the swap receiver.

Total Return Swaps During and Post Lehman

The credit crisis of 2008 highlights the importance of understanding the terms of a leverage facility, especially given leverage providers' rights to terminate the facility. The crisis was as close as one can get to the "perfect storm" in testing the robustness of financing lines. The financial markets were in trouble, and financial institutions, particularly banks, were one of the key sources of the turmoil (and the main recipients of much of the negative impact, due to a self-feeding mechanism that took place). Banks were under heavy motivation to secure their liquidity as well as their solvency, and business units were under severe pressure to de-risk quickly. TRS desks were no exception. They had to bring back the loans made to "risky" counterparties, which in this case meant hedge funds.

In the meantime, credit hedge funds were seeing the value of their investments rapidly declining in value. We saw large, liquid loans marked down 3 to 5 points within a day. Contrast this with historical volatility of the asset class prior to this period when loans were exhibiting 3 to 5 percent volatility per annum. Combine the unprecedented price volatility with leverage, and credit hedge fund NAVs were rapidly declining. In many TRS agreements, if the hedge fund assets under management (AUM) drop beyond a certain level within a given period, whether due to poor performance or redemptions, this would be deemed to qualify as a termination event. When this happens, the TRS payer has the right to terminate the TRS agreement. Typically there is a notification period as specified in the ISDA agreement. The length of the notification period is at least a day. The financing provided by the TRS payer to purchase the reference assets becomes due in full. The TRS receiver has two options: repay the TRS payer in cash or the payer will sell the underlying assets in order to generate the cash.

Assume the case of a TRS with an AUM trigger with the hedge fund as the swap receiver. If the hedge fund loses more than a certain amount of AUM within a certain period as a result of negative performance and/or investor redemptions, a termination event may be deemed to have taken place and the liquidation trigger is hit. The financing provided by the swap payer is immediately due in full. The swap receiver either has to provide the cash or the swap payer has the right to seize and sell the underlying collateral. When bank loan prices declined in 2008, widespread forced selling took place as total return swap lines were unwound and the assets liquidated via the "bids wanted in competition" (BWIC) process.[11] In 2008, the BWIC process was part of a vicious cycle that drove asset prices ever lower as many of the trades occurred at extremely depressed prices. Certain players in the market (broker-dealers and hedge funds, among others) gamed the market when it became public knowledge that certain assets would be available for sale. The dramatic fall in price led to more event of default triggers being hit, which led to more assets available at firesale prices, and so on.

After 2008, the immediate reaction of many investors was to forsake leverage altogether, including TRS. Given where asset prices were and the potential for attractive unlevered return, a new temporary market equilibrium was reached where leverage was neither necessary nor available at an attractive price. However, prices of corporate bonds and loans soon rose to a point where some demand for leverage started to come back into the market. Around the same time, new leverage providers and existing players that saw their balance sheets stabilized came into the market and started to offer leverage facilities. Over time, the demand and supply of capital to finance credit portfolios will continue to determine the cost of financing as well as the term of the facilities. As such, credit hedge fund investors need to be comfortable that their hedge fund managers are fully aware of the rights and obligations of both parties in a financing agreement.

Investors that are familiar with credit hedge funds, particularly those that invest in bank loans and use leverage via a TRS, will be familiar with the fact that the terms of the TRS are contained in an ISDA agreement. ISDA stands for International Swaps and Derivatives

Association.[12] The ISDA establishes guidelines on how parties will trade in a bilateral contract on derivatives. The terms of the swap are contained in a set of documents including the term sheet, the ISDA Master Agreement and Schedule to the Master Agreement, and the Credit Support Annex.

Key terms of the agreement include definition of events of default and termination events. Examples of events of default include failure to meet a margin payment, noncompliance with certain requirements of the portfolio (such as the limitation on lower rated assets), and bankruptcy.

Of related importance to the events of default provision are the ability to cure, the cure period, the grace period, and the notice period. This is important because triggering an event of default does not necessarily lead into a termination of the swap agreement if the default can be cured. The event of default and termination event are important to hedge funds in two different ways. First, hedge funds care about what can happen in the event that their swap counterparty defaults (as in the Lehman scenario) and the fund's rights in that scenario. Second, hedge funds are interested in the scenarios that may cause the fund to be deemed in default under the swap agreement and how this may have an impact on the portfolio. The cure and notice periods provide credit hedge funds with valuable time and options that can possibly delay or deter forced liquidation from happening.

Post Lehman, many credit hedge funds have adopted the best practice of managing cash collateral, which is not to accumulate too much cash in excess of the required margin with the swap. If an event of default is triggered, the counterparty will be able to seize all the posted collateral including the amount in excess of the maintenance margin. This means that one needs additional operational resource to keep up with the counterparty and the swap lines and to meet margin calls in a timely manner.

 ## Key Takeaway on Excess Margin

You wouldn't walk into a bazaar and negotiate by telling the merchant how much money you have in your pocket. Similarly, don't leave too much excess margin with your financing provider.

Right after Lehman Brothers, seeing what happened to Lehman's swap counterparties that lost their posted collateral and positive mark-to-margin (the unrealized gains of the swap), there was much talk about having the cash collateral in a swap held by an independent custodian. At the moment, the idea has not been widely adapted by the market participants. The broker-dealer community has not changed the current practice of having the broker-dealer hold the cash collateral, while the hedge funds have not embraced the additional operational burden involved with this practice.

 ## Key Takeaways on Trade-offs in Cash Management

The most conservative cash management technique is to leave only the exact amount of margin required with the counterparty and meet margin calls daily. However, keep in mind that the frequency of cash sweeps should balance the need to manage counterparty risk and costs associated with very frequent cash sweeps, such as additional burden on the back office and the interest earned on the cash balance.

Whether via PB financing, TRS, or repo, incurring a noncompliance trigger in the financing agreement is clearly not a positive thing. However, under normal market conditions, this very seldom leads to the disastrous event of a fund blowup. The grace period and ability to cure gives the hedge fund manager some breathing room, as it will have some time to come back into compliance. The longer the grace and cure period, the better for the hedge fund. In practice, if the fund is expected to breach a trigger, a conscientious credit edge fund manager will communicate with the counterparty regarding its plan to bring the fund back in compliance, such as by reducing borrowing, selling assets, changing the mix of assets used as collateral, or sending additional margin payment.

 ## Key Takeaway on Negotiating Financing Agreements

When it comes to leverage, almost everything is negotiable. Make sure that your credit hedge fund manager can show that they have done sufficient due diligence to compare the terms offered by the PB or other leverage provider.

REPURCHASE AND REVERSE REPURCHASE AGREEMENTS

One way to finance bonds and hybrid instruments such as convertible bonds is through repurchase agreements or repos. Repo is not used for bank loans due to ownership and transfer issues. Repos are commonly used for higher quality assets, such as investment grade fixed-income instruments, particularly Treasuries and agency mortgage-backed securities. Repo can also be used for select types of sub-investment grade credit instruments such as mortgage-backed securities.

A repurchase (repo) agreement is basically an agreement to borrow or lend money with collateral backing the loan. Borrowers of capital post collateral in exchange for cash—in other words, the borrower is a net seller of asset. At the end of the repo term, the borrower buys back the collateral, paying cash to the lender at a prearranged level, which is the borrowed amount plus interest. Institutional investors and commercial banks typically are net borrowers of funds (net sellers of asset) while money market funds and corporations are on the opposite side of the table.

The cost of financing through repo can be higher or lower than financing via prime brokers, depending on conditions in the repo market. The relative cost is dependent on what the repo market is currently offering at the time and supply and demand for PB financing. For credit hedge funds that largely traffic in leveraged credit, use of repo for financing is not commonly seen. It is often cheaper for the manager to finance the portfolio via prime brokers. Logistically, repo financing is provided on an asset-by-asset basis (compared to prime brokerage lending, where the collateral is a portfolio of assets), so a credit hedge fund that relies largely on repos as a financing mechanism is likely to need a repo trader to roll the repos on the individual collateral as they come due.

Figure 10.3 shows the flow of funds and collateral in a simple two-party (bilateral) repo transaction between hedge fund A and a repo dealer. From the dealer's perspective, this is a repo transaction, and it's a reverse repo from the hedge fund's perspective. From hedge fund A's perspective, a reverse repo finances its short position via collateralized lending, while a repo finances its long position through collateralized

A Repo

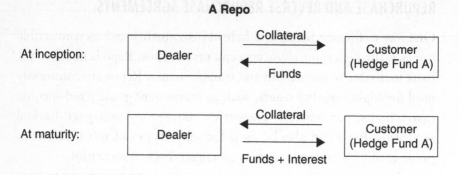

This is a repo from the dealer's perspective and a reverse repo from Hedge Fund A's perspective.

A Reverse Repo

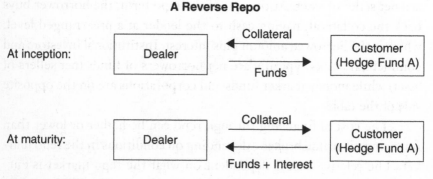

This is a reverse repo from the dealer's perspective and a repo from Hedge Fund A's perspective.

Figure 10.3 Illustration of bilateral and reverse repo
Source: PAAMCO

borrowing. In many cases, the dealer faces another customer and takes the reverse position. The dealer earns a bid-ask spread when it runs a matched book as illustrated in Figure 10.4.

Credit hedge funds use reverse repo for shorting instead of the explicit purpose of earning additional yield on their cash. For example, in order to fund the "borrow" against $10 million of short exposure to a corporate bond, hedge fund A enters into a reverse repo where it buys $10 million worth of the bonds and agrees to sell them back at the end of the repo term.

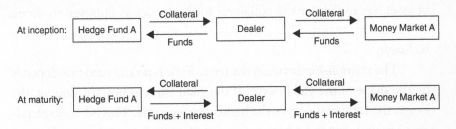

Figure 10.4 A Dealer's matched repo book
Source: PAAMCO

The price of borrowing money through a repo arrangement, the repo rate, fluctuates according to the supply and demand of capital and collateral in the repo market. The terms of a repo and reverse repo agreement are documented in a Master Repurchase Agreement or Global Master Repurchase Agreement (MRA or GMRA), a Custodial Undertaking, and a Securities Lending Service Agreement. Repo agreements are customizable depending on the needs of the borrower and the lender of funds. Repo rate can be fixed or floating, with periodic reset for the floating rate. The parties can also agree to acceptable substitutes for posted collaterals and frequency of substitution allowed. Borrowers of funds can take advantage of longer-term financing relative to PB financing and/or more advantageous cost in the repo market. Lenders of funds benefit from mitigated credit risk due to lending on a collateralized basis and overcollateralization through the use of haircuts.

Determinants of repo rate include the quality and liquidity of the collateral, availability of collateral, delivery method, term of the repo, and the current federal funds rate. Higher quality and more liquid collateral will require a lower repo rate. Similarly, collateral that is less available also requires a lower repo rate. If the collateral in question happens to be difficult to borrow, it is often said to be "on special" or "hot." The lenders of capital (aka the buyers of collateral, in this case, hedge fund A) are eager to get their hands on the collateral and thus may be willing to lend capital at a lower repo rate. Delivery method also plays a role—as we will discuss later, if the borrower of capital/seller of asset has to deliver the collateral to the lender as opposed to doing an intrabank transfer between custodial accounts, the repo rate will be lower.

The relationship between the term of the repo and repo rate depends on the shape of the yield curve. If the yield curve is upward sloping, the longer the term of the repo, the higher the repo rate. This is because lenders of capital demand a higher amount of interest to make a loan over a longer period of time. If the yield curve is inverted, lenders of capital will receive higher compensation for providing short-term capital. Last, the repo rate usually fluctuates with changes in the federal funds rate.

Example of a simple repo transaction with no haircut assumption: Credit hedge fund A has bought a corporate bond with $10 million face value at par and wished to finance the bond via repo. In order to borrow additional capital to invest in more assets, hedge fund A would enter into a repo agreement with the dealer. The hedge fund agrees to "sell" (deliver) $10 million worth of the bonds to the dealer in exchange for $10 million cash and simultaneously agrees to buy back these bonds from the dealer 30 days later (assume the term repo lasts for a month). If the repo rate is 5 percent, at the end of the term, the hedge fund will "repurchase" the bond for $10,041.667. Here the original principal amount is $10 million and the dollar interest of financing the corporate bond purchase is $41,667. The dollar interest amount is calculated as principal amount multiplied by the repo rate and the number of days in the repo term divided by 360 days.[13]

In practice, repo dealers impose haircut or margining on the value of the collateral posted. If the market value of the collateral falls such that the variation margin trigger is hit,[14] the repo is now undercollateralized and hedge fund A would be facing a margin call. There are two ways a margin call could be effected, but in both methods, effectively hedge fund A (the borrower of capital/asset seller) restores the margin to its initial level. One method is for hedge fund A to deliver additional collateral in the form of cash or securities, the latter of which may be subject to haircut. Another method is known as "close out and repricing"; effectively the original repo is closed out and a new repo with new terms is opened.

Bilateral repo carries counterparty credit risk. After the trade is put on, if hedge fund A fails to come up with the principal amount plus interest to repurchase the bond and the price of the collateral has fallen, then the repo counterparty is stuck with collateral that is worth less than the amount it is owed. Capital lenders mitigate their counterparty credit risk by overcollateralization, requiring posting of collateral that has higher value than the amount of the loan. The haircut amount differs by asset type and quality of assets; riskier assets such as high yield corporate bonds require higher haircut (higher margin and overcollateralization) than Treasuries.

RISKY REPO?

There have been great losses for investors in repo transactions due to the combination of high leverage on a directional bet as opposed to due to counterparty default. The default of Orange County in 1994 was a prime example of this scenario.

The county had leveraged itself by short-term borrowing via repurchase agreements and invested in longer-term bonds paying higher interest. This trade contains an inherent directional bet on the direction of interest rates. When rates fell, the trade was highly profitable. When the interest rate rose, the value of the longer-term bonds fell. The county also saw losses in inverse floaters—another type of interest rate derivative whose value fell as the interest rate rose. The county faced margin calls it could not meet and filed for bankruptcy.

Another way to mitigate counterparty risk is to engage in tri-party repo. In the example given above between hedge fund A and the repo dealer, there will be a third party. Figures 10.5 and 10.6 show the flow of funds and collateral at the beginning and ending of the tri-party repo transaction. The borrower of the cash does not have to deliver out the collateral. Instead, the lender will have a custodial account at the borrower's clearing bank, and the collateral is delivered to this custodial account. This practice increases ease of transaction and reduces collateral delivery cost because the process only involves a transfer in the borrower's clearing bank. This third party is responsible

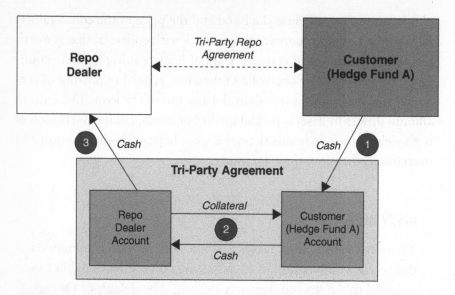

Figure 10.5   **Illustration of a tri-party repurchase agreement at inception**
Source: PAAMCO

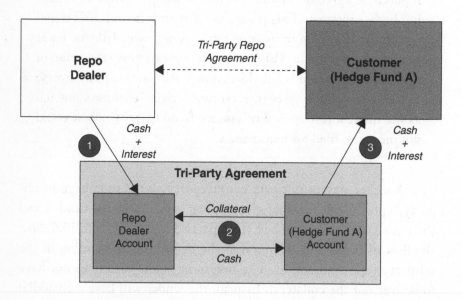

Figure 10.6   **Illustration of a tri-party repurchase agreement at maturity**
Source: PAAMCO

for taking collateral custody, monitoring, marking to market, margining, and reporting. For less liquid corporate bonds, although the setup carries additional costs, the dealer's counterparties may take additional comfort from the fact that the marking to market and margining are done by an independent third party. In a bilateral repo, the repo dealer is in charge of marking the portfolio and portfolio margining.

Repo Market During and Post Lehman

One of the risks of financing via repo is inability for the borrower of funds to roll the repo and having to sell its positions, potentially before the trade has the time to work. One way to mitigate this risk is to pay attention to the notice period of the repo agreement. In the example given above, hedge fund A is borrowing funds through a one-month repo. If the notice period is 15 days, then 15 days before the repo term matures, hedge fund A has the ability to request the rolling of the repo (exiting from the existing repo and entering into a new repo expiring 30 days away).

Should the repo roll request be refused, for example due to a dislocation in the repo market such as the one seen surrounding Lehman Brothers' bankruptcy, hedge fund A has three options. The first is to renegotiate with the existing counterparty to enter into a new contract, potentially with a higher haircut, shorter term, and higher cost. The second option is for hedge fund A to enter into a new repo contract with another counterparty. This option is likely to be open only if hedge fund A already had an existing relationship with the new counterparty. Even so, the process of negotiating the terms, documentation, and on-boarding associated with a new repo agreement takes time. What may take weeks during normal business course may be extended to months during a market downturn. The third, and usually least preferable, option is for hedge fund A to unwind the position.

Another way to mitigate the risk of having broken repo financing is by controlling the limit of leverage on the portfolio. What constitutes acceptable leverage depends on the type of the asset and the liquidity of the asset. However, high leverage combined with lower liquidity assets can translate into large losses if liquidity for the asset dries up because it combines the need to find a large amount of financing combined with assets whose values are hard to ascertain for broker-dealers. From the perspective of the lender of funds, if the lender cannot put a value on the collateral asset with a certain amount of confidence, not only would the asset make for a poor collateral (it may be stuck holding a low valued asset) but it may also not be able to put a margin and overcollateralization amount on the asset that it would be comfortable with.

At the time of the writing, we have also started to see repo agreements with NAV trigger as an event of default. If the NAV of the fund falls below a certain level within a predetermined period, the counterparty will have the right to terminate the swap. In a sense, repo agreements are moving toward the way of the ISDAs, with NAV-based event of default. Hedge fund managers tend not to be in favor of these new provisions because during times of market volatility, similar to the scenario in a TRS, this gives the repo counterparty the right to liquidate the trade and potentially seize collateral. Similar to several TRS agreements, one negotiation point may be to exclude investor flows from NAV calculation (i.e., the NAV change is solely limited to performance). This way, should a large investor redeem due to non-performance-related reasons, the fund is not in danger of having its repo lines being withdrawn. However, this may cut both ways—assuming the manager is correctly expecting a large negative performance, he may be able to add a subscription (e.g., from friends and family or his own capital) so that the NAV-based event of default trigger is not breached. If the NAV calculation excludes redemption or subscription in the NAV calculation, then this option is not there.

CREDIT DERIVATIVES

Derivatives such as futures, forwards, options, and swaps are unfunded or partially funded instruments and thus provide implicit leverage. A credit hedge fund can get economic exposure to a much larger amount of assets via fixed-income derivatives compared to if the cash margin were put to use to purchase the assets directly on an unlevered basis. Examples of types of derivatives that may be used by credit hedge funds both on the long and short books include interest rate futures, single-name credit default swaps and indices, currency forwards, as well as options on swaps (swaptions). Using the example of a hypothetical single-name credit default swap with $10 million notional, a protection seller has long exposure to the credit and its risk is similar to owning $10 million of the cash bond. If credit spread rises, the protection seller will see mark-to-market losses on its long protection exposure via CDS. However, if the margin requirement is 5 percent, the CDS exposure requires the investor only to come up with $0.5 million of cash margin to obtain similar exposure to credit risk compared to $10 million required for a fully funded purchase of the cash bond.

There are three types of derivatives by standardization of terms and trading venue: over-the-counter, cleared, and exchange-traded. See Figure 10.7 for a comparison of the features of these three types of derivatives. The most liquid and standardized are exchange-traded derivatives, also known as listed derivatives. Futures and option on futures such as interest rate futures and future options are example of exchange-traded derivatives. The terms for exchange derivatives, such

OTC	Cleared	Exchange-traded
• Trades negotiated over-the-counter	• Trades negotiated over-the-counter	• Trades executed on organized exchanges
• Customized contracts are broken down by trading desk into tradable risks and hedged in liquid markets	• Trades limited to standardized contracts	• Trades limited to standardized contracts
• Traded between dealers as principals	• All trades are booked with clearinghouse, which is counterparty to all trades	• All trades are booked with exchange's clearinghouse, which is counterparty to all trades
• Dealer is normally counterparty to all trades	• Mandatory margin requirements	• Mandatory margin requirements
• Margin (collateral) often exchanged but subject to negotiation between counterparties	• Initial margin	• Initial margin
	• Variation margin	• Variation margin
	• Daily settlement (mark to market) and margin calls	• Daily settlement (mark to market) and margin calls

Figure 10.7 **Comparison of various types of derivatives**
Source: ISDA

as contract size, quoting convention, tick value,[15] contract maturity, and delivery mechanism are standardized across contracts. Trading is conducted on an exchange, which serves as a centralized marketplace for buyers and sellers to meet, and trades are booked with a clearinghouse. A clearinghouse is also known as a central counterparty (CCP) and serves as a "buyer to every seller and a seller to every buyer"[16] to mitigate counterparty risk. On the other end of the spectrum are over-the-counter (OTC) derivatives. The terms of OTC derivatives are not standardized and instead are privately negotiated over the counter between the parties in the agreement. Given the bespoke nature of the contracts, trading is bilateral (between the parties involved in the original contract), and no clearinghouse is involved.

OTC Derivatives During and Post Lehman

Swaps are OTC derivatives. Credit default swaps, interest rate swaps, and currency swaps are examples of swaps often used by credit hedge funds. Between the two, there are also cleared derivatives, also known as OTC cleared; similar to OTC transactions, these contracts are negotiated over the counter and the contracts are not traded on an exchange. However, the contracts are partially standardized and the trades are booked with a clearinghouse after the trade is completed. Credit default indices (CDX) are an example of OTC cleared derivatives that are commonly used by credit hedge funds. Starting in March 2013, mandatory clearing as required by the Dodd-Frank Act was effective for interest rate swaps and credit default swap indices.[17]

When a credit hedge fund buys exchange-traded derivatives and OTC cleared derivatives, it has essentially exchanged the credit risk of specific counterparties with the credit risk of the clearinghouse. The natural next question of a hedge fund investor is, which system is preferable and why? In Figure 10.8, the left diagram shows a market without a central counterparty, where banks or dealers are involved in multiple bilateral contracts with one another. In this scenario, should one of the banks default, the other banks (and their

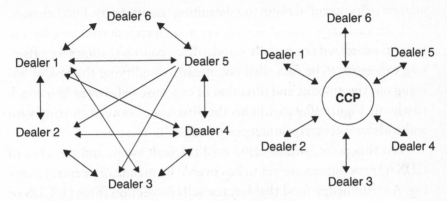

Figure 10.8 Comparison of market with or without a CCP
Source: PAAMCO

customers) are at risk. The right diagram shows a market structure with a clearinghouse in the middle, where it is the counterparty to the trades with all market participants. In this scenario, should one of the banks default, losses are contained between the defaulting party and the clearinghouse, mitigating potential losses to the other banks and their customers.

 Key Takeaways on Clearing Requirement on Derivatives

Many credit hedge funds are supportive of the new clearing requirement for OTC derivatives such as interest rate swaps and credit default swaps. Credit hedge funds expect to benefit from increased liquidity, better transparency, standardized pricing, and better bid-ask spread.

While the use of a clearinghouse is not a panacea to completely protect against losses from counterparty default, clearinghouses have adopted certain risk mitigation practices to improve their standing. The two key practices are mandatory margining and daily marking to market or margin calls. Although these practices may not completely protect the CCP should many of its counterparties default at the same time, they do mitigate the CCP's exposure to losses by reducing the amount of its potential claim to a defaulting counterparty. Furthermore, for both exchange-traded derivatives and cleared derivatives, having fully standardized or partially standardized contracts allows for offsetting exposures to be cancelled out, greatly simplifying the task of figuring out the amount and direction of exposure (who owes how much to whom). Figure 10.9 highlights the difference between clearing with and without a central counterparty ("CCP").

At this point, single-name credit default swaps and tranches of CDX/iTraxx indices are yet to be covered by mandatory central clearing. A credit hedge fund that buys or sells protection through CDS or credit indices is still exposed to the risk that its swap counterparty fails to meet certain financial obligations. This risk was illustrated perfectly during the credit crisis of 2008 and the collapse of Lehman Brothers. Many hedge funds that had bought protection on single-name CDS from Lehman lost their posted collateral as well as the unrealized gain on their swap.

Dealer A and B enter into a swap

| Dealer A's customers exposed to losses. | Dealer A is owed mark-to-market gains from Dealer B on the swap. Dealer B posts no margin. | | Dealer B defaulted. | Dealer B's customers exposed to losses |

No central counterparty

| Dealer A's customers are protected. | Dealer A is owed mark-to-market gains from Dealer B on the swap. There is daily margin posting and initial margin with the CCP. | Clearinghouse acts as a central counterparty and sits on a pool of margin. | Dealer B defaulted. | Dealer B's customers are protected. |

With a central counterparty

Figure 10.9 **Clearing with and without a central counterparty (CCP)**
Source: PAAMCO, FT

Terms of a credit default swap, like other swap agreements, are specified in an ISDA agreement. Ways for a credit hedge fund to mitigate the risks of its swap contracts include master netting agreements, margin or collateral requirement, periodic cash resettlement, and other forms of bilateral credit enhancements. With a master netting agreement, when a credit hedge fund has multiple swaps with one counterparty, its exposure to the counterparty is mitigated when positive mark-to-market gains are offset by the losses owed to the counterparty. Bilateral margin posting also mitigates counterparty risk because the counterparty's margin offsets the amount of exposure the credit hedge fund has to the swap counterparty. Periodic cash resettlement also offsets risk when the trade is working in favor of the credit hedge fund because it sweeps back cash instead of letting cash accumulate with the counterparty. In practice, even after Lehman, there are trade-offs to these risk mitigation techniques. For example, in theory, one can ask for daily cash sweep. However, in practice, it may get operationally cumbersome (especially for funds with multiple swap counterparties), and there is an opportunity cost of the interest on the cash. Monthly or quarterly cash sweep is more commonly seen.

CONCLUSION

- The type of financing mechanism used by credit hedge funds varies by the type of instrument.
- A credit hedge fund can borrow from an entity (prime brokerage) or via instruments (swaps and repos).
- Each financing mechanism comes with its own unique features and risks; however, some best practices such as margin netting and sweeping excess margin apply to most of them.
- The collapse of Lehman Brothers changed many industry practices on financing. Some are market driven; others are mandated by regulation (the Dodd-Frank Act). There are trade-offs associated with different methods of financing

and between asset security and factors such as cost, amount of leverage, and flexibility. In the post-Lehman world, it is imperative that investors understand the type of financing that's appropriate for their portfolio and the terms the financing comes under.

Notes

Chapter 1

1. Imogen Rose-Smith, "The Great Hedge Fund Experiment," *Institutional Investor*, June 2011.
2. Adam Richmond and Jason Ng, "Morgan Stanley Leveraged Finance Insights, XYZ or ETFs," October 16, 2012.
3. Examples in late 2007–2008 include SIVs and hung bridge loans on banks' balance sheets, mark-to-market CLOs, event of default on PB, and TRS financing surrounding Lehman bankruptcy.
4. Lehman Brothers Holdings Inc. Chapter 11 Proceedings Examiner's Report, Jenner & Block, http://lehmanreport.jenner.com/docs/BARCLAYS/LBEX-LL%202165164–2165176.pdf.
5. S&P LCD, Markit, JP Morgan, September 2011.
6. Transaction conventions have largely been standardized (e.g., on quoting convention, yield calculation method, trading units, trade agreement format, settlement cycles, settlement instruction format, master repurchase agreement). Source: Noritaka Akamatsu, The World Bank, "Improving Infrastructures for Corporate Bond Market," September 27, 2007. It is presented in Shanghai, China.

Chapter 2

1. The other groups are U.S. Treasury and federal government agencies. For a detailed overview on the various types of fixed-income securities, see *The Handbook of Fixed Income Securities*, edited by Frank J. Fabozzi with Steven V. Mann (7th ed., New York: McGraw-Hill, 2005).
2. Livingston and Zhou (2002) estimated that 80 percent of issuance in the U.S. high yield bond market was done under Rule 144A.
3. Source: Credit Suisse, Leveraged Finance Strategy, data includes $U.S. and non-$U.S. denominated bonds, data as of February 28, 2013.

4. Fidelity Investments, "Looking for Income? Think Global," July 13, 2011.
5. Ibid.
6. For more information on convertible securities, see Fabozzi, "The Handbook of Fixed Income Securities."
7. Examples of electronic trading platforms for bonds and OTC derivatives include MarketAxess, TradeWebb, and Bloomberg BondTrader.
8. Block trades typically refer to large trades. However, in some markets such as the coal futures market, the minimum size for a block trade is as small as five contracts. See http://www.cmegroup.com/clearing/trading-practices/NYMEX-COMEXblock-trade.html for block trade minimum thresholds.
9. The Financial Industry Regulatory Authority (FINRA) is the largest independent regulator for all securities firms doing business in the United States. FINRA's mission is to protect America's investors by making sure the securities industry operates fairly and honestly. All told, FINRA oversees nearly 4,560 brokerage firms, about 163,465 branch offices, and approximately 630,820 registered securities representatives. See http://www.finra.org/AboutFINRA.
10. Option adjusted spreads (OAS) factor in any embedded puts or calls in the high yield bond.
11. This makes sense given investors have to be compensated for taking risk, as investors are generally risk averse. However, the point is that degree of risk aversion varies, which is manifested in different levels of corporate credit risk premia across time and in different market conditions.
12. "Hedge Fund vs. Ireland, Round 2—Aurelius Capital Battles Over Its Allied Bond Holdings," *Wall Street Journal*, April 21, 2011.
13. The fixed charge coverage measures the company's ability to meet its fixed obligations, such as interest rate and lease.
14. High yield CDS trades with standard 500 bps coupon, and the difference between the market yield and 500 bps is paid in points up front.
15. Correlation trade was commonly seen expressed on structured credit portfolios with various types of underlying assets ("reference obligations") including corporate bonds and residential mortgages.

Chapter 3

1. Having to file Chapter 11 twice is referred to as "Chapter 22." Some distressed practitioners referred to the Hostess situation as "Chapter 33," referring to the two Chapter 11 filings and the eventual liquidation.
2. Fitch refers to this as "Restrictive Default." Moody's includes exchange offers in its definition of default.
3. GAO Report to Congressional Committees, "Financial Market Regulation: Financial Crisis Highlights Need to Improve Oversight of Leverage at Financial Institutions and Across System," July 2009.

4. "Bear Stearns's Cayne Admits Leverage 'Was Too High,'" Telegraph.co.uk, May 5, 2010.
5. A comparable example would be a negative-amortization mortgage.
6. Martin J. Whitman and Fernando Diz, *Distress Investing: Principles and Technique*. Hoboken, NJ: Wiley, 2009.
7. There are some exceptions such as set-off and critical vendor exemption. This exemption allows the debtor to pay prepetition arrearages to suppliers whose goods and services are deemed essential to the continued operation of the debtor during the restructuring process, and who might not otherwise continue to sell to the debtor. Most critical vendor arrangements require the vendor to provide normalized payment terms, which enhances the debtor's working capital.
8. Cases filed on or after October 17, 2005, are subject to BAPCPA.
9. Limited to claims incurred within 180 days of the petition date and capped at $11,725 per employee.
10. There is no separate bankruptcy trustee in Chapter 11.
11. From www.uscourts.gov: "In North Carolina and Alabama, bankruptcy administrators perform similar functions that U.S. trustees perform in the remaining 48 states. The bankruptcy administrator program is administered by the Administrative Office of the United States Courts, while the U.S. trustee program is administered by the Department of Justice. For purposes of this publication, references to U.S. trustees are also applicable to bankruptcy administrators."
12. Often referred to as the "section 341 meeting" in a Chapter 11 case.
13. www.uscourts.gov.
14. www.pacer.gov.
15. Exchange Act 10b, rule 10(b)5 and Securities Act 17a.
16. A "big boy letter" is an agreement between the two sides of a private trade and makes clear that the party without access to inside information considers itself a sophisticated investor able to examine and bear the potential risks associated with entering into a trade with a party with a potential informational advantage. The big boy letter discloses that one party has access to material nonpublic information, but it does not disclose the information itself. The big boy letter has two major components: first, the unrestricted party acknowledges that it is aware that the other party is in possession of material nonpublic information. Second, the unrestricted party waives its rights to assert legal claims against the restricted party related to its possession of nonpublic information.
17. This term is the author's and is not an industry convention.
18. For more on revolvers, please refer to Chapter 4 on Leveraged Loans.
19. "Hostess Plans to Liquidate After Mediation Fails," *New York Times*, November 20, 2012.
20. Vitro Press Release, April 12, 2011.
21. Chapter 15 in the U.S. Bankruptcy Code deals with cross-border bankruptcy cases.

22. From www.otcmarkets.com: "The OTC Marketplace is comprised of over 9,000 securities not listed on a U.S. stock exchange. They represent a broad and diverse group of companies with a variable level of financial strength, disclosure availability, and management quality with market capitalizations ranging from micro-cap start-ups to large cap multi-national companies. The OTC is a broker-driven marketplace where brokers can trade using Pink OTC's electronic interdealer quotation and trading system. The OTC market is not a listed marketplace; therefore, companies cannot apply to be listed in the OTC market. To be quoted in the OTC market on Pink OTC Markets' electronic quotation and trading system, at least one market maker who is a FINRA member must be willing to quote a company's stock. A market maker must file a Form 211 with FINRA or meet one of the exemptions to SEC Rule 15c2–11 in order to begin quoting a new security."

23. Some buyers of distressed assets choose to forgo access to inside information to preserve their trading flexibility.

24. The information on the bankruptcy filing such as the date of filing and the court where the petition was filed can be found in SEC form 8-K on Edgar.

25. According to the SEC, "[C]ompanies in bankruptcy are not relieved of their reporting obligations. Neither the United States Bankruptcy Code nor the federal securities laws provide an exemption from Exchange Act periodic reporting for issuers that have filed for bankruptcy. However, the SEC generally will accept the monthly reports an issuer must file with the Bankruptcy Court under Rule 2015 in lieu of Form 10-K and Form 10-Q filings. The issuer must file each monthly report with the Commission on a Form 8-K within 15 calendar days after the monthly report is due to the Bankruptcy Court." "Researching Public Companies Through EDGAR: A Guide for Investors." http://www.sec.gov/investor/pubs/edgarguide.htm

26. www.pacer.gov.

27. Jim Rutenberg and Bill Vlasic, "Chrysler Files to Seek Bankruptcy Protection," *New York Times*, April 30, 2009.

28. In order to be considered a QIB, an institutional investor needs to meet a minimum asset requirement of $25 million of investable assets and a professional money manager needs to have at least $100 million under management at firm level.

29. For simplicity, assume no transaction costs.

30. For a detailed discussion on OID, see Chapter 4.

31. Unless the DIP lenders agree to a different treatment.

Chapter 4

1. Prior to 2004, bank loans had no CUSIPs (i.e., they had no common identifiers). In January 2004, the Loan Syndications and Trading Association (LSTA) and Standard and Poor's, operator of the CUSIP Service Bureau,

launched a service that provides CUSIP numbers for bank loans. Although the industry has yet to consistently adopt the usage of one set of common identifiers across the board, the process of standardization of identifiers for loans helped with secondary loan market trading.

2. Bankruptcy would include corporate reorganization (commonly referred to as Chapter 11) or liquidation (commonly referred to as Chapter 7) in the United States. In this book, we focus on the legal system in the United States to illustrate our point. The concept of seniority applies across the globe; however, the details and application of bankruptcy laws differ across the various legal jurisdictions within the European and Asian loan markets. Investors are advised to consult legal counsel with relevant expertise.

3. Mariarosa Verde, "Loan Preserver: The Value of Covenants," Fitch, March 4, 1999.

4. Select bonds are traded on an exchange.

5. Industry convention defines par value of a bank loan at 100.

6. Historically, loans trading below 80 were considered distressed. However, the LSTA no longer uses price as an indicator for distressed loans because under that definition, almost the entire universe of large leveraged loans would have been considered distressed at one point in 2008 regardless of the health of the underlying borrower. Currently, whether a loan trades on par or distressed documents depends on several factors including potential for restructuring or bankruptcy, likelihood of impending default, downgrade, and balance sheet trends.

7. Generally an event of default in a CLO structure means that the "controlling class" (typically the most senior outstanding notes) has the right to demand accelerated repayment of their principal and direct the liquidation of the underlying assets.

8. Includes U.S. dollar–denominated non-investment grade bank debt.

9. "The Loan Syndications and Trading Association promotes a fair, orderly, and efficient corporate loan market and provides leadership in advancing the interests of all market participants." Source: www.lsta.org.

10. www.lsta.org.

11. The remaining equity tranches are often retained by the CLO manager.

12. See the section "Investment Strategies in Bank Loans" for more information.

13. "The Russell 1000 Index measures the performance of the large-cap segment of the U.S. equity universe. It includes approximately 1,000 of the largest securities based on a combination of their market cap and current index membership. The Russell 1000 represents approximately 90 percent of the U.S. market." Russell 1000 Index Fact Sheet, www.russell.com.

14. Cleary, Gottlieb, Stein & Hamilton, "IRS Chief Counsel Memo on Loan Origination by Foreign Entities," Alert Memo, September 23, 2009.
Kaye Scholer, LLP, "IRS Issues Guidance on U.S. Lending Activities by Non-U.S. Investor," Tax Department, October 2009.

15. European Loan Primer, Standard and Poors, January 2010.

16. Covenant-light (also known as "covenant-lite" or "cov-lite") refers to loans with fewer or less restrictive covenants than the typical loan.
17. Loan credit default swaps have similar structure to regular (corporate) credit default swaps. The first meaningful difference between them is that the underlying reference obligation is a bank loan as opposed to a bond. The second key difference is that a loan credit default swap contract is cancelled if the underlying loan is called by the issuer.
18. ISDA published standardized documents for LCDS on June 8, 2006.

Chapter 5

1. "US Banks Issue Preferred Shares in Rush to Plug Capital Shortfall," *Financial Times*, November 20, 2012.
2. Philippe Jorion, *Financial Risk Management Handbook*, 6th ed. New York: John Wiley & Sons, 2011. Chapter 14.

Chapter 6

1. Financial Markets Series, Bond Markets, theCityUK, July 2011.
2. Kenneth S. Rogoff and Carmen M. Reinhart, "The Forgotten History of Domestic Debt," NBER Working Paper 13946.
3. www.nakheel.com/en/corporate.
4. Gwen Robinson, "Markets Reel over Nakheel Default Fears," FT.com/ Alphaville, November 26, 2009.
5. "Sukuk" bonds are IOUs issued in compliance with Islamic laws or principles, under which interest payment is prohibited.
6. For more details on the different structures of the CDS for corporate, sovereign, and municipal borrowers in various jurisdictions, see the ISDA Credit Derivatives Physical Settlement Matrix, http://www.isda.org/c_and_a/ Credit-Derivatives-Physical-Settlement-Matrix.html.
7. "Greek Sovereign Debt Q&A" (update), ISDA statement dated October 27, 2011.
8. Defined as leverage obtained by borrowed funds (i.e., not leverage obtained).
9. The Markit iTraxx SovX family of indices include indices of the following region: Western Europe, CEEMEA, Asia Pacific, Global Liquid IG, G7, and BRIC. Source: Markit Partners.
10. The iTraxx SovX Western Europe is made up of 15 equally weighted sovereign constituents out of a universe of 18 European countries whose sovereign debts are traded on Western European documentation. The 18 countries are Austria, Belgium, Cyprus, Finland, France, Germany, Greece, Ireland, Italy, Luxembourg, Malta, Netherlands, Portugal, Spain, Denmark, Norway, Sweden, and the United Kingdom.

11. Euro Summit statement, Brussels, October 26, 2011.
12. Eurobonds are debt obligations that are backed by all EU member countries. Samuel Diedrich, "Three Potential Outcomes for Europe—Investor Positioning and Outlook," *PAAMCO Viewpoint*, June 2011.

Chapter 7

1. The author cannot emphasize enough that this structure is intended for U.S. nontaxable investors and should not be construed as a suggestion for U.S. taxable investors to commit tax evasion. U.S. taxable investors invest in hedge funds through onshore vehicles. The onshore funds are typically structured as Delaware limited partnerships, and they issue K-1 statements annually to reflect investors' gains and expenses.
2. Technically, in a participation, because the participant is not a lender of record, he or she does not have any voting rights. However, in practice, participants may contractually restrict the swap seller from voting on amendments or waivers and maintain voting rights on terms that often require unanimous lender consent such as rate, amortization, term, and collateral or security—RATS).
3. According to section 864(b)(2)(A)(ii) of the U.S. tax code, a foreign corporation can trade in securities or stocks for its own account without being subject to ECI (i.e., "securities trading safe harbor"). Satyajit Das, *Risk Management*, 3rd ed., Hoboken, NJ: John Wiley & Sons, 2006
4. www.irs.gov/Individuals/International-Taxpayers/Fixed,-Determinable,-Annual,-Periodical-%28FDAP%29-Income.
5. One of the arguments for a winding up petition on just and equitable grounds is the loss of substratum argument.

Chapter 8

1. SEI and Greenwich Associates, "The Shifting Hedge Fund Landscape Part I and II, The Fifth Annual Global Survey of Institutional Hedge Fund Investors," December 2011.
2. Julie Steinberg, "SEC Digging Into Fund Fees," *Wall Street Journal*, March 19, 2013.
3. Carlos Ferreira and Marc Towers, "Are Hedge Fund Managers Prepared for Centralized Clearing," *PAAMCO Perspectives*, second quarter, 2012.
4. Miguel A. Segoviano and Manmohan Singh, "Counterparty Risk in the Over-the-Counter Derivatives Market," IMF Working Paper, November 2008.
5. Ferreira and Towers, "Are Hedge Fund Managers Prepared for Centralized Clearing?" by Carlos Ferreira and Marc Towers. PAAMCO Perspectives, 2nd Quarter 2012.

6. U.S. Commodity Futures Trading Commission, "CFTC Issues Clearing Determination for Certain Credit Default Swaps and Interest Rate Swaps," Press Release, November 28, 2012.

7. Nick Rice, "Compliance: A Key Cornerstone of Operational Due Diligence," *PAAMCO Viewpoint*, October 2011.

8. Susan Pulliam and Gregory Zuckerman, Wall Street Journal, "Galleon Clients Abandon Ship", October 21, 2009.

9. Joshua Barlow, "Expert Networks: What to Expect from Hedge Funds Today," *PAAMCO Viewpoint*, May 2011.

Chapter 9

1. Philippe Jorion, "Coping with 'Unknown Unknowns,'" *Canadian Investment Review*, October 18, 2010.

2. There are many reasons why the spread of the CDS of a particular issuer is not the same as the spread of the cash bond of the same issuer. Some reasons include different funding cost for cash versus CDS, the fact that the CDS is long 'cheapest-to-deliver' option, perceived counterparty risk of a CDS, and different liquidity profile of cash bonds versus CDS. For a more detailed discussion, please see Mayer Cherem, "Basis: Corporate Bonds and Credit Default Swaps," PAAMCO Research Paper, July 2009.

3. A simple risk analysis should show the directional interest rate risk in this portfolio. Exposure-based reports alone (e.g., report shows 120 percent long exposure in bonds and 120 percent short exposure via CDS/CDX) are not sufficient.

4. This assumes that the credit hedge fund with the swap sweeps the mark-to-market gains back and posts mark-to-market losses daily, which minimizes counterparty risk.

5. David A. Stawick, CFTC/AIMA letter to SEC, February 22, 2011, http://www.sec.gov/comments/s7–39–10/s73910–33.pdf.

6. Another improbable, but possible, risk is jump to risk-free—for example, if a risky entity gets bought by the government or a quasi-government entity and the reference obligation (the bond related to the CDS) is swapped for the bond of the acquirer, the spread of the reference entity is expected to narrow to the spread level of the acquirer. Note that this risk is not the same for shorting the cash bond, whose price is capped at par. This is an extreme scenario. For small movements in spread, cash-CDS position is going to be hedged.

7. "Coping with 'Unknown Unknowns,'" by Philippe Jorion. *Canadian Investment Review*, October 18, 2010.

Chapter 10

1. Leverage is measured as the amount of gross long exposure divided by NAV.
2. Prime brokers also exercised their contractual rights and notified credit hedge funds that the prime brokerage accounts would be closed within 45 days.
3. Accounts with U.S.-based broker-dealers are also covered by insurance by the SIPC (Securities Investor Protection Corp.). In its simplest form, this insurance is similar to the FDIC insurance on depository accounts. The SIPC is a nonprofit membership corporation with broker-dealers as members. In the event of a PB failure, the SIPC is tasked with returning consumers' securities to the owners and will pay assets up to $500,000 per type of account. The protection provided by the SIPC is valuable; nonetheless, given the monetary limit it is more relevant for individual investors. A hedge fund is likely to have assets with a prime broker that are significantly in excess of the $500,000 protection limit.
4. From www.sec.gov: "According to Regulation T of the Federal Reserve Board, you may borrow up to 50 percent of the purchase price of securities that can be purchased on margin. This is known as the 'initial margin.' Some firms require you to deposit more than 50 percent of the purchase price. Also be aware that not all securities can be purchased on margin."
5. From FINRA website: "The Financial Industry Regulatory Authority (FINRA) is the largest independent regulator for all securities firms doing business in the United States. FINRA's mission is to protect America's investors by making sure the securities industry operates fairly and honestly. All told, FINRA oversees about 4,270 brokerage firms, about 161,765 branch offices and approximately 630,345 registered securities representatives."
6. In the period immediately after Lehman Brothers' Chapter 11 filing, the recovery rate of a general unsecured claim on various Lehman entities including the U.K. broker-dealer was estimated at 10 to 15 cents on the dollar, similar to what the Lehman unsecured high yield bonds were trading at.
7. Securities and Exchange Commission, Rule 15c3-3: Reserve Requirements for Margin Related to Security Futures Products.
8. Between 1992 and 2007, the highest annual volatility of the Credit Suisse Leveraged Loan Total Return Index was 4.4 percent (2007), and the second-highest annual volatility was 4.01 percent (2002). The volatility of the index spiked to 15.19 percent in 2008, and registered 8.5 percent in 2009.
9. The number of days required as notice period can be found in the ISDA agreement.
10. Leverage is measured as market value of asset divided by equity.
11. In a loan BWIC, a list of bank loans will be offered for sale for a limited amount of time via a loan broker-dealer, who will collect the bids from interested parties.

12. The group comprises of global participants in the OTC derivatives market. Its members include "a broad range of OTC derivatives market participants: global, international and regional banks, asset managers, energy and commodities firms, government and supranational entities, insurers and diversified financial institutions, corporations, law firms, exchanges, clearinghouses and other service providers." ISDA website: http://www2.isda.org/about-isda.

13. Convention in the U.S. market for repo assumes 360 days per annum. Outside the United States, some countries use 365 days convention.

14. The variation margin trigger determines the level of margin below which a margin call is made. Variation margin trigger has to be agreed on by parties of the repo before trading begins.

15. The minimum increment price increase for a particular type of contract.

16. Jeremy Grant, "Financial Reform: Conduits of Contention," FT.com, June 15, 2011.

17. Mandatory clearing applies to North American and European Untranched CDS Indices. "CFTC Issues Clearing Determination for Certain Credit Default Swaps and Interest Rate Swaps," CFTC Press Release, November 28, 2012.

Key Takeaways and Questions

Chapter 1 - Hedge Funds and the Credit Market

 Takeaway on Corporate Structures

When investing in a corporate structure, understanding the value of a credit instrument involves understanding where value lies within the capital structure of a business unit as well as among different business units.

 Key Questions on Corporate Structures

If you are investing in the loan or debt of a subsidiary, what are the assets of that subsidiary? Does that subsidiary have assets beyond the assets on its own balance sheet such as parent guarantee or guarantee from another subsidiary? Does that subsidiary have off-balance-sheet liabilities or provide guarantee to the parent or other units?

Chapter 2 - High Yield Bonds

 Key Takeaway on the Naming Convention of Bonds

Assuming where a bond lies in the pecking order based only on its brief description can sometimes result in an incorrect analysis. The key point is for fund managers to understand the pecking order of the bond they are holding relative to other "IOUs" of the issuer and the asset coverage relative to that pecking order.

 Key Takeaway on Different Market Practice Regarding Seniority

As an example of how market practices change over time, many convertible bonds issued after 2008 are pari passu to bonds of the same issuer.

Key Takeaway on Relative Attractiveness of Different Credit Asset Classes

For managers who focus on high yield debt, it is important to be aware of the relative attractiveness of the loan market, as many issuers will issue wherever it is cheaper. The relative cheapness of either market may be dependent upon macroeconomic factors. There is a strong correlation between the level of issuance and secondary market liquidity.

Key Takeaway on Bond Terms

The terms of each new bond issuance can vary dramatically, and many things such as covenants, cash vs. payment-in-kind coupons, and conversion rights are negotiable.

Key Takeaway on the Importance of Primary Market

Pay attention to the primary market even if the portfolio only invests in bonds traded on the secondary market. There is a strong correlation between the liquidity of the secondary market and the level of primary issuance.

Key Takeaway on Trading Private Placements

When investing in hedge funds with less than $100 million under management, be sure to understand whether they qualify as a qualified institutional buyer (QIB) and thus can trade private placements.

Key Takeaway on the Use of Historical Analysis

When looking at historical performance data (either actual or back-tested), be aware that in many parts of the credit markets, trading patterns and liquidity can vary dramatically between periods. Thus, future volatility, opportunities, and sources of mispricing may differ significantly from historical periods.

Key Takeaway on Interest Rate Risk

High yield bond managers, sometimes for the first time in their entire careers, now have to worry about managing their interest rate risk.

 ## Key Questions on Hedging

- How is the amount of hedge determined? How do you determine which instruments are best used as hedges?
- Are these calculations based on normal or stressed risk exposures? What are the scenarios?
- Note that there is no correct answer. Hedging may be inadequate. Actual stress test or scenario analysis based on past events may not appropriately reflect current market risks.

 ## Key Questions on Position Sizing and Shorting

- Do you have a maximum position size? At cost or at market? Is it a hard limit?
- What is the current largest position in your portfolio? How has the size changed over time?
- How do you maintain your borrow? Will you use credit index hedges? Equity puts or calls?

 ## Key Takeaways on Stop Losses

Due to its liquidity profile and the way technicals affect the high yield bond market, stop losses can be difficult to implement and may result in selling the position at or near market bottom. Unlike equity hedge funds, credit hedge funds with a fundamental investment approach tend not to employ stop losses.

 ## Key Questions for the Short Side of the Portfolio

- How do you prefer to express your short view—cash or synthetics?
- Is your portfolio negative carry?

- How do you think about the cash-synthetic basis in your portfolio?
- What is the liquidity of the CDS of (a particular bond)?

 ## Key Questions for Event Credit Managers

- How do you define an "event"?
- Give me an example of a soft event you would not invest on.
- What are the time horizons of the events in the portfolio?
- How frequently is the thesis reevaluated? What if events do not materialize as expected?

 ## Key Questions for Capital Structure Arbitrage

- Which side of the portfolio—long or short—has been the main return generator for the past quarter/12 months/X years?
- Do you think of the short side as a hedge or as an alpha generator?
- If the company files for bankruptcy, which positions will be hurt?
- How do you manage the cash-synthetic basis risk (if at all)?

 ## Key Questions for Trading-Oriented Strategies

- What are the reasons behind the technical dislocation?
- Who are the market makers for the bond X?
- What are potential reasons that may cause the technical dislocation to persist?
- What is the bid-ask spread for situation X?
- How long would it take for the portfolio to exit a trade in normal scenario? In a distress scenario?

 ## Key Questions for the Levered Long Strategy

- What are the terms of the leverage?
- Why this method of financing rather than others?
- Under what circumstances can the leverage lines be pulled? Is there a cure provision in the event of a breach of covenant?

- How do you monitor your leverage lines? Who is responsible, and how often is it done?
- If credit spreads rise, how do you protect the portfolio?

Chapter 3 - Stressed and Distressed Investing

 ### Key Takeaway on Timing in Distressed Investing

The opportunities in distressed investing typically follow a spike in default and like defaults; distressed investing tends to be cyclical. Post the 2008 credit crisis, we see an increase in large distressed situations related to large leveraged buyouts.

 ### Key Takeaway on the Definition of Distressed

Given the ratings, spread, and price-based definitions above, the market can regard a security to be distressed long before it files for protection under bankruptcy laws. Be clear as to whether the manager is talking about actually defaulted securities or merely securities trading at a wide spread.

 ### Key Takeaway on Price as an Indicator of Opportunity

Beware the manager who has a low average price as a selling point for a fund (implying a potentially high expected return). Consider the risk—these are often pure operational turnarounds. While on the surface the portfolio may seem cheaper than a well-diversified portfolio containing both operational and financial restructurings, it should be cheaper given the greater risk level.

 ### Key Takeaways on Evaluating Distressed Hedge Funds

One technique for evaluating and comparing the depth and quality of hedge fund manager research is to look at the current portfolio, choose several "stressed," prebankruptcy companies and ask about the likelihood of an out-of-court restructuring. Strong answers include analyses of current market conditions for various types of securities the company could issue; current creditors and their motivations; as well as traditional financial statement analysis.

 ## Key Takeaway on Claim Name as Indicator of Rights

The name of the claim (e.g., "senior unsecured notes") by itself is not a sufficient indicator of its contractual rights and potential subordination.

 ## Key Takeaway on Comparing Distressed Hedge Funds

Be careful when comparing how different hedge funds position in the same bankruptcy. Pay particular attention to exactly which bond or bonds they own both in terms of seniority and in terms of issuer. Holding a secured opco bond may result in a very different view of the situation from a hedge fund that has been providing DIP financing.

 ## Key Takeaway on Where Filing is Done

Watch out for "forum shopping" by debtors, i.e., filing the bankruptcy in the court that is expected to be most favorable to the debtor or management. A good distressed manager should be able to demonstrate familiarity with previous rulings of the relevant bankruptcy court and/or a particular judge.

 ## Key Takeaways on Creditors Committee

Typically, an official creditors' committee is made up of investors with significant holdings. If you invest in a manager who is on a creditors' committee, your liquidity and redemption rights may effectively be restricted beyond what the manager may have agreed with you, the investor.

 ## Key Takeaway on Unofficial Committees

Investors who do not wish to be part of the official creditors' committee can still benefit from partnering with other investors who share similar goals in unofficial or ad hoc committees.

Key Takeaways on Stressed vs. Distressed Investing

Stressed investing can be a subset of event-driven credit investing and is sometimes referred to as special situations investing. Think of stressed and special situation investing as "distress-lite."

 ## Key Takeaways on Liquidity of Distressed Assets

Be aware that although there are some large bankruptcies where there is an active trading market for the distressed bonds (the Lehman bankruptcy comes to mind), in most cases, even though they may be supported by a "broker quote," most distressed bond prices are nothing more than educated guesses, and it is rare that size may be traded without significantly moving the market.

 ## Key Takeaway about "Timing the Market"

Many distressed hedge funds accept the fact that being a little early or a little late to buy or sell is a risk. However, if they are right on their investment thesis and execution as well as generally judicious in their purchase, the upside is expected to far outweigh the cost of not being able to perfectly time the market.

 ## Key Takeaways about Fund Liquidity Terms vs. Actual Portfolio Liquidity

Understand what the liquidity of the portfolio is through time—this is what drives your end liquidity. Not understanding the likely exit horizon for bankruptcies for which your manager is involved may lead to unanticipated lock-ups.

 ## Key Takeaway on Jurisdictional Risk

The ruling was done by a U.S. court, and involved U.S. guarantors—the jurisdiction risk is not because Vitro was a Mexican company. Process and legal risk are not uniquely limited to non-U.S. jurisdictions—there may be plenty of it in U.S. courts too!

Key Takeaway on Equity Risk in Credit Hedge Fund Portfolios

Many distressed managers have significant long-only equity positions as they retain the post-reorganization equity. Don't be surprised to find significant equity risk in these "event oriented" credit portfolios.

Key Takeaway on Information Efficiency in the Distressed Market

In distressed investing, the difficulty in finding timely and reliable information presents a significant barrier to entry to select investors.

Key Takeaway on the Nature of Available Information in the Distressed Market

Complexity in distressed situations means that even when information is publicly available and readily accessible, there are significant time commitments, expertise requirements, and additional out-of-pocket costs associated with collecting and interpreting the information.

Key Takeaway on Activism in the Distressed Space

Be careful not to assume direct positive correlation between size of a firm or a hedge fund and size of influence in the restructuring process.

Key Takeaway on Evaluating Distressed Funds Using Past Investments

Distressed investing is a very specific to each situation. Do not assume that the current portfolio characteristics will be reflected in the future.

Key Questions for a Distressed Fund

- Describe a distressed situation you have been involved in.
- At what stage did you decide to enter into a position?
- What is your exit plan? What if the restructuring does not go as planned?

- What is the typical size of a position at cost? At market? What is your maximum position size? Is it a guideline or a hard limit?
- Do you tend to take on an activist role in restructuring? Describe an involvement.
- How are trades allocated? (for managers who have multiple funds or managed accounts)
- How are positions valued?
- For fair valued positions, what is the methodology used? What are the comparables used, and how were they selected?

Key Takeaways of the Trade-Offs between Liquidity and Volatility

For tradable distressed assets, there is a trade-off between liquidity and mark-to-market volatility. Many distressed assets including post-reorganization equities have a "kink" in their beta profile—it is idiosyncratic to the market when the market is up, but has a high beta when the market is down.

Key Questions for Trading Oriented Positions

- What is the typical time horizon for a trade?
- Describe some of the catalysts that are currently in the portfolio.
- What if a catalyst does not materialize in a timely manner? Give an example.

Chapter 4 - Bank Loans

Key Takeaway on the Loan Market

Unlike bonds, there are no public bank loans. All bank loans are privately negotiated contracts.

Key Takeaways on CLO Event of Default

Collateralized loan obligations (CLOs) are not all created equal. The likelihood of an event of default (EOD) leading to the unwinding of the structure depends on two key factors. First, whether the EOD is dependent on a single factor being breached (such as a drop in market value of the assets) or on multiple factors. Second, whether there is a cure provision should a breach takes place.

 ## Key Questions on Loan Managers

- How are you holding your loans (assignments versus participations)?
- How long would you expect to take to liquidate your entire portfolio in the current market scenario?

 ## Key Takeaway on Settlement Risk

There is larger settlement risk for loans, particularly distressed loans, than for high yield bonds. Having the right trading and back office expertise are crucial parts of the investment thesis.

 ## Key Takeaway on Investment Grade Bank Loans

Investing in investment grade par or near-par loans, on a long-only or predominantly long basis, particularly if using low leverage or unlevered, should be done via traditional mandates and not hedge funds (investors should not pay hedge fund fees).

 ## Key Investment Questions for Standard Leveraged Loan Strategy

The key here is to gauge the quality of the manager's research and trading process.

- Who is responsible for idea generation?
- What is the key driver of performance: Fundamental research? Distressed loans? Trading? Hedging?

- Describe the short side of the portfolio. How actively traded are the shorts?
- What is the average price and typical annual carry of your loan portfolio?

 Key Financing Questions for Standard Leveraged Loan Strategy

- What are the terms of your financing?
- Under what circumstances can the financing be revoked? Describe the process to monitor and manage the financing lines.
- How much of the attribution is due to LIBOR arbitrage?
- What happens when the LIBOR floor goes away?

 Key Takeaways on the Cyclicality of Distress in the Loan Market

The supply of distressed loans is cyclical. The cycle typically looks like this: increased volume of issuance corresponding with looser lending standards leads to higher default, which leads to restructuring and recovery—rinse and repeat.

 Key Takeaway on Loans as the Fulcrum Security

As a higher proportion of indebtedness on a company's balance sheet comes in the form of bank loans, it is more likely that the loan, not the bond, is the fulcrum security in a restructuring.

 Key Questions for the DIP Strategy

- Describe your sourcing of the DIP opportunities.
- If the manager is starting a new DIP fund and sourcing comes from an existing loan position largely held by an existing fund—how do you allocate DIP between the existing and new fund?
- What is the sweet spot for the size of this fund?

Chapter 5 - Convertible Bonds

 Key Takeaways on Convertible Bond Features

Convertible bonds come with a wide range of features, some of which can add significant complexity to the bond. Specific features relating to take-over protection such as ratchet clauses or make-whole provision are often key parts of the investment thesis for hedge funds, which are able to benefit by taking either a long or short position depending on the situation.

 Key Takeaway on Gamma

Positive gamma can be interpreted as delta increasing at an increasing rate and decreasing at a decreasing rate. Gamma is highest for short-term, at-the-money options.

 Key Takeaway on Implied Volatility

Think about implied volatility as the "going rate" for option price. All else equal, option price goes up as implied volatility rises.

 Key Takeaways on the Seniority of Convertible Bond in a Corporate Capital Structure

Structurally a convertible bond may be more junior than a senior unsecured bond. However, if the convertible bond has a puttable date earlier than the maturity date of the bond, the contractual ability to demand payment before others gives the convertible bond an advantage over the structurally more senior bond. Just like dinner time at the family table, in order to claim the most desirable parts of the roast, seniority helps but is not a guarantee. One also needs to get to the table quickly.

 Key Takeaway on Convertible Arbitrage

In a delta neutral convertible arbitrage, the credit hedge fund manager is less concerned about whether the underlying equity price moves up or down. As long as the underlying equity price moves, i.e., shows some volatility, the manager is happy.

 ### Key Takeaways on The Risks of Shorting

The shorting ban in 2008 is a great example to illustrate this risk. The speed and ferocity of the shorting ban, in the middle of a very chaotic market environment with little clarity, hurt many convertible bond arbitrage managers as they were forced to cover their shorts at losses. To make matters worse, an arbitrageur who is unable to put on a short position is faced with either keeping an unhedged long position or liquidating the long convertible bond exposure. Many chose the latter, crystallizing loss at a very inopportune time in the market.

 ### Key Takeaways on "Busted" Converts

Negative gamma is a phenomenon often seen with "busted" converts. With negative gamma, the convertible bond price sensitivity to the stock price rises as the stock price falls and falls as the stock price goes up. In other words, the worse the stock price gets, the worse the impact of stock price on bond price gets.

Chapter 6 - Sovereign Debt

 ### Key Takeaway on Different Features Among Sovereign CDS

When investing via sovereign CDS, investors need to keep in mind that the structure of the CDS agreement varies for different sovereigns. For example, the Multiple Holder Obligation applies to Western European sovereign CDS but not emerging European or Middle Eastern sovereign CDS. The Multiple Holder Obligation states that in order for a restructuring to trigger a credit event, when the restructuring goes into effect, the debt obligation needs to be held by three or more debt holders that are unaffiliated with one another, and if it's a loan, at least two-thirds of holders (66.67 percent) need to consent to the event.

Key Takeaway on Credit Event of CDS

When hedging the risk of a bond default using a credit derivative such as a CDS, keep in mind that a bond default in itself does not necessarily trigger a credit default event of the sovereign CDS.

 Key Questions On Sovereign Debt Exposure

- How do you size your sovereign debt positions?
- How do you measure the macroeconomic risk in your portfolio?
- How do you weigh the risk of policy intervention in your sovereign debt positions?
- What do you expect will happen to the portfolio if the government implements changes such as capital control or monetary intervention? What's your plan in this case?

 Key Takeaway on Two Types of Sovereign Debt

When discussing sovereign debt, credit hedge funds may be referring to internal or external debt. Historically, hedge funds largely traffic in external debt, which is likely offered in U.S. dollar, U.K. sterling, or euro and is referred to as "hard currency" debt.

 Key Questions Regarding Hedging Sovereign Debt Risk

- What types of instruments are you using to hedge the portfolio? Why?
- How much is being spent in premium? How much is the maximum amount that can be spent?
- Will the hedges be actively traded?

 Key Questions on Basis Risk

- What are the basis risks inherent in your investment strategy?
- How did you get comfortable with this basis risk?
- In the worst-case scenario where the basis moves against you, what is the expected loss in this portfolio?

Key Takeaway on Short Dated Credit Derivatives

The spread DV01, or the measure of sensitivity of the credit derivative to every basis point change in the credit spread of the underlying sovereign bond, may decline dramatically as the maturity of the sovereign CDS or CDX comes near.

 ## Key Takeaway on How Macro Winds Influence Fundamental Investment Strategy

The strong component of fundamental or default risk in a directional long/short strategy means that many credit hedge fund managers whose expertise is in analyzing corporate and not sovereign credit chose to stay away from this strategy during the European sovereign crisis.

 ## Key Takeaway on Navigating a Macro-Driven Environment

Investors should be aware that for any given period, value added from fundamental research may be overcome by macro-driven fears. Credit hedge funds can mitigate this risk by adding value via trading and tactical shorts as well as active risk management.

Chapter 7 - Legal and Structuring

 ## Key Takeaways on Commonly Used Investment Structures

The three most commonly used structures are: side by side, master feeder, and mini master structures. The side by side structure is the simplest and least expensive to set-up but tracking error can be an issue. The master feeder structure gives ease of allocation but involves additional costs. The mini master structure offers relative simplicity and cost benefit to the master feeder structure, while mitigating tracking error.

 ## Key Takeaway on Minimum Size

Due to the additional set-up, legal, back-office, and monitoring costs associated with a separate account, it does not make economic sense to have a separate account for less than $50 million. The amount may be higher for more complex strategies.

 ### Key Takeaway on Replicating Service Provider Terms for the Commingled Fund

Replicating the terms of the commingled fund's service agreements for the separate account is practically impossible in most cases. This is due to several reasons, one of which is the confidential nature of the service agreements. Another reason is that service provider terms vary depending on current acceptable market level at the time of contract negotiation.

 ### Key Takeaway on Minimum Account Size

The minimum bite size for many credit instruments is another reason why a managed account does not make sense for accounts below a certain size. A managed account that's too small is also likely not to get the proper amount of attention from service providers.

 ### Key Takeaways on Liquidity and Separate Accounts

When evaluating the liquidity profile of a hedge fund portfolio, be sure to include the investments made via the separate accounts in addition to the investments in the commingled fund.

 ### Key Questions On Steering Clear of Insider Trading Rules

- Do you commonly opt to receive private information? Why or why not?
- How do you mitigate the risk of trading positions for which you possess material non-public information?
- How would your trader know what he can or cannot trade? Walk me through the process.

 ### Key Takeaways on Liquidity Management Tools

Gates and Side Pockets have received plenty of negative press, some of it well deserved. There are particular situations and types of instruments where the use of gating and side pockets is not only justifiable, but also necessary to protect remaining investors from the impact of exiting investors. Constant monitoring, deep understanding of the true nature of one's investment portfolio, and knowledge of market condition are crucial in determining whether gates and side pockets have been used and managed appropriately.

Key Takeaway on Suspension

In cases where suspension is inevitable, managers who offered reduced or no management fee and / or gave investors the option to stay or redeem (with attractive terms for investors who elect to stay) tended to maintain goodwill with their investors throughout and after the liquidity crisis.

Chapter 8 - Operational Due Diligence Program for Credit Hedge Fund Investing

Key Takeaway on Creating Stable and Effective Operational Due Diligence Program

Three legs to a stable and effective operational due diligence program are independence, proper resources, and organizational commitment.

Key Takeaway on the Importance of Testing

In order to "peel the onion," ODD personnel need to test the processes that the manager has put in place to understand how they are being put to work in the day-to-day activity of running the fund.

Key Takeaway on Valuation

The administrator may not provide valuation on all the positions in the fund. Ask your manager for situations where they have overridden the administrator's pricing and for supporting documents.

Key Takeaway on the Role of Administrator

Common pricing practice in the industry is for the administrator to follow the policy outlined in the fund documents. Two funds with the same administrator owning the same level 3 asset may have different pricing if the funds have different pricing policies per the fund offering memorandum.

Key Takeaways on Central Counterparties ("CCP")

There are multiple CCPs for different geographies, and they are competing entities with different coverage for different assets. Different asset coverage and margin requirement across CCPs add complexity to how a credit hedge fund manager manages cash.

Key Takeaway on Different Clearing Rules for Different Jurisdictions

Another complexity associated with central clearing is the differences in the rules adopted by different jurisdictions. For example, the U.S. and European regulators used different starting points as the basis of the new rules surrounding the central clearing of derivatives.

Key Questions on Service Providers

- Ask your manager about the selection process for the fund's service providers.
- Have they worked with this firm before?
- Have they worked with the specific professionals that will be servicing the account?
- What are some of the criteria that the manager used to make the selection?
- Can the manager show you their documentation of the interviews with the various service providers, which may include a questionnaire or a "scoring sheet" on various metrics.

Key Takeaway on Systems

If the manager uses a system that is not widely compatible with those of trading counterparties or administrators, it may result in discrepancies and opens the door to human oversight or error. For example, some credit managers are trying to "fit a square peg into a round hole" by using equity-based systems on their credit portfolio, which may necessitate constant manual adjustments.

Key Questions on Compliance

- Who are the relevant regulators?
- Who are the individuals responsible for compliance? Whom do they report to?
- Is there an external compliance consultant? What is the extent of the external consultant involvement in day-to-day compliance monitoring? Is it appropriate?

Key Takeaways on Trade Allocation

A fair trade allocation process is key, particularly in capacity constrained trades. A concern of investors, for example, is that the manager may allocate more of the opportunity to accounts where the trade has a higher probability of earning incentive fees for the manager.

Key Questions on Trade Allocation

- Ask managers for a written trade allocation procedure.
- Select a few trades and ask the operations personnel how these trades were allocated across accounts.

Key Takeaway on Regulatory Breaches

Any significant regulatory breach is generally part of public record. Investors should take care to review the firm's disciplinary history on regulators' websites as well as general searches for stories in the financial press.

Key Takeaways on Use of Expert Networks

Review of the information received from experts can include having the CCO or the compliance officer being present during conversations with experts. Alternatively, the conversations should be documented or recorded and the record should be available to the CCO or compliance officer for his or her review.

Chapter 9 - Risk Management

 Key Takeaways on Mark to Market Risk vs. Permanent Loss

When discussing risks with a credit hedge fund manager, investors should be specific whether it refers to permanent impairment of capital or mark-to-market risk. Be aware that in a volatile credit market, efforts to minimize mark-to-market risk can result in selling at or near market bottom, turning a mark-to-market loss into a permanent loss.

 Key Questions on Portfolio Risk

- How has the risk changed in the portfolio over the past few years?
- Where are the most attractive opportunities currently, both on the long and the short side?
- What have you learned from the credit crisis of 2008?

 Key Takeaways on Historical Return

Solely using historical return to make forward looking investment decision is akin to driving forward while looking at the rear view mirror. It is also important to analyze how the portfolio is expected to perform going forward based on current risks in the portfolio.

 Key Questions on Concentration Risk

- How large are the top 5 or top 10 positions in the portfolio?
- What's the largest issuer in the portfolio, and how has the position size changed over time?
- Are there hard caps or guidelines on position or issuer size?

Key Questions on Measuring Credit Risk in the Portfolio

- Do you think spread or interest rate duration is useful to measure the risk in your credit portfolio?
- If not, why not?
- What is the current spread duration and rate duration of your portfolio?

 ## Key Takeaways on The Risk of Rising Rates

The portfolio manager of a long-only or long-biased credit portfolio used to focus on managing credit risk rather than interest rate risk. However, given rates at an all-time low, interest rate risk has now moved from secondary to primary importance. The longer the duration of the portfolio, the higher the interest rate risk.

 ## Key Takeaways on Non-Linearity of Credit Instruments

Although linear risk factors such as equity beta capture the sensitivity of the portfolio for small market moves, investors should be cautious of extrapolating these numbers for large market moves given the nonlinear nature of the expected return of many credit instruments. During extreme market volatility, stress tests may be more helpful in illustrating the risks to the portfolio.

 ## Key Takeaway on Liquidity Risk

Investors should consider the trade-off between flexibility to invest in smaller, less liquid or niche opportunities and the liquidity risk in a portfolio.

 ## Key Questions on Liquidity Risk

- How long do you expect to take to liquidate the entire portfolio under normal circumstances? Under stressed scenarios?
- What measures do you use to monitor the liquidity of your portfolio?

Key Takeaways on Modeling Liquidity Risk

Liquidity for credit instruments is notoriously difficult to model before the fact (ex-ante). The over-the-counter market translates into a liquidity that can be defined as "it's there until it's not." Size of issuance, ownership as percent of issuance, and the number of active dealers trafficking in the name are some of the liquidity proxies commonly used. Investors should also ask their credit manager the time required to liquidate the portfolio during normal and stress scenarios.

 Key Takeaways on Stop Losses as a Risk Management Technique

Stop losses are more difficult to implement and less effective as a risk management tool for less liquid credit due to higher mark-to-market volatility and wider bid-ask spread.

 Key Questions on Modeling the Risks of a Distressed Portfolio

- How do you model the distressed positions in your portfolio? Distressed managers are, by definition, investing in idiosyncratic risks, which are difficult to map.
- Are there any positions that are modeled using a proxy in the risk model?
- When the fulcrum security is turned into equities, what is your view on the directional equity risk of this exposure? Do you think it makes sense to hedge that risk?

 Key Takeaway on the Volatility of Lower Priced Credit Instruments

Lower priced corporate loans and bonds are usually more volatile. When evaluating the portfolio of a credit hedge fund, ask for the weighted average price of instruments for both the long and short portfolio.

Key Takeaway on False "Risk Neutral" Claims

A portfolio with risky long positions hedged with an investment grade index may look neutral on net exposure basis, but it is not neutral to credit spread risk—it will lose money when credit spread widens.

 ## Key Portfolio on Hedging Interest Rate Risk

A credit portfolio where the long side consists of cash instruments and the short side consists of synthetic instruments is taking interest rate risk. Just because the net exposure of the credit is neutral or low, do not assume that the portfolio is hedged against interest rate risk.

 ## Key Questions on Instruments With Payment-in-Kind Feature

- How much of the exposure in the portfolio is to bonds with payment-in-kind (PIK) feature?
- How much of the NAV is from payment-in-kind interest?
- How are PIKs accounted for in the portfolio, and is the PIK amount included in calculating fees paid by investors?

 ## Key Takeaways on The Limits of Risk Models

A risk management exercise worth doing is to focus on how the manager expects these positions to behave "out of model"—how it will actually behave in a current crisis compared to predefined stress tests. Before coming to visit credit managers, spend a few days to research some of their niche or idiosyncratic positions.

 ## Key Takeaways on Shortcomings of Credit Risk Models

Watch out for basis risk between an instrument and its proxy. In order to get a long period of historical data, fixed-income instruments are usually mapped to a particular bucket. For example, the risk of a particular B-rated bond is mapped to a basket of B-rated bonds. However, if the issuer of the bond in the portfolio is smaller than the average bond in the basket, it may be impacted more heavily in a scenario of economic downturn and the basket may not sufficiently capture the risk of the bond being modeled.

 ### Key Takeaways on Risk Models

Credit instruments are more difficult to model than equity instruments. Modeling the risk of credit instruments may involve a greater degree of complexity to capture features such as convexity. Investors should keep in mind that a complex, shiny risk engine should not distract from the intuitive understanding of what the models are trying to do and the limitations of modeling.

Chapter 10 - Financing

 ### Key Takeaways on Financing

Many investors intuitively seek the cheapest financing. However, investors should not focus solely on managers with the least expensive financing. Financing providers may offer cheaper financing in exchange for stricter and less flexible covenants.

 ### Key Takeaways on The "Right" Amount of Leverage

The right amount of leverage (which can be none) depends on the volatility of the instruments and the terms of the leverage, not the expected arbitrage profit. Increasing leverage when arbitrage profit narrows in order to reach a target return is a very risky strategy.

 ### Key Takeaways on How Mark-to-Market Loss Becomes Actual Loss

The risk of leverage is in its ability to turn mark-to-market loss into actual and permanent loss of capital. Term financing, cure provision, and non-mark-to-market are features that mitigate this risk.

Key Takeaways on Financing "Basis" Risk

There is basis risk associated with different ways long and short portfolios are exposed to different financing lines. Managers who thought they were hedged by buying CDS protection from Bear and Lehman as counterparties found themselves with significant net long exposure when both firms went belly up in 2008.

 ## Key Takeaways on Financing Mechanisms for Credit Instruments

Investors tend to be most familiar with prime broker financing. Nonetheless, there are a variety of financing methods available for different credit instruments. For example, bank loans are typically levered through total return swaps (TRS) and not prime broker financing. As such, if investors ask to review a PB agreement, a credit hedge fund predominantly invested in bank loans may not be able to show this. Investors should ask to see the ISDA agreement instead.

 ## Key Takeaway on Excess Margin

You wouldn't walk into a bazaar and negotiate by telling the merchant by how much money you have in your pocket. Similarly, don't leave too much excess margin with your financing provider.

 ## Key Takeaways on Trade-offs in Cash Management

The most conservative cash management technique is to leave only the exact amount of margin required with the counterparty and meet margin calls daily. However, keep in mind that the frequency of cash sweeps should balance the need to manage counterparty risk and costs associated with very frequent cash sweeps, such as additional burden on the back office and the interest earned on the cash balance.

Key Takeaway on Negotiating Financing Agreements

When it comes to leverage, almost everything is negotiable. Make sure that your credit hedge fund manager can show that they have done sufficient due diligence to compare the terms offered by the PB or other leverage provider.

 Key Takeaways on Clearing Requirement on Derivatives

Many credit hedge funds are supportive of the new clearing requirement for OTC derivatives such as interest rate swaps and credit default swaps. Credit hedge funds expect to benefit from increased liquidity, better transparency, standardized pricing, and better bid-ask spread.

Index